ATLANTIS

and the Kingdom of the

NEANDERTHALS

100,000 Years of Lost History

COLIN WILSON

Bear & Company
Rochester, Vermont

Bear & Company
One Park Street
Rochester, Vermont 05767
www.BearandCompanyBooks.com

Bear & Company is a division of Inner Traditions International

LIBRARY OF CONGRESS CATALOGING-IN-PUBLICATION DATA

Wilson, Colin, 1931–
    Atlantis and the kingdom of the Neanderthals : 100,000 years of lost history /
Colin Wilson.
        p. cm.
    Summary: "The history of Neanderthal influence from Atlantis to the
contemporary era"—Provided by publisher.
    Includes bibliographical references and index.
    ISBN-10: 1-59143-059-3
    ISBN-13: 978-1-59143-059-9
1. Atlantis. 2. Neanderthals. I. Title.
    GN751.W556 2006
    569.9'86—dc22

                                                        2006008994

Printed and bound in the United States by Lake Book Manufacturing, Inc.

10   9   8   7   6   5   4   3   2   1

Text layout by Virginia Scott Bowman
This book was typeset in Sabon with Ellington as the display typeface

To send correspondence to the author of this book, mail a first-class letter to the
author c/o Inner Traditions • Bear & Company, One Park Street, Rochester, VT
05767, and we will forward the communication.

CONTENTS

ANALYTICAL TABLE OF CONTENTS

One: Hapgood's Unsolved Mystery

Rand Flem-Ath proposes a collaboration. Hapgood tells him that a civilization with "high levels of science" existed 100,000 years ago. Hapgood dies in a car accident before he can explain himself. Hapgood's career: Did the slippage of the Earth's crust cause the destruction of Atlantis? Teotihuacan's Way of the Dead. Hapgood and the ancient maps. The Piri Reis map and Antarctica. Hapgood's *Maps of the Ancient Sea Kings*. Von Daniken. The islands of St. Peter and St. Paul. John West and ancient Egypt. Did ancient Egyptian culture come from Atlantis? Graham Hancock and Rand Flem-Ath. Robert Bauval and *The Orion Mystery*. Was Atlantis destroyed 10,500 BC? Making a TV program on The Flood. The attempt to solve Hapgood's riddle. Neanderthal man?

Two: A Trip Down the Nile

How was the Great Pyramid built? Frank Domingo investigates the Sphinx. Eratosthenes measures the size of the Earth. Hapgood's students establish that the center of the Piri Reis map is Syene. Agatharchides of Cnidus. The French meter. Joy and I sail down the Nile. The Temple of Edfu. The positioning of ancient sites. The "earth force" at Carnac. Emil Shaker on the Temple ritual. "The ritual activates the Temple." Michael Baigent gets lost. Chris Dunn's sounding-box theory. David Elkington:

the Pyramid is "alive." John Reid discovers that vibrating sand creates Egyptian religious symbols. The Valley of the Kings. A spermatozoon? Precession of the equinoxes. Who built the Oseirion? Chatelain's *Our Cosmic Ancestors*. The mystery of the Nineveh number. The Great Constant of the Solar System? The Sumerians. Neanderthal brain was bigger than ours. Benjamin Blyth: a six-year-old "super-computer." Primes and the New York twins. Critchlow and the Babylonians. Alexander Thom and the Megalithic Yard. Robert Graves and heightened intuitive awareness. "It occurred to me that I knew everything."

Three: Ancient Technologies

An ancient worldwide culture? Petrie and Naquada. Hapgood and the mystery of the Libyan desert glass. Lord Rennell and John Dolphin. An atomic blast? Rennell's pure gold necklace. Lakes in the Sahara? Rennell contacts Hapgood. Farouk El-Baz and the "natural pyramids." Yull Brown and the gas that can vaporize metals. Verne's *The Mysterious Island*. Water as a fuel. Did the ancients use Brown's Gas? The Baghdad Battery. Howard-Vyse and the iron plate in the Great Pyramid. Aztec gold. The gods of Tula. The Temple of the Morning Star. Lake Titicaca and its sea creatures. What wrecked Tiahuanaco? The Akapana pyramid. Posnansky's 15,000 BC. Oswaldo Rivera changes his mind. "Tiahuanaco was built by a lost civilization."

Four: The Flood

The harbor at the top of a mountain? What split the Gate of the Sun? Were the Andes formed 13,000 years ago? The four Great Floods. Claudius Rich looks for ancient Babylon. The Tower of Babel. Botta finds the palace of Sargon II. Why the Assyrians vanished. Layard excavates Nimrud. Rawlinson reads cuneiform. George Smith discovers the *Epic of Gilgamesh*. The Gilgamesh Flood. J. E. Taylor excavates Tell al Muqayyar. Where did the Sumerians come from? Ur of the Chaldees. Leonard Woolley. Queen Shubad. The layer of clean clay. The Biblical Flood? The Black Sea Flood.

Five: More Catastrophes

The big melt-down of 12,000 BC. Alexander Tollmann and the Flood of 7545 BC. The "Seven Burning Mountains" of Enoch. *Cosmic Winter*. The Chicxulub strike—the "star that killed the dinosaurs." The four other "great strikes." The Oort Cloud. Tree rings reveal another impact. Deucalion's Flood of 2200 BC. *When the Earth Nearly Died*—the impact of 9500 BC. The Tiahuanaco flood myth—Adam and Eve. The Haida Indians. How Hapgood became interested in Atlantis. Stephen Oppenheimer's Sundaland. Svetlana Balabanova and the Cocaine Mummies. Did Egyptians sail to Peru? Hapgood and the Hadji Ahmad map—Asia and Alaska joined. What turned our ancestors into Sea Kings? Ivar Zapp and the Stone Balls of Costa Rica. John Michell and ley lines. The Stone Balls as navigational aids. The Olmec heads. Columbus in Costa Rica.

Six: The Mystery of the Maya

Maurice Chatelain and the Quiriga numbers. The discovery of the Maya. Was Mayan science a legacy? Mayan blood sacrifices. Maurice Cotterell on Maya astronomy. Gauquelin and his statistics. Cotterell and sunspots. Did sunspots cause the decline of the Maya? AD 2012—the End of the World? *Maya Cosmogenesis* by John Major Jenkins. The sun and Milky Way conjunction. My visit to Monte Alban. Carvings of massacre. What happened to Teotihuacan? Batres uncovers the Pyramid of the Sun. Cotterrell and his "supergods." The Pyramid of Sipan in Peru. The tomb robbery. Heyerdahl and the plundered tomb. The Tucume pyramids. The Moche and human sacrifice. Heyerdahl and the Guanches of Tenerife. The black stone "pyramids" of the Canaries. Is the Sipan pyramid the tomb of Viracocha? Cotterell at Palenque. The sarcophagus and its lid. Cotterell cracks its visual code. Eidetic vision—Tesla. The *Popol Vuh* myth: "Let their sight reach only that which is near."

Seven: The Shamanic Vision

Ross Salmon goes to South America. Wakchu and the condor. Rider Haggard's statuette. Psychometry. Colonel Fawcett vanishes. Nazca and its lines. The forty-year drought that destroyed the Moche and the Nazca. Runways for alien spacecraft? How could the Nazca Indians see the drawings from overhead? Can shamans leave their bodies? Manuel Cordova. Shared visions. Harry Wright and the Leopard Dance of Dahomey. Arthur Grimble and the porpoises. Miriam Starhawk on stone age hunters. "Willing animal sacrifice." Jacquetta Hawkes and the pygmy hunters. The archpriest Avvakum on Siberian shamans. Training of a shaman. Eliade and shamanism. A fisherman's daughter receives "the call." Knud Rassmussen and the Eskimo shaman. "Shamanism takes the existence of spirits utterly for granted." *Shamans through Time*. Thurn and the peaiman. Voices from above the roof. Sieroshevski on Yakut shamans. "Doomed to inspiration." The shaman's drum. Gordon Wasson popularizes shamanism.

Eight: A More Powerful Reality

Eliade on techniques of ecstasy. Michael Harner and the Jivaro. Hallucinogens as "teachers." Jeremy Narby and the Ashaninca of Peru. "Two gigantic boa constrictors." What is a shaman? The "third eye" and serotonin. Jung and his visions. DNA: intertwined snakes. Keith Critchlow and the shamans' ladder. The world axis. The number 7. The notion of teleology: Does life have a purpose? The Yage Drinker shuns sorcery. Illness as the result of sorcery. An energy vampire. Decoding the secret language of shamans. Max Freedom Long and the Kahunas. The Death Prayer. Man's three souls. Myers and the superconscious self. The low self and the death prayer. Ghosts. Changing the future. The Hawaiian boy and the death prayer. The secret of the Egyptian temples, and the Princess Ahhotep. William Reginald Stewart and the Witch of Atlas. The Quahunas of the Sahara. Their move to Hawaii. Guy Playfair in Rio. Edivaldo's magical stomach operation. Umbanda.

Nine: Enoch's Burning Mountain

James Bruce in search of *The Book of Enoch*. Solomon and Sheba. *Uriel's Machine*. New Grange and Callanish. Gerald Hawkins decodes

Ten: The Magic Landscape

Eleven: Primal Vision

Twelve: The Old Ones

ACKNOWLEDGMENTS

Many people have given me help and advice with this book. My chief debt of gratitude goes to Robert Lomas, who suggested that I should write it, and who has given much valuable advice.

Jerome Sigler of San Francisco introduced me to the work of Joseph Jochmans, who wrote *The Hall of Records* in 1980, long before the revival of interest in ancient Egypt triggered by Graham Hancock's *Fingerprints of the Gods* and Robert Bauval's *The Orion Mystery*, and in many ways anticipating their discoveries. Mr. Sigler also went to the trouble of duplicating for me a second copy of the book when I mislaid the first, and for this I offer my grateful and apologetic thanks.

David Elkington drew my attention to the work of John Reid on the importance of sound in understanding the role of the sarcophagus in the King's Chamber of the Great Pyramid.

I owe my discovery of Maurice Chatelain's important work on the Nineveh number to Gurth and Maria Walton, as recounted in chapter 2.

The account of Yull Brown and his extraordinary discoveries was provided by Shawn Montgomery.

My old and now deceased friend Ross Salmon was responsible for the astonishing story of the condor at the beginning of chapter 7.

It was Michael Baldwin, of the Baldwin Institute in Marion, Massachusetts, who drew my attention to the work of Jeremy Narby.

Special thanks to Henry Lincoln, the man who was originally responsible for investigating the mystery of Rennes-le-Château, who drew my attention to Berriman's *Historical Metrology*, and to the work of Harald Boehlke on Norwegian landscape geometry.

My old friend Eddie Campbell lent me Henri Bortoft's book on Goethe and has provided many important comments on the ideas of chapter 11.

I wish to thank Stephen Phillips, expert of subatomic particles and on the Kabbalah, and author of *Extrasensory Perception of Quarks*, for providing me, in correspondence, with additional material of which I have made use in chapter 11.

It was Michael Baigent who told me the story and showed me the photograph of the half-million-year-old polished wooden plank that has since disappeared.

I can hardly overemphasize the importance of the work of Stan Gooch on Neanderthal man and on the psychology of the paranormal and can only hope that my own comments on it help to bring him the attention he has long deserved.

Finally, it will be obvious to the reader that the work of John Michell on the Platonic "canon" has been one of the major influences on the writing of this book, and I wish to thank him for his friendship and support over a quarter of a century.

PREFACE

In 1956, anthropologist Michael Harner went to live among the Jivaro Indians of Ecuador, on the eastern slopes of the Andes. He discovered that, while willing to talk about most aspects of their culture, the Jivaro were unwilling to discuss their religion. This reluctance was not reticence but was an inability to express their faith in words. They finally told Harner that if he wanted to learn, he would have to drink the drug called ayahuasca, made from a vine. Harner agreed.

The village elder, Tomas, spent the day making the potion. That evening, in a communal hut with the whole tribe watching, Harner drank the potion from a gourd. He reported that it tasted bitter. Then he lay down. Lines of light began to appear in the total blackness above him. Then they burst into brilliant colors. A roaring noise, which sounded like a waterfall, came from far away, and grew louder until it filled his ears.

The lines above his head formed into geometric patterns, like stained glass, and became a kind of celestial cavern. Then Harner was surrounded by a carnival of demons, in the center of which was a huge crocodile's head from whose jaws gushed a flood of water. The water rose until it became a sea, with a blue sky overhead. A galleon with square sails came toward him, and he could hear the sound of singing coming from crowds of bird-headed humans who filled the decks, reminding him of gods in ancient Egyptian tomb paintings. As his body seemed to turn to concrete, he became convinced he was dying, and that the boat had come to carry away his soul.

He then began to see more visions, which he felt were reserved for the dying. He was shown the Earth as it was eons ago, with a barren sea and land. Then he saw hundreds of black specks in the sky, flying toward him. They were shiny black creatures with pterodactyl wings and whalelike bodies. As they flopped exhausted onto the Earth they explained to him in thought-language that they were fleeing from something in space.

Finally, he was shown how these creatures had created life, so they could hide among its many forms. They were inside all forms of life, including man. (In 1956, Harner had never heard of DNA, but he was struck by this idea later.) These creatures told him that they were the "true masters of humanity" and that man was their servant.

While Harner had felt no fear of the bird-headed humans on the galleon, he was afraid that his soul might fall into the hands of these shiny black creatures, the "ancient ones." He struggled against them and finally managed to croak the word: "medicine," meaning antidote. When this was poured into his mouth, the ancient ones disappeared and he was back in the communal hut.

This experience inspired Harner to become a shaman, like the village elder, Tomas. He was overwhelmed by the sensation that what he had seen was not some kind of illusion, but the very reality that underlies existence. The remainder of his book *The Way of the Shaman* describes the disciplines he underwent to become a shaman.

Jeremy Narby, another anthropologist who drank ayahuasca among Peruvian Indians, was also convinced that what he saw was "a more powerful reality" than our everyday kind. And in his book *Supernatural*, Graham Hancock has described how, after drinking the African plant extract iboga, he also saw visions that he insists were real, not illusory. He adds the interesting information that when Francis Crick was working with James Watson to uncover the structure of DNA, he had also been experimenting with the drug LSD.

Mythology abounds with stories of earlier human beings who understood this more powerful reality that we have forgotten, the most persistent account being that of the lost continent of Atlantis.

In writing about Atlantis in two earlier books, I concluded that the reality behind Atlantis has something in common with the reality reported by Harner and Narby. There was a time when our remote ancestors possessed a different kind of knowledge than that explored by modern science. Intimations of this knowledge can be sensed in the immense "Nineveh number," fifteen digits long, that was found on a tablet in the library of Ashurbanipal in the mid-nineteenth century—and that turned out to be the number of years in the cycle of the precession of the equinoxes, but expressed in seconds—and in the two even greater numbers found in the sacred ruins of Quiriga, in Central America. It is clear that our ancestors knew far more than we do today.

ONE

HAPGOOD'S
UNSOLVED MYSTERY

In the summer of 1998, I received a letter from a friend named Rand Flem-Ath, suggesting that he and I should collaborate on a book about Atlantis. His proposal sounded so fascinating that I agreed without hesitation. The book was to be called *Blueprint for Atlantis*.

The idea for the book was based on a paper that Flem-Ath had written some time prior, which suggested that the site of Atlantis was the South Pole, or rather, the continent of Antarctica. To many people, this suggestion sounds absurd since Antarctica is thousands of miles south of the mid-Atlantic, which Plato claimed was the location of Atlantis. But Flem-Ath's theory was based on a suggestion that had been made by Charles Hapgood, a New England professor of history, who declared that the earth's crust is subject to periodic shifts that can cause the continents to change their positions.

His apparently unlikely theory gained the support of Albert Einstein, who, just before he died in 1955, had written a foreword to Hapgood's book *Earth's Shifting Crust*, which was published in 1958.

Flem-Ath sent his paper to Hapgood and was delighted to receive a warm reply that called it "the first truly scientific exploration of my work that has ever been done."[1] Oddly enough, Hapgood did not comment on Flem-Ath's notion that Atlantis might be in Antarctica. But Flem-Ath was nevertheless encouraged enough to continue with his investigations. He and his wife went to London, where he pressed on with his studies in the British Museum Reading Room.

In October 1982 Flem-Ath wrote to Hapgood to update him on his progress with the "shifting crust" theory and, in reply, received a letter that left him staggered. Hapgood stated that he had recently made some exciting discoveries that showed that civilization, with a highly developed level of scientific knowledge, was at least one hundred thousand years old. He said that he intended to publish his discoveries in a new edition of his book *Earth's Shifting Crust*.

It has been generally accepted that civilization started in the Middle East about ten thousand years ago—in approximately 8000 BC—not a hundred thousand years ago. But Hapgood had written to Flem-Ath of "a whole new cycle of civilization"—in other words, a civilization that existed before our present one.[2] It sounded like science fiction. But Hapgood had always been a sober, hardworking professor of history, without even a touch of the crank in his character.

Understandably, Flem-Ath was excited and wrote to Hapgood saying, in effect, "Quickly, tell me, tell me."

His letter was returned a month later stamped "Deceased." Hapgood had walked in front of a car and had been killed.

Flem-Ath then tried hard to solve the mystery of the "exciting discoveries." He visited the Hapgood Archives at Yale but left empty-handed. He wrote to all Hapgood's relatives and to many of his friends asking if Hapgood had mentioned his "discoveries" to any of them. No one could help him and finally he gave up.

The question then became: was it worth continuing to try to solve this mystery and include the results in our Atlantis book, and could I fare any better than Flem-Ath had with the search. I decided to go back to Flem-Ath's starting point, Hapgood's 1958 book *Earth's Shifting Crust*, to see what I could discover.

Hapgood began the book with the question: is there any proof that the Earth's crust has "slipped"?

His answer was: yes. The Earth's crust is full of iron ore. And since the Earth is a magnet, all the molecules of iron oxide point in the same direction, like tiny arrows. And since they all point toward the North Pole, it is quite easy to see if the position of the pole has altered since the ore solidified, for in that case, the iron oxide molecules (the "arrows") will be pointing in the wrong direction. And that is precisely what has happened. The "arrows" in a great deal of the Earth's crust are pointing too far south, which shows that the pole must have since moved north.

However, Hapgood explained, the pole itself had stayed where it was; it was the Earth's crust above it that had slipped south, a little like a schoolboy's cap being pulled down over his eyes. It had slipped south by about two thousand miles. According to Hapgood, Hudson Bay used to be right above the North Pole. Then the crust slipped, and Hudson Bay—together with Canada and North America—moved two thousand miles south.

The various indicators revealed that the great slippage had occurred about twelve thousand years ago, at the end of the last Ice Age.

Hapgood also noted the fact that Plato, in *Timaeus*, had pointed to that date as the time when Atlantis was destroyed "in a day and a night."[3] Plato mentions that his ancestor, the statesman Solon (who lived around 600 BC) said that Egyptian priests had told him that Atlantis had disappeared about nine thousand years earlier. That date is close to 10,000 BC.

Although Hapgood had never dared to admit this, he had experienced a lifelong fascination with Atlantis, which was why he began to study the question: what kind of catastrophe could destroy a continent "in a day and a night"?

A possible answer came to him when the washing machine in his kitchen malfunctioned. The wet laundry had bunched into a tight bundle, so that as the drier spun round, the drum began to shudder and bump until it ripped the bolts out of the floor. This led Hapgood to wonder if the earth would also shudder and bump if one of the continents (say Antarctica) became lopsided.

A quick look at the map seemed to support the idea: Antarctica *is* lopsided (i.e., off-center). But then a colleague who was a mathematician did the calculation and pricked Hapgood's bubble. The mathematician determined that even if Antarctica were made of solid lead, it could not give the Earth a lopsided spin.

But Hapgood pressed on. When he discovered the iron-ore evidence, proving the Earth's crust had slipped, he felt he had found the basic solution. The Atlantis catastrophe had occurred because the Earth's crust had moved, creating roughly the same effect as a movement of the San Andreas fault, but one of a thousand times greater force. Hapgood had no idea why the crust had slipped (perhaps it was the result of the impact of a giant meteor); all he knew was that it had.

Considering all this, Flem-Ath felt that to include this material in the book we were writing, some evidence was needed to convince nongeologists. He stumbled on this by accident when his wife brought home a library book called *Archaeoastronomy in Pre-Columbian America*, by Dr. Anthony Aveni. In the book, Flem-Ath found a vital clue: that no fewer than fifty different religious sites in Mexico seem to be misaligned from true north.

For example, Mexico's most famous religious site is Teotihuacán, formerly called Tenochtitlan, a city that was once as large as ancient Rome. This site includes a long avenue running from north to south, known as the Way of the Dead. But for some odd reason, it does not run precisely from north to south. It is 15.5 degrees off true north. When Flem-Ath learned that forty-nine additional sacred sites were similarly misaligned, he began to feel that he was on to something.

He took a tape measure and tried extending the Way of the Dead in a straight line. The line passed through Hudson Bay.

What this appeared to mean was that when Teotihuacán was first built, the Way of the Dead pointed due north. Then the Earth's crust had slipped, taking Teotihuacán and the Way of the Dead with it, but twisting it sideways slightly as it did so, so that it now pointed 15.5 degrees away from true north.

The same thing had apparently happened to forty-nine other religious sites, which seemed to rule out the possibility that the architect of Teotihuacán was drunk when he designed the site.

The implications of this insight are hair-raising. If true, it means that Teotihuacán must have been built before the crust's great shift of 10,000 BC. Yet according to historians, no human civilization existed as early as that. Besides, most archaeologists still believe that Teotihuacán was built much more recently. Some suggest 4000 BC, while a few even think it was built as recently as 150 BC.

That, however, would not affect the argument as much as one might suppose, for we know that most significant religious sites are built on older religious sites. Many great temples are built on the ruins of half a dozen earlier temples.

If all this is correct, it means there must have been a civilization before 10,000 BC. It is true that Plato said that Atlantis was destroyed around 10,000 BC. But that is supposed to be a legend. What Flem-Ath seems to have proved is that it was a fact.

Hapgood also believed that Atlantis was a reality, but he came to that conclusion by a completely different route. His speculations about Earth's shifting crust had suggested a mechanism to explain how a continent might vanish overnight but had done nothing to demonstrate that it had actually happened. On August 26, 1956, a broadcast from Georgetown University in Washington threw new light on the problem.

A panel of experts was arguing about the so-called Piri Reis map, which had been found in the Topkapi Palace in Istanbul in 1929. A copy of this map was also with the Library of Congress in Washington, D.C. Piri Reis was a Turkish admiral and one-time pirate who had, in 1513, set out to construct a map of the Atlantic Ocean, showing Europe and the New World. This was difficult because America had been discovered very recently and few maps existed. Piri Reis reported relying on many old maps, including one used by Columbus.

The Piri Reis map of 1513 showed not only the whole coast of South America—in impressive detail—but also a fragment of Antarctica in the extreme south. What was so startling was that, given the fact that the coast of Antarctica had undoubtedly been covered in ice in 1513 and for thousands of years before that, the map showed certain bays on Antarctica's coast.

In 1949 an expedition had used radar to penetrate the ice there and show the land underneath. Core samples they took were six thousand years old, i.e., from 4000 BC.

But although civilization existed in 4000 BC, when the Middle East was dominated by the Sumerians, no one had yet invented writing—and a map is useless without writing on it.

It looked as if there must have been an even more ancient civilization than any before known to history. Plato's Atlantis began to seem less and less like a myth.

Hapgood wrote to the Library of Congress to ask if any more similarly ancient maps were stored there. The library replied that it had hundreds. Such maps were called portolans, which means "from port to port," and were used by mariners to sail by the shortest route.

The Library invited Hapgood to come look at its collection. What he saw took his breath away. Among the dozens of maps laid out on trestle tables, some showed the whole of Antarctica. Yet Antarctica was not officially discovered until 1818. These maps meant that ancient mariners must have sailed all around it. But the sailors must also have explored the continent from end to end, for other maps showed Antarctica without the ice, including rivers and mountains in the interior. The maps were so detailed, in fact, that it seemed fairly clear they must have been made by the inhabitants of the continent, since sailors, no matter how hard-working and conscientious, could never have conducted such extensive explorations.

Other maps, which included Russia and China, made it clear that these mysterious explorers must have penetrated nearly every corner of the globe. But who were they? Hapgood enrolled the help of his students at Keene State College, in New Hampshire, to help him study the maps and try to work out the dates of their origin.

The results were summarized in Hapgood's book *Maps of the Ancient Sea Kings*, subtitled: *Evidence of Advanced Civilization in the Ice Age*. In this book Hapgood concluded that the old maps proved beyond doubt the existence of a worldwide maritime civilization around 7000 BC. His arguments were all so well documented that no one could seriously doubt that Hapgood had proved the existence of a forgotten civilization.

What Hapgood took good care not to mention was the word Atlantis. He wanted to give his fellow academics no chance to dismiss him as a member of the lunatic fringe.

Unfortunately, through an appalling piece of bad luck, this happened anyway. Serious works of scholarship usually take a while to break out of the closed circle of academia and become known to a wider audience. But this slow pace failed to apply to Hapgood because the Piri Reis map was already regarded as the happy hunting ground of cranks. In 1960, six years before Hapgood published his book, a book called *The Morning of the Magicians*, by Louis Pauwels and Jacques Bergier, became a worldwide bestseller.

This argued that the Piri Reis map showed such detailed knowledge of the coast of South America that it could only have been observed from the air by a spaceship. So Hapgood already had a hostile academic audience prepared to dismiss his findings as fantasy.

In 1967, the year after the publication of *Maps of the Ancient Sea Kings*, Hapgood was mentioned with approval in a book called *Memories of the Future*, written by a Swiss hotelier named Erich von Daniken. Translated as *Chariots of the Gods*, it went on to sell more copies than the Bible. Daniken argued that all the Earth's greatest monuments, from the pyramids to the statues of Easter Island, were built by visitors from outer space.

The book was full of inaccuracies. Daniken had, for example, multiplied the weight of the Great Pyramid by five and then had argued that the Nazca lines in Peru were built as runways for spaceships (when anyone can see that they are merely scratched on the surface of the desert). And Daniken praised Hapgood for asserting that the Piri Reis map must have been based on an aerial photograph taken by these space visitors—which Hapgood certainly hadn't.

With that, his last chance of being taken seriously evaporated. Hapgood must have felt bemused. He had written two of the most important books of the midcentury, and they had both been dismissed. *Earth's*

Shifting Crust had run into trouble because his fellow academics objected that Hapgood was not a geologist and said that he had no right to venture outside his field. But *Maps of the Ancient Sea Kings* was his field, the history of science. It should have made him world famous. Instead it was ignored or derided.

After a period of discouragement, during which he retired from Keene State, Hapgood again took up the problem of the whereabouts of Atlantis. On the Piri Reis map, he had noted an island in the mid-Atlantic, opposite the coast of Venezuela. It has now vanished, but since it appears on two other ancient maps, it cannot have been a mistake. Nowadays all that remains in that location are two tiny islands balanced on the mid-Atlantic ridge. They are known as the islands of St. Peter and St. Paul, and they are obviously the tips of submerged mountains. These, Hapgood was convinced, were all that remained of Atlantis.

Hapgood continued to hope that someone would back his hunch and go look. He even approached President Kennedy in 1963, hoping the president would send a naval craft to explore the spot. Kennedy agreed to see him—Hapgood had once worked for the Secret Service—but Kennedy was assassinated in Dallas not long before the appointment was due. And when Hapgood's attempts to interest Walt Disney and Nelson Rockefeller also came to nothing, he gave up.

This explains why Hapgood never commented on Flem-Ath's theory that Atlantis might have been Antarctica: because he was convinced that he had already pinpointed the site of Atlantis.

Hapgood died in 1989, after being hit by a car. But by then others had taken up the quest where he had left off. One of these was a maverick Egyptologist named John Anthony West, who became convinced that the Sphinx had been eroded by rainfall rather than by wind-blown sand. He persuaded an academic geologist, Robert Schoch, to go with him to Egypt to examine the matter more closely and was delighted when Schoch agreed that the Sphinx was water-weathered. Their conclusion was announced at a conference of the Geological Society of America in 1993, where they convinced many other geologists of their findings, which suggested that the Sphinx was built in 7000 BC, not 2500, as is usually accepted. (This date, of course, is the same as that suggested by Hapgood for his worldwide maritime civilization.)

By this time, I had also become fascinated by the controversy, my interest sparked by a request by film producer Dino de Laurentiis to write a film script about Atlantis. As a result, I met John Anthony West in New York and learned that two other writers were working on the same subject. One was Canadian librarian Rand Flem-Ath (this was my first introduction to him), who had written an as yet unpublished book, *When the Sky Fell*, coauthored with his wife, Rose, arguing that Atlantis was Antarctica. The other was Graham Hancock, who was writing a book called *Fingerprints of the Gods*, whose thesis was that civilization is many thousands of years older than historians believe.

I contacted them both, and when Flem-Ath told me that he could not find a publisher for his *When the Sky Fell*, I offered to read it and write a preface for it. Perhaps this did the trick, as the book was soon thereafter accepted for publication.

Graham Hancock also sent me a warm reply, followed by the typescript of the original version of his book. My first reaction was to wonder whether Graham had left me anything to write about, but I soon noted important points that he had left uncovered, such as ancient India, and I returned to planning my own book, which I was then calling *Before the Sphinx*.

Graham's *Fingerprints of the Gods* appeared in the spring of 1995 and became an instant bestseller, making him a millionaire. The Flem-Aths' book, which had appeared a few months earlier, was also warmly received, although it had nothing like the same impact. My own book, the title of which had been changed to *From Atlantis to the Sphinx*, came out in May 1996 and sold out its first printing before publication.

One result was that in September 1996, I was invited to a symposium on ancient knowledge at the University of Delaware. Hancock, West, and Schoch were also there. So was Robert Bauval, a Belgian engineer, whose remarkable book *The Orion Mystery* had thrown a completely new light on the Atlantis problem. In the Cairo Museum, Bauval had seen an aerial photograph of the pyramids of Giza and had idly

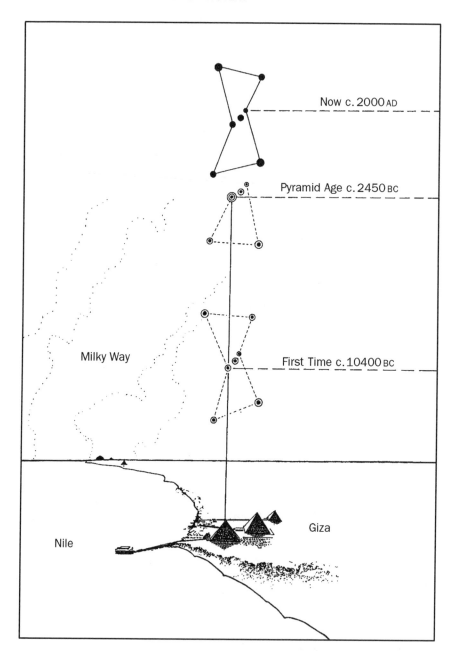

The Giza pyramids and the constellation of Orion.

noted their oddly unsymmetrical arrangement on the ground. The two main pyramids—Cheops and Chefren—were arranged, so to speak, in a line. But the smallest pyramid, Men-kau-ra, had slipped well out of the line. That seemed odd for builders as obsessed with symmetry as the Egyptians were.

Some time later, camping in the desert, Bauval noticed that the three stars of the belt of Orion have precisely the same unsymmetrical structure, with the third, and smallest star, out of line. And since he knew that the ancient Egyptians had regarded earth as heaven's mirror, he wondered if the Giza pyramids were built as a reflection of Orion's Belt.

In our own time, this reflection is not exact. Due to a phenomenon called "precession of the equinoxes," it is as if someone has twisted the mirror slightly askew.

Bauval consulted his computer and discovered that the last occasion when the stars and pyramids "reflected" each other was about 10,500 BC. But why should the ancient Egyptians have wanted to memorialize that particular date?

Then it struck him—Atlantis! He recalled the legend that ancient Egypt was settled by Atlantis survivors. That surely had to be the answer to the Orion mystery. Rand Flem-Ath and his wife, Rose, were also present at the Delaware Symposium; Flem-Ath was about to deliver his first public lecture.

This was our first face-to-face meeting and I took to him immediately. He was a bullet-headed, bearded man who gave an impression of strength and determination, yet made me feel oddly protective—perhaps because he reminded me of my younger brother, Barry. Rose, who was writing a novel, was a charming and intelligent girl, and I could see they formed an ideal partnership.

That weekend I was approached by a producer of TV programs named Roell Oostra, who wanted to know if I would act as the presenter of a program called *The Flood*. This would maintain that the "great flood" recorded in so much ancient literature was the catastrophe that destroyed Atlantis. If I accepted, I would have to travel to Mexico, Egypt, and South America. Being a typical Cancer, I hate travel, but my wife, Joy, loves it, so I agreed to go if I could take her. Roell agreed, provided I paid her fares myself.

The first leg of the journey, to the "tar pit of La Brea" in Los Angeles and then to the Library of Congress in Washington, would only take a weekend, so I went alone. And, to my delight, I met Flem-Ath again—at the Library of Congress—and was confirmed in my view that he was one of the nicest people I had ever met. As I finally said good-bye to him on my way to the airport I felt a twinge of sadness at the thought that I might never see him again, given that I lived in England and he in Canada.

The program took six months to make and was broadcast in the spring of 1998. I wondered if Flem-Ath had seen it and e-mailed to ask him. When he replied that he hadn't, I sent him a copy. It was a few weeks later that I then received the letter from him asking me if I would be willing to collaborate on his book about Atlantis (which would eventually be called *The Atlantis Blueprint*). His letter was accompanied by a magazine article he had published about his theory.

The theory, quite simply, was that before the great Atlantis catastrophe, ancient scientists had become aware, from volcanic eruptions, that the earth's crust was beginning to split and drift. Aware that this had happened before, they constructed "markers" at various points along the lines of strain so they would be able to anticipate disaster. These markers were laid out symmetrically all over the earth's surface (for the Atlanteans had a worldwide civilization).

After the catastrophe (which Flem-Ath, like Plato, dated to 9600 BC), later civilizations discovered the markers and assumed they had been placed there by gods or superhuman beings. So they treated them as sacred sites and built temples on them, which is why sacred sites are placed so symmetrically all over the world.

This latter element was the essence of Flem-Ath's theory. He concluded that sacred sites have been built at certain definite latitudes and longitudes, and often in a grid pattern. The patterns are evidence that the earth was once covered by a great pre-Atlantean civilization.

The latitudes and longitudes are in round figures, like 50, 40, 25, 10, and so on. Our modern measurements disguise this, for they might give the longitude of a sacred site as 127.153. But all we have to do is to measure from the Great Pyramid, which Flem-Ath believed the ancients used as their line of 0 degrees longitude, and we immediately see that other sacred sites—say Delphi or Teotihuacán—fall into neat, round figures.

I was totally convinced and agreed to collaborate with Flem-Ath. Our first task was to find a publisher and get the book commissioned. I approached Bill Hamilton, who was Graham Hancock's agent, and he suggested that we should do a series of "presentations." Flem-Ath and I would go to various publishers, and give short lectures, accompanied by slides, presenting the Blueprint Theory. Then we would accept the offer of the highest bidder.

The presentations would involve having Flem-Ath come to the UK, which he did. After a few days in my home in Cornwall, during which we rehearsed our act, we went to London and did our presentations to half a dozen publishers. The offers were larger than we had anticipated, and we were both well satisfied. Then we went to New York and did it all over again. Once more, the offers were higher than we expected. So we signed contracts, and a collaboration agreement, and began writing the book in December 1998. The delivery date was January 2000. We had a vast amount of material and I felt that all we had to do was to arrange it in an orderly fashion.

There was still, of course, one major problem: Hapgood's letter to Flem-Ath asserting that he was convinced that civilization was more than one hundred thousand years old. I felt that unless we could prove Hapgood's point, the theoretical arch we were constructing would lack a keystone. But I didn't let this worry me too much; we had almost a year in which to solve this problem.

Despite the fact that Flem-Ath had already contacted Hapgood's friends and relatives in his own quest to solve the mystery, I decided to try as well. These individuals included Hapgood's cousin Beth and his friends Elwood and Daria Babbitt. None of them were able to help me track down the missing notes that might explain the claim of a hundred-thousand-year-old civilization. The notes were obviously essential, for without them, the book would remain a kind of unfinished detective story. But as the weeks turned into months without result, I felt my optimism begin to fade.

Nevertheless, I worked on steadily. I made interesting discoveries along the way, such as the amazing story of the "Nineveh number," which internal evidence shows to have been discovered about sixty-six thousand years ago.

Then, suddenly, my luck changed. It was February 28, 1999.

The previous day I had received an e-mail from a friend of Hapgood's, telling me he had mislaid the material I had sent him; so I sent it again. That morning, a Sunday, he had written to thank me and had mentioned, as a postscript, that it might be worth contacting a retired academic who lived in New Hampshire, and who also had known Hapgood. Accordingly, when I had finished my day's work, chapter 3 of *Blueprint*, and was preparing to take my dogs for a walk, I gave him a ring.

The phone was answered by a man with a pleasant New England voice. I explained about Hapgood's last letter to Flem-Ath and said that I was trying to find out how Hapgood had become convinced that civilization was more than a hundred thousand years old.

The man on the other end of the line said, "Oh, sure, that was me."

The admission was so casual that it took a moment to sink in. "What was you?"

"I gave Charlie Hapgood the information that persuaded him that civilization was a hundred thousand years old."

My heart skipped a beat.

"And what did you say?"

"Well, to begin with, I told him that Neanderthal man had calculated the equivalent of Thom's megalithic yard, and Cro-Magnon inherited it from him."

"And what made you think so?'

"Lots of things. To begin with, the La Quina disc, the disque en calcaire."

The astronomer Alexander Thom had claimed that megaliths all over the world were built using the same basic measurement, the megalithic yard. What amazed me was this man's assertion that Neanderthal man had used this same basic measurement, too (as evidenced by the fact that these measurements were shown to date back to the La Quina disc, carved by a Neanderthal man a hundred thousand years ago).

I stayed on the phone for over two hours that afternoon, and when I hung up, I felt slightly stunned. My new acquaintance was bewildering erudite and supported his argument about the antiquity of civilization, which he claimed was proved by its system of measurement, with linguistic evidence in Greek, Semitic, Sumerian, and Sanskrit, which he went on to quote.

His theory and its corollaries were incredibly complex, involving music, planetary distances, archaeology, and atomic numbers. His published articles, which he promised to send me, ranged from the Great Pyramid, Ice Age art, and the archaeology of Chaco Canyon to alchemical symbolism.

Although much of what he said was above my head, much of it made sense, for an old friend of mine, the psychologist Stan Gooch, had written a book called *Cities of Dreams*. This book had argued that Neanderthal man was a highly intelligent creature who had created his own civilization. It had left me in no doubt that Neanderthal was far more intelligent than we have given him credit for, while the claim that ancient measurements proved the existence of some great ur-civilization had been argued in a remarkable book called *Historical Metrology* by A. E. Berriman in 1953.

So there was little doubt in my mind that I had solved the problem of Hapgood's hundred-thousand-year-old civilization. I now knew who had given Hapgood the evidence that had convinced him—the disque en calcaire and the ancient measurements—and that when Hapgood had looked at this evidence, he had seen as clearly as I had that the answer had to lie in Neanderthal man.

I was understandably quite keen to include in *The Atlantis Blueprint* the insightful information that I had gleaned from this extremely knowledgeable retired New Hampshire academic. However, Flem-Ath had a different opinion, and because this was an issue that, ultimately, he and I were unable to resolve, this information did not make it into the pages of that book.

The story could have ended there, but Hapgood's ideas were, and still are, too intriguing and potentially significant not to warrant further examination. Indeed, in the six years that have elapsed since publication of *The Atlantis Blueprint*, even more evidence of the high level of intelligence of Neanderthal man has arisen, strengthening Hapgood's supposition and the arguments that Stan Gooch presented in *Cities of Dreams*.

In what follows I shall tell the story of my ten-year investigation into the question of the age of civilization.

TWO

A TRIP DOWN THE NILE

In November 1998, Joy and I set out on a visit to Egypt. We were going to sail down the Nile with a group of writers who were interested in ancient civilizations. Our fellow travelers included John West, Robert Bauval, Robert Temple, Michael Baigent, Ralph Ellis, and Yuri Stoyanov, an expert on the ancient religion of Dualism. It was my intention to gather material for *The Atlantis Blueprint*, which I was due to start writing soon after our return.

We flew to Cairo and took a taxi to our hotel, the Mena House, located within half a mile of the Sphinx. The following morning, we were up at half past five, to go and watch the sun rise behind the pyramids.

Looked at in a photograph, the pyramids do not seem at all mysterious. They are basically huge piles of stones. But when you stand directly in front of the Great Pyramid, you see the problem. It would not be difficult to lay the first, second, even third course of granite blocks weighing between two and six tons each; this task could be done by sheer manpower.

But you still have another two hundred courses to go. How do you get the blocks up to, say, tier 150? Build a sloping ramp and drag them up? But to get them to that height, you would need as much material in the ramp as in the pyramid itself. Moreover, to avoid collapse it would have to be of solid stone.

Could portable lifting gear be used to raise the stones a block at a time, as Herodotus said the builders did? Using this method, it would take a day to raise and position just one block, and even at twenty-five blocks a day, the pyramid would take 274 years to complete. (Remember, it contains 2,300,000 blocks.) Herodotus said it only took 20 years to build, an obvious impossibility, unless the builders had some secret that we have forgotten.

Hire a giant crane? We have none in the modern world that could do the job.

How about wind power? An American scholar, Dr. Maureen Clemmons, has conducted a series of extraordinary experiments to try to show that wind power could have been utilized in the construction of the pyramids. In 2004, Dr. Clemmons demonstrated that stones and obelisks weighing many tons apiece could be raised into the air, using giant kites, and then guided into position from wooden scaffolding. But she admits that she has no idea of how certain blocks weighing 80 tons were maneuvered into position in the heart of the Great Pyramid. Any tourist who has seen these blocks will agree that the problem of raising them simply defies imagination.

In the 1980s, a remarkable scholar named Joseph Jochmans, who wrote under the name "Jalandris," produced a bold and wide-ranging book about the challenge. In the book, he addressed the "impossible engineering feats—stone blocks that were placed into positions where no crane, lever or sheer human strength alone could have put them."

"In 1978," Jochmans wrote, "the Nippon Corporation of Japan received permission from the government of Egypt to construct a 'mini-pyramid,' which was to be located just to the southeast of the Third Pyramid at Giza. The aim of the project was not for size, but technique: the Japanese endeavored to complete the pyramid building task by utilizing the same methods supposedly employed by the ancient Egyptians—or at least the methods claimed they employed by modern archaeologists.

"The Japanese objective was to quarry the stone out of nearby hills, float them by raft across the Nile, drag them to the building site by the 'heave-ho' method of large numbers of men pulling on the stones with ropes, and finally lifting and placing the stones into the pyramid structure with simple levers.

"But no sooner had work begun on the pyramid, when the planners found themselves faced with insurmountable problems. First, the rock for the stones resisted most of the hand tools that tried to cut them, so the workmen had to resort to air jackhammers. Then the quarried blocks could not be safely floated on the Nile River by wooden raft, so finally they were ferried across by steamboat. Once ashore, the stones were tackled by large teams of Arab workmen hired by the Japanese—but the stones would not budge, sinking instead into the river silt and desert sands. Again, modern technology had to be called upon, and heavy trucks were strained to their limits in transporting the stones to the pyramid site.

"As a last straw, neither could the great number of workmen lift the large weights using ropes, levers or pulleys, and large power cranes and helicopters had to come to the rescue. Even then—employing the most powerful lifting equipment known to today's technology—the work of placing the stones into the pyramid was slow and tedious, with the blocks left greatly out of alignment, and many broken and battered by the difficult and clumsy handling.

"At this point, the Egyptian government intervened, and fearing that the unauthorized heavy equipment was destroying the desert environment, ordered what little of the Japanese pyramid had been built to be torn down and removed."[1]

The Sphinx is perhaps slightly less problematic. But only slightly.

Unlike most visitors, we were allowed inside the Sphinx enclosure. Before the sun rose, it was uncomfortably cold; then, as the light flooded across the desert landscape, intolerably hot. I was particularly anxious to get a close look at the Sphinx enclosure, because although this was my second visit, I had been made to keep my distance with the other tourists on the first. Now I was able to see the weather erosion that had convinced John West that it was thousands of years older than it was supposed to be.

West was not the first to say so. Before that, an eccentric French alchemist named René Schwaller de Lubicz had suggested the same idea.

Schwaller had spent much of his life trying to understand how the red and blue glass of Chartres Cathedral had been stained without pigment. He became obsessed by the art of medieval craftsman, and by the question of where those artisans acquired their knowledge. In the mid-1930s, Schwaller went to Egypt with his wife Isha. There they saw the tomb of Rameses VI, with a wall decoration showing the pharaoh as the hypotenuse of a right angle triangle whose sides are three, four and five. This proved that the ancient Egyptians knew the Pythagoras theorem nearly a thousand years before Pythagoras. Suddenly, Schwaller was convinced that the knowledge of the medieval craftsman dated back to ancient Egypt.

As soon as Schwaller saw the Sphinx and its enclosure, he recognized that its erosion was due to water, not wind-blown sand. If a rock surface is "sand blasted," it will erode in layers, with the harder rock projecting and the softer rock worn away. If it is "rain blasted," it is again worn into layers, but also into vertical fissures where the water has run down. And the walls of the Sphinx enclosure show both kinds of weathering, vertical as well as horizontal.

This was quite clear to us as we stood in front of the wall. The rock was rounded into curves like a baby's bottom. But Egypt has very little rain. Schwaller—and West—reasoned that the last time significant rain fell in the region was at the end of the last ice age, about 10,000 BC. This factor seemed to support the view that the Sphinx was carved by survivors from Atlantis.

The Sphinx, which gazes east, originally had two temples in front of it, one to the right and one to the left. Only the right hand one, the so-called Sphinx temple, is now complete. Its 200-ton limestone blocks were actually sliced straight out of the ground on either side of the Sphinx, and we still have no idea of how they were raised into position. Geologists speculate that the Sphinx was originally a great lump of hard rock, projecting out of the limestone, and that at some remote time, this rock was carved into the semblance of a head, possibly a lion (which would make sense if it was carved in the age of Leo, 10,000 BC).

Then someone decided to add a lion's body, so a deep trench was cut into the limestone, creating blocks. This created a wall around two sides of the Sphinx. At some point, a later king decided to put his own face in place of the lion's, but this involved making the head smaller. It still looks absurdly small compared to its vast body.

Since we know the Sphinx was buried up to its neck in sand when early explorers came to Egypt, we can assume that it has been protected by a shroud of sand for thousands of years. According to a stele found between the Sphinx's paws, the pharaoh Thutmose IV had a dream in about 1425 BC in which he was asked by the sun god to clear away the sand.

The Sphinx is 240 feet long and 60 feet high. We walked to its rear end, which has been repaired with great stone blocks. This repair, apparently, was done by the pharaoh Chefren, son of Cheops (Khufu), who built the Great Pyramid. But since Chefren lived around 2500 BC, it seems a little odd that he was already having to repair a monument that, according to archaeologists, was built by his father about fifty years earlier. Surely, from the rate at which it weathered, the Sphinx must have been at least centuries old at the time of Cheops and Chefren?

By half past nine in the morning, it was getting atrociously hot, and we were longing for a long, cool drink, so we sneaked off back to the hotel, along with John West, who was also heading there for breakfast. Over the meal, John reminded us how he had been able to prove that the face of the Sphinx is not that of the pharaoh Chefren, as orthodox archaeologists insist. West's discovery arose from a small statue found buried in the Sphinx temple, which the archaeologists declared to be that of Chefren. John thought the Sphinx's face looked nothing like Chefren, and he asked a police forensic artist named Frank Domingo to come from New York and take a look.

After studying the two faces, Domingo declared that he found no resemblance between them. He even did a scale drawing of the head of Chefren, and another of the battered face of the Sphinx (which looks as if it had been used for cannon practice at some time in its history). Domingo showed that the chin of the Sphinx is far more prominent than Chefren's, and that a line drawn from the Sphinx's ear to the corner of its mouth sloped at an angle of 32 degrees, while a line from Chefren's ear to his mouth only sloped at 14 degrees. That discrepancy was conclusive.

After breakfast, we all went to the Cairo Museum and looked at the statue of Chefren that had been found in the Sphinx temple. Joy and I agreed it looked nothing like the Sphinx. In the entrance hall of the museum, we also saw the aerial photograph of the pyramids that had so impressed Robert Bauval and had formed the basis of his theory that the Giza pyramids were built as a reflection of Orion's Belt. Bauval pointed out that the Nile stands in exactly the same relationship to the pyramids as the broad band of the Milky Way stands to the stars of Orion's Belt. The "mirroring" effect is exact.

The following morning we took a plane to Aswan, five hundred miles down the Nile, where the river emerges from Ethiopia. I was anxious to see the ancient town because it had played an important part in the Hapgood theory. It had originally been called Syene and was where a genius named Eratosthenes established the size of the earth.

Eratosthenes happened to know that the sun was reflected in the depths of a deep well in Syene at midday on Midsummer's Day. That fact meant, of course, that the sun was precisely overhead, so that towers did not cast a shadow. But in Alexandria, five hundred miles south, the towers did cast shadows. All Eratosthenes had to do was measure the length of the shadow of a tower in Alexandria at precisely midday on June 21. This told him the angle of the sun's rays at Alexandria at the same moment when they were also falling vertically on Syene. This angle was 7 degrees. If 7 degrees represents 500 miles of the earth's curved surface, it is easy to see that 360 degrees amounts to 24,000 miles—a remarkably accurate assessment for 240 BC.

Due to a slight miscalculation of distance, Eratosthenes increased the size of the earth by 4 degrees. Hapgood discovered that if he allowed for this miscalculation, the Piri Reis map became even more accurate.

Since the earth is a sphere but a map is flat, today mapmakers use Mercator's "projection," based on division into latitude and longitude. The ancient mapmakers used a method that was more complicated but just as effective. They chose a center, drew a circle round it, then subdivided it into sixteen slices, like a cake. Then they drew a series of squares around the circumference of the cake, extending outward.

The original center of the Piri Reis map was in Egypt, but was way off the map. Alexandria seemed to be the obvious place for the center. But more calculation showed it had to be further south.

In fact, it proved to be Syene.

This discovery, Hapgood realized, had some interesting implications. When the mapmakers of Alexandria set out to make a new map, it is unlikely that they actually sailed to the various places they were mapping. They probably used older maps. And without the 4-degree error, these old maps must have been remarkably accurate, which suggests that the pre-Alexandria mapmakers possessed a more accurate and advanced mapmaking science than the Greeks had.

In fact, interesting evidence exists proving that this was so. Toward the end of the second century BC, the Greek grammarian Agatharchides of Cnidus, who was a tutor to one of the Ptolemy kings of Egypt was told that, according to ancient tradition, the base of each side of the Great Pyramid was precisely one-eighth of a minute of a degree of the earth's circumference. (A minute is a sixtieth of a degree.) The pyramid's base is just over 230 meters.

Now if we test that statement by multiplying 230 by 8, to get it into minutes, then by 60, to get it into degrees, than by 360, to get the size of the earth, the result is just under four hundred thousand kilometers, or just under twenty five thousand miles, an amazingly accurate estimate of the length of the equator. So it seems that the architect of the pyramids already knew the size of the earth in 2500 BC.

Indeed, this is proved by the Great Pyramid itself. Not only is its base in exact proportion to the equator, but also its height is in the same exact proportion to the "height" of the earth, from its center to the North Pole. The Egyptians would probably have preferred to construct a huge geodesic dome to represent the earth, but that kind of construction would have involved losing some of the fascinating geometry of a pyramid, so they did the next best thing.

When Napoleon invaded Egypt in 1798, one of the learned men he took along with him, Edmé-François Jomard, studied the Great Pyramid carefully and made some important discoveries: the four sides of the pyramid point to the four points of the compass—north, south, east, and west—with incredible accuracy. The pyramid is ten miles from Cairo, which is at the base of the Nile Delta, so called because it is a triangle of streams running into the sea, and if diagonals are drawn from the pyramid, they neatly enclose the delta. Moreover, a line drawn from exactly halfway along the north face slices the delta into two exact halves. All of these facts indicate that the ancient Egyptians had some extremely precise method of measuring long distances and did not do it by rough guesswork.

The French meter is supposed to be precisely one ten-millionth of the distance from equator to pole. Jomard's study of the pyramid convinced him that the Egyptians had also used a measure based on the earth's size, in this case, two hundred and sixteen thousandths of the equator. (216,000 is sixty cubed.)

This information is astonishing. How could a fairly primitive agricultural civilization know the size of the earth? What is equally hard to understand is why this knowledge had to be rediscovered by Eratosthenes more than two thousand years later, unless we recall that until Columbus sailed to America, the general belief was that the earth was flat. Knowledge can be lost very easily, as Hapgood emphasized at the end of his book, *Maps of the Ancient Sea Kings*.

Where did the Egyptians learn all this knowledge of distances and measurements? We could understand if they were great seafarers, like the Vikings, but they weren't. They were inclined to stick to their own land and their own sea. So they can only have learned it from some earlier civilization. Hapgood concluded that their "evident knowledge of longitude implies a people unknown to us, a nation of seafarers, with instruments for finding longitude undreamed of by the Greeks."[2]

Joy and I didn't get a chance to see the famous well of Eratosthenes, for the simple reason that no one knows where it is. It probably vanished centuries ago. Instead, we went on board our boat, the Sun Queen, and had an excellent dinner.

As we sailed down the Nile, we were amazed by the richness and greenery of the landscape between the river and the desert. Our destination was the temple at Edfu, one of the oldest and best-preserved in Egypt, and also one of the most impressive (although not on the same scale as Karnak). What makes it so important is a picture narrative of the battle between Horus and Set, which is inscribed on the outer walls, and some texts, known as the Building Texts, that are associated with it, which tell us about the building of the temple and offer us a glimpse into a remote period in history.

According to the Egyptians, the world was destroyed by a flood at some time in the distant past, which they call zep tepi, the "first time." The date given for this first time seems to be about 10,000 BC, and so could easily be the flood that was caused by the destruction of Atlantis. The original mythical temple dated from this remote time and only later was given physical form in stone and brick. Edfu is one of the most sacred sites in Egypt.

On the matter of sacred sites, I was in basic disagreement with Flem-Ath. He thought they were simply ancient "markers" laid down to indicate earthquake zones. My own investigation of ancient sites—like Stonehenge and Carnac—had instead convinced me that they were chosen as sacred because they contain whirlpools of some earth force that can literally produce magical effects. As vice-president of the Ghost Club Society, I have noted again and again how often hauntings are associated with whirlpools of earth force, and when writing a book on UFOs, I have noted how frequently UFOs were seen in such areas. When approaching the megaliths at Stonehenge with a dowsing rod, I have actually felt this force. It is like walking into a powerful magnetic field.

In certain places the force can produce an unpleasant effect, making one feel disoriented, as if suffering from a slight fever. I once felt this at Carnac, in Britanny, and noticed that it became almost tangible in a small field with many standing stones, where my dowsing rod twisted in my hands as if it were alive.

Our guide at Edfu was Emil Shaker, an authority on ancient Egypt. He was convinced that sound played an important part in the mystery of the temples. In 1998, scientists at Southampton University discovered that the megaliths at Stonehenge have acoustic properties and could have acted as gigantic amplifiers for drums during festivals, their flat surfaces accumulating and reflecting sound over a wide area. And we discovered that temples had the same effect, functioning almost like an echo chamber. We stood in a doorway in a temple courtyard and made a deep humming sound, and it was amplified by the stone.

Emil pointed out hieroglyphics on the wall close to the "sanctuary." Those, he said, specified the number of times the temple ritual had to be performed. In this case it was three. "The ritual must be chanted three times, or it will not work," he said. The ritual involved chanting a hymn to the sun, and presenting the god with offerings.

I asked, "But what does the ritual actually do?"

"It activates the temple," Emil said.

"You mean like switching on a light?" I said, giving voice to the first image that came into my head.

Emil nodded. "Exactly like switching on a light."

So a ritual that involved chanting could somehow "switch on" the temple. It seemed almost like the sequence of actions we have to perform to send an e-mail.

The "sanctuary," which occupied the place where a visitor would expect an altar, was a kind of enormous box of gray granite, turned on its side. I started to walk toward the back, facing the temple wall, but found this narrow passage blocked by someone who was obviously meditating, with his forehead against the stone of the sanctuary. I recognized our fellow traveler Michael Baigent, who has collaborated on a number of books on the Templars and Rennes-le-Château.

I backed away quietly and joined John West, who took us to look at the Building Texts, which refer back to the "first time," when the Seven Sages are believed to have designed the temple and the pyramids. Then we strolled out to the courtyard at the back (actually the front) and enjoyed the sunshine. A brisk wind was blowing up the river.

Summoned to the bus, we were taken back to the Sun Queen for lunch. An hour later, Robert Bauval came to tell me that Michael had not returned with the rest of us. Since Michael was due to lecture at 3:30, Robert wondered if I would step in and give Michael's lecture instead, which I did. We were all worried about Michael, for we were in "bandit country," and since visiting Aswan, we had been escorted by the military, in case of terrorist attack. Only a short time ago, German tourists had been machine-gunned at the temple of Hatshepsut, in the Valley of the Queens.

About two hours later, Michael turned up in a taxi. I asked him what had happened.

"I don't know. I was meditating for a few minutes. Then I found you'd all gone."

But I knew that it wasn't just a few minutes since I had seen him meditating for at least twenty. When I told him so, he was surprised.

"It only seemed a few minutes."

What happened to Michael puzzled me for a long time. Obviously, he had tuned in to the vibrations of Edfu, and time had stood still. But was that the whole truth, a purely mechanical process, like switching on a light? I had a strong feeling that there was more to it than that. But it was not until six years later, when I was writing this book, that I stumbled on what must surely be the true solution. (See chapter 8.)

My suspicion that the secret of the temples lay in sound vibration was supported by an American engineer named Chris Dunn, who was convinced that the Great Pyramid was a kind of gigantic sounding-box. Dunn had bribed the guard to allow him to remain in the King's Chamber when everyone else had left and had struck the sarcophagus with his fist and recorded its frequency, then hummed the note. When he played back the tape later he found that his humming had caused sympathetic vibrations in the chamber. When he went outside, leaving the tape recorder running, and called for the guard to turn off the lights, his shout was recorded just as loudly as if he were still in the chamber, proof that the chamber had unusual acoustic properties.

Another friend, David Elkington, stumbled on something equally fascinating. In his book *In the Name of the Gods*, he describes how in Giza he met a sound engineer named John Reid, to whom he explained his theory that the Pyramid was somehow "alive," and responded to sound. Reid verified this observation with a curious experiment. He made a temporary repair of the broken corner of the sarcophagus with an aluminium corner, then stretched a plastic membrane over the top of the sarcophagus, and sprinkled sand on it. A small loudspeaker was connected to a sine-wave oscillator, which was then switched on. The sand quickly began to arrange itself into patterns, like sand on a drum.

To Reid's amazement, the sand began to form a whole series of Egyptian religious symbols: the Pharaoh's ritual headdress, the Ankh, and the sacred eye of Horus, bringing an entirely new meaning to the Masonic phrase, "the eye in the pyramid." Photographs of these patterns are printed in Elkington's book, and they leave no doubt that our guide Emil Shaker was right: the secret of ancient Egypt is connected with sound patterns. Elkington describes the sound-rituals of the temples and pyramids as "an acoustic Eucharist."[3]

In the Valley of the Kings the following day we went into the splendid tomb of Rameses VI. I was fascinated when Emil pointed out a design that was unmistakably that of a sperm cell on the wall of the long descending corridor. But how could the ancient Egyptians have known about sperm? Had they invented the microscope? It was not until the following year, when I was reading Jeremy Narby's book *The Serpent Power* that I came upon a plausible solution, which I shall describe later.

My pleasure in the temples was undermined by the first rumbles of some stomach bug that caused vomiting and diarrhea. (If I had been superstitiously inclined I might have blamed it on a visit to the tomb of Tutankhamen.) It also removed most of the pleasure from the Valley of the Queens, although nothing could diminish the splendor of the temple of Hatshepsut—even the guards with machine guns.

The bug was still around the following morning, and a prebreakfast visit to the Karnak temple—although, as usual, I was overawed by those vast, elaborate columns—proved to be a little too early even for me, who normally rise at 5:30.

It certainly spoilt a visit to the temple at Dendera—which was a pity, since I had wanted to see this for many years, ever since I had written about it in a book called *Starseekers*. The ceiling contains a famous zodiac, which, as Schwaller de Lubicz pointed out, proves that the Egyptians knew all about the precession of the equinoxes.

Precession is due to a slight wobble on the earth's axis, reminiscent of a spinning top. Imagine the axis as a giant pencil that sticks through the earth from pole to pole, and then imagine that the ends of the pencil are searchlights that penetrate into space. If you think of the heavens as a flat ceiling, the searchlight would describe a circle on it. It takes 25,776 years to complete this circle, so it is hard to imagine how the ancients knew about this snail-paced phenomenon, let alone become so obsessed by it.

Precession's practical effect is to make the constellations appear to move backwards. We all know how the year progresses from Aries through Taurus, Gemini, and Cancer until it reaches Capricorn, Aquarius, and Pisces. But in the stars, every spring starts a little earlier. If precession was thousands of time faster, the spring would rise in Pisces one year, Aquarius the next, Capricorn the next, and so on, moving backwards, west instead of east.

The ancients noted this odd backward movement of the heavenly clock and attributed tremendous importance to it. It seemed to them a glimpse into the mind of the gods, and they pondered what it meant. Every civilization knew about it: Eskimos, Icelanders, Norsemen, Finns, Hawaiians, Japanese, Persians, Romans, Greeks, Hindus. It almost seems as if our ancestors did nothing but gaze at the night sky.

At Dendera, there are, in essence, two zodiacs carved one on top of the other. One has its east-west axis passing through Pisces, showing it was constructed at the beginning of the Age of Pisces, about 2,100 years ago. But two hieroglyphs on the edge of the zodiac suggest a second axis that passes through the beginning of the Age of Taurus, more than 4,000 years earlier. So the builders of Dendera knew Taurus would give way to Ares and then Pisces. In other words, they knew about precession.

So it looks as if the Egyptians not only knew the precise size of the earth, down to the meter, but also knew about the past 26,000 years.

We made one more major stop before we flew back to Cairo, and it was the one I looked forward to most of all: a visit to the mysterious Oseirion, the "tomb of Osiris," which was built behind the temple of Osiris at Abydos. The temple was built by the pharaoh Seti I, father of Rameses II, who figures as the oppressor of the Israelites in the Bible.

The Oseirion is a small temple built of megalithic blocks, like the Sphinx temple of Giza, and the bareness and bleakness of the architecture makes it look completely unlike the temples of Karnak or Luxor, with their elaborate wall decorations. The reason I was so eager to see it was that I suspected that it had been built by Atlanteans, the same people who had carved the Sphinx and built the Sphinx temple.

It was found early in the twentieth century, as Flinders Petrie and his assistant Margaret Murray were clearing away deep sand behind the temple of Seti I. With thousands of tons of sand to remove, they finally left the job to Professor E. Naville, who in 1912 realized that this was quite unlike the architecture of the temple of Seti I. The megalithic style gave it a resemblance to a miniature Stonehenge with trilithons.

Naville's work was interrupted by the First World War, then a young archaeologist named Henri Frankfort took over and completed the operation. He found the name of Seti I written on the stone, not carved, and a broken potsherd inscribed: "Seti I is of service to Osiris." The potsherd seemed to confirm Frankfort's research; he decided that the Oseirion was built by Seti I as a temple to Osiris.

Margaret Murray pointed out that the pharaohs were fond of adding their names to monuments of the past, so the inscription by Seti proved nothing—any more than the statue of Chefren proved he had built the Sphinx temple. And this temple, with its vast blocks—one of them 25 feet long—was certainly quite unlike the temple of Seti I above it. But by then, Margaret Murray had begun to get herself a bad name in the academic establishment with her eccentric views—for example, that the medieval witches were really priestesses of a cult dedicated to the horned God Pan—and so no one paid much attention.

A far more straightforward scenario was possible: that the Oseirion was built long before the temple of Seti I, and that Seti had chosen that same spot to built his temple, hoping to curry favor with Osiris, whose servant he declared himself.

At all events, Naville had a real flash of intuition when he announced that the Oseirion could well be "the most ancient building in Egypt." It could indeed. There is something very mysterious about this building which, when we went to see it, looked more like a swimming pool, due to rising waters. Naville even speculated that it might be some primitive water works. But although that water was due to the rising water table, the deep trench around Oseirion's central platform was undoubtedly intended as a kind of moat. Behind the moat were seventeen man-sized cells, hinting at a monastery. Now, seven years later, both moat and platform are flooded.

The Oseirion was built on a man-made mound, reminding us of the Giza pyramids, and the presence of water seemed to hint at the primeval creation myth. Did priests sit in those cells, gazing on the still water and meditating on the "first times"?

I walked down the slope, to get as close to the water as I could, and was fascinated by its green depths. I stood there so long that Joy had to shout to say that the others had left, and the gatekeeper was about to lock the door to the temple. And as I hurried back into the temple, with its thirteenth-century carvings and inscriptions, I felt as though I was entering the modern world again.

The Oseirion is undoubtedly one of the most powerful places in the world. It is as well it is so inaccessible, for a stream of visitors would suck away its power, as tourists have sucked away the energy of the great menhirs of Carnac, so that only the smaller and more remote stones preserve their primitive force.

By evening we were back in Cairo and, twenty-four hours later, back at home in Cornwall.

But I have almost forgotten to mention one of the most important discoveries I made on that trip down the Nile—a staggering piece of evidence that appears to show that our ancestors knew about precession more than sixty thousand years ago.

In the cabin next to ours was a charming South African couple named Gurth and Marie Walton. After my lecture, they asked me if I knew of a book called *Our Cosmic Ancestors* by French space scientist, Maurice Chatelain.[4] When I said I didn't, they lent me their copy. Within a few hours, I knew I had come upon a discovery that seemed to support Hapgood's assertion that a sophisticated science existed a hundred thousand years ago.

In 1843, a Frenchman named Paul Emile Botta, who was consul at Mosul in Iraq (then Mesopotamia), began digging at a mound called Kuyundjik, near the upper Tigris, and came upon the library of the Assyrian king Assurbanipal (669–626 BC). Among the clay tablets, he discovered one containing a vast number: 195,955,200,000,000. The name of the ruined city in the mound was Nineveh.

At that time, even the concept of a million was rarely used in the west, so Botta was perplexed. What on earth could the ancient Assyrians want with a number so vast?

Using a computer, Chatelain discovered that this figure is not as arbitrary as it looks. It is 60 multiplied by 70 to the power of seven.

In his book, Chatelain recalled an obscure piece of information: the Sumerians, who invented writing, did their calculations in sixties rather than tens. (They invented sixty seconds to the minute and sixty minutes to the hour.) Suddenly, in a flash of inspiration, Chatelain wondered if this huge figure could be in seconds. He worked it out to be 2,268 million days, or somewhat over 6 million years.

The Sumerians had also been great astronomers, who had compiled tables of the motions of all the planets, including Uranus and Neptune. Did they, Chatelain wondered, know about the precession of the equinoxes? The time it takes for the earth to complete its precessional cycle is just under 26,000 years. He tried dividing this into the Nineveh number, and was delighted to find that it was exactly 240 precessional cycles—or "Big Years."

Now he found himself wondering if this giant number might be what astrologers and occultists used to refer to as "the great constant of the solar system," a "highest common factor" into which all other numbers—planetary orbits, and so on—will divide. He proceeded to calculate the cycles of the planets and their satellites in seconds and found that each would divide exactly into the Nineveh number.

This was staggering. Modern science assumes that these ancient astronomers were interested in the heavens for purely superstitious reasons. But if the Nineveh number was what Chatelain suspected, it proved that the Chaldean astronomers understood our solar system as well as Isaac Newton did.

To test this still further, Chatelain compared the period of the earth's rotation with the figure obtained from the Nineveh number. He was slightly puzzled to find a slight discrepancy in the sixth decimal place. Admittedly, this inconsistency was only a twelve-millionth of a day per year. But the Nineveh number had proved itself so accurate that he could not understand even such a tiny difference.

Then the answer dawned on Chatelain. We now know that the earth is slowing down very slowly. In twelve million years, a year will be shorter by a day.

For the Nineveh number to fit our earth's rotation with total accuracy, it is necessary to assume that it was calculated 64,800 years ago. But surely no intelligent beings existed that long ago?

Yet according to the Nineveh number, human beings were not only here but were as scientifically sophisticated as any that followed many millennia later.

If so, then who were they? We may take our pick. They may have been Neanderthals, who were still around then. Or they may have been our own kind, Cro-Magnons. Or perhaps they were Daniken's space visitors, which was Chatelain's view. It was why he titled his book *Our Cosmic Ancestors*, and why he begins:

"Most American space flights, from Mercury and Gemini to Apollo, were followed by unknown spacecraft that could have come from another civilization in outer space. . . . Every time the incident occurred, the astronauts informed Mission Control, who then ordered absolute silence."[5]

Chatelain mentions a Cro-Magnon skull, found near San Diego, that dated from between 50,000 and 65,000 years ago, and he cites two scientists who agreed that that its brain size indicates "the highest intelligence," and that the man "could have been capable . . . of observing and registering astronomical cycles."[6]

Chatelain has forgotten—or perhaps did not know—that the Neanderthals' brain-size was far greater than ours.

But another possibility must be taken into account, that ordinary human beings like you and me possess quite extraordinary brainpowers. One of my favorite examples concerns a six-year-old child named Benjamin Blyth, who in 1826 was out for a walk with his father when the child asked: "What time is it?"

"Seven fifty AM," said the father.

They walked on for five minutes. Then Benjamin said: "In that case, I must have been alive . . . ," and he gave the number in seconds, about 190 million. His father wrote it on his cuff, and when they got home, worked it out on paper. He said that he was 172,800 seconds off. "No," said Benjamin, "you've forgotten the two leap years."[7]

How can such things be possible? Mathematical agility is something that human beings have only developed after thousands of years of civilization. Yet apparently complex math can be done by people without any kind of intellectual sophistication. In fact, they often do it far better than the rest of us. Since even people who are mentally defective or unsophisticated can do these things (people known as idiot savants), it would seem to follow logically that humans must be possessed of two sorts of brain skills: the kind needed by a great philosopher, and the kind utilized by mathematical prodigies such as Benjamin Blyth, who might be regarded as a kind of supercomputer.

But that explanation doesn't work either. Numbers known as primes—numbers like five, seven, eleven—cannot be divided by any other number without leaving a remainder. No mathematical shortcut exists to discover whether some huge number is a prime or not—one simply has to keep on dividing every other number into it to find out. Even a computer has to do it the long way. Yet mathematical prodigies are often able to see at a glance whether a huge number is a prime or not. The psychiatrist Oliver Sacks described a pair of subnormal twins in a New York mental hospital who amused themselves by swapping twenty-four-figure primes. It is as if the mind of the twins could hover in the air, like a hawk, over the whole number field, and pounce on prime numbers as if they were rabbits.

According to architect Keith Critchlow in his book, *Time Stands Still* (whose title makes me think of Michael Baigent's experience at Edfu), this method is the one the Babylonians used to work out a right-angle triangle whose size ran to thousands of feet. It probably also explains the Nineveh number studied by Maurice Chatelain.

Critchlow is also deeply interested in ancient megaliths and stone circles, and in the work of Professor Alexander Thom. In 1933, Thom had moored his sailing yacht near the island of Lewis, in the Hebrides. When he went ashore at dusk to look at the megalithic stone circle of Callanish, he noticed that the circle's main north-south axis pointed directly at the Pole Star, but he knew that the Pole Star was not in the same position when the circle was built about five thousand years ago.

As Thom studied Callanish and other stone circles, he came to recognize that some of these circles were not circles, but were shaped like eggs, or like a letter D. Thom eventually recognized that the builders had created these irregular shapes with the use of Pythagorean triangles, which, when we recall the Great Pyramid, sounds like more than coincidence. He concluded that the men who had built them were highly intelligent or, as he called them, "prehistoric Einsteins."

Thom also noted that the same basic measure was used in all these circles: he called it "the Megalithic yard." It was 2.7272 English feet. (The basic measure was, in fact, half that, but Thom doubled it to make it closer to the yard.) A Megalithic foot proved to be equal to the Egyptian measure used in the Great Pyramid, known as the Ptolemaic foot. One commentator in the Thom tradition, B. L. Van de Waerden, said that there must be a pre-Babylonian source of geometry and algebra, from which Greece, India, and China all drew their knowledge.

Critchlow explained that a culture does not need to be highly complex and technological to be sophisticated. It does not need skyscrapers and great metal bridges. Highly civilized people can live very simply. Yet their knowledge can be as profound as that which created the Nineveh number.

Once more we face the question: how could our remote ancestors have been capable of working out a number that is fifteen digits long, and that, if Chatelain is correct, amounts to 2,268 million days expressed in seconds?

Our observations on calculating prodigies at least offer us a glimpse of an answer. Perhaps our ancestors could calculate such numbers as easily as five-year-old Benjamin Blyth, or Oliver Sacks's two "subnormal" twins.

My suggestion about two types of brainpower might also be relevant here. The kind of brainpower needed by a lightning calculator is mechanical. But the kind required by a great philosopher depends upon something else—the power that was once called inspiration. This power is similar to what Mozart utilized when he composed the Jupiter Symphony.

When I was in Majorca in 1969, I asked the poet Robert Graves his own experience of inspiration, and he advised me to read his short story, "The Abominable Mr. Gunn."[8] In this story, Graves describes the odd ability of a schoolfellow named F. F. Smilley, who was a calculating prodigy. The master, Mr. Gunn, had set the class with a complicated mathematical problem. Smilley simply wrote down the solution and then sat gazing out of the window. Asked how he did it without written calculation, Smilley replied, "It just came to me." Mr. Gunn said, "You mean you looked up the answer in the back of the book?" Smilley replied this was not so and said that, anyway, the back of the book got two figures wrong. Mr. Gunn then sent him to the headmaster with a note saying Smilley was to be caned for cheating and gross impertinence. This reminds Graves of his own experience when, sitting on a roller behind the cricket pavilion, he received a sudden "celestial illumination."

"It occurred to me that I knew everything. I remembered letting my mind range rapidly over all its familiar subjects of knowledge, only to find that this was no foolish fancy. I did know everything. To be plain, though conscious of having come less than a third of the way along the path of formal education, and being weak in mathematics, shaky in Greek grammar, and hazy about English history, I nevertheless held the key of truth in my hand, and could use it to open the lock of any door. Mine was no religious or philosophical theory, but a simple method of looking sideways at disorderly facts so as to make perfect sense of them."

Graves explained that he tried out his insight on "various obstinate locks: they all clicked and opened smoothly." The insight was still intact when he woke up next day. But after morning lessons, when he tried to record the insight in the back of an exercise book, "My mind went too fast for my pen, and I began to cross out—a fatal mistake—and presently crumpled up the page." Later, when he tried to write it down under the bedclothes, "The magic had evaporated and the insight vanished."

Writing about his experience, he said that what struck him at the time was "a sudden infantile awareness of the power of intuition, the supra-logic that cuts out all routine processes of thought and leaps straight from problem to answer."[9]

Before the end of this book I shall make an attempt to reconstruct what Graves meant.

THREE

ANCIENT TECHNOLOGIES

The last chapter of Hapgood's *Maps of the Ancient Sea Kings* is called "A Civilization That Vanished," and it begins by repeating the author's conviction that the ancient maps suggest "the existence in remote times, before the rise of any of the known cultures, of a true civilization . . . a worldwide culture."[1] Hapgood then wrote a word of warning:

"When I was a youth I had a plain simple faith in progress. It seemed to me impossible that once man had passed a milestone of progress in one way that he could ever pass the same milestone again the other way. Once the telephone was invented it would stay invented. If past civilizations had faded away, it was just because they had not learned the secret of progress. But Science meant permanent progress, with no going back. . . . This process would go on forever."[2] The ancient maps, however, had taught him otherwise, he said; progress can go backwards, ancient knowledge can be forgotten.

My trip down the Nile taught me the same thing, that the ancient Egyptians knew far more about certain things than we do now, and that most of this knowledge has been forgotten.

The archaeologist Flinders Petrie stumbled upon a puzzling example in the 1890s. Excavating a village called Naquada, on the Nile, he found pottery and vases of such sophistication that he decided they probably dated from the eleventh dynasty, about 2000 BC (which is five hundred years later than the Great Pyramid). Since there was no sign of such people in dynastic history, he coined the term "New Race" to describe them.

But when he found the same pottery in tombs dating from 3000 BC, he decided to drop Naquada from his chronology rather than face the embarrassment of trying to explain how "primitives" could produce such fine ceramics.

A similar problem was encountered in the long-necked vases found in the Step Pyramid at Saqqara, built about 2650 BC. The vases had been carved out of crystalline materials such as quartz, diorite, or basalt. Archaeologists were puzzled by how craftsmen had carved the insides of the vases. Such craftsmanship would require not only a long drill to reach down the neck, which was too narrow to admit a child's finger, but also an instrument to cut out the inside with delicate precision. We are forced back to the improbable hypothesis that the craftsmen had some method of softening the crystal to the consistency of clay, or perhaps of melting it like glass. The ancient Egyptians clearly had technology that has since been lost.

In 1957, Hapgood was called in to give advice on a very similar problem: the mystery of the Libyan desert glass. This glass had come to light a quarter of a century earlier, in December 1932, when two Englishmen were driving along a sand-free corridor in the desert (which is actually in Egypt). They were Patrick Andrew Clayton, of the Egyptian Desert Survey, and Professor Leonard Spencer, the Keeper of Minerals in the British Museum. As they were driving, they noticed the glitter of shining objects on the ground. These objects proved to be beautiful pieces of glass, which ranged from the size of a pea to the size of an egg. Spencer assumed they were tektites, a kind of glass that probably arrives on earth in the form of meteorites. The puzzling thing, however, was that the tektites were on the surface, which seemed odd, since a meteor would bury itself in the sand.

The scientists collected about a hundredweight of this beautiful substance—valued by Arab craftsmen for making jewelry—and took it back to Cairo.

Closer examination revealed just how strange their find was. Some of the pieces had fractures that looked as if they had been produced deliberately, like the flakes of flint found near prehistoric hand-axes. What was also odd was their sheer quantity: tektites are relatively rare, not found by the hundredweight.

Chemical analysis proved they were not tektites, but were made of the same silicon as the desert sand. But what had melted it? There was no sign of a crater.

One interesting piece of evidence suggested a strange alternative. One fragment, about the size of a lemon, had a neat hole running right through it, looking as if someone had poked it with a metal rod while it was still molten. Two other "bore holes" penetrated the glass for only a short distance. So it looked as if the glass had been made by human hands. The few bubbles in it were elongated, as if the glass had been turned while it was still molten.

When Clayton and Spencer presented their evidence to the Royal Geographical Society in 1933, one member of the audience was particularly interested. He was Francis James Rennell, who later became Lord Rennell of Rodd (as well as President of the Royal Geographical Society).

He had been a staff officer in Egypt during the First World War, and later been involved in Sahara exploration. He was fascinated by the mystery of the Libyan desert glass.

What kind of men had manufactured it? Rock carvings in the area dated to about 5500 BC. It had been assumed that the artists had been nomads, but if they had made the glass, then there must have been a fairly sophisticated level of civilization in this area in the sixth millennium BC.

In the late '50s, Rennell spoke of the mystery to Dr. John R. V. Dolphin, the chief engineer of the British Atomic Energy Authority, and Dolphin remarked that he had seen something similar in the Australian desert. But he knew just how it had been created: by an atomic bomb test.

Dolphin showed some of the Australian glass to Lord Rennell, who agreed it looked astonishingly like the Libyan desert glass. Like the Libyan specimen, Dolphin's Australian glass contained virtually no water, because of the tremendously high temperature at which it had been formed—Dolphin thought about 6000 degrees Celsius.

That added another dimension to the mystery. Colored glass was one of the preoccupations of the alchemists, and alchemy was studied in Graeco-Roman Egypt, as well as ancient India and China. But would alchemical experiments have produced such quantities? Or could the glass have been the by-product of some industrial process?

That seemed to suggest that the predecessors of the ancient Egyptians possessed something like atomic power. Could it have got out of hand and caused an explosion?

Lord Rennell took this suggestion seriously, for he himself was in possession of a necklace of pure gold from ancient Egypt. It is impossible to make pure gold by any normal metallurgical process, because it is impossible to remove all the impurities. Gold can be made nowadays by a chemical process that was unknown in the ancient world. Another method of production these days involves heating the gold until it vaporizes, like liquor in a still, and then is allowed to cool, leaving behind its impurities. But this method again requires immensely high temperatures.

Industrial processes requiring high temperatures need lots of water, and the Libyan desert is waterless. But has the desert always been so dry?

Rennell contacted an expert on such matters, Charles Hapgood, in 1957, for Hapgood was also a member of the Royal Geographical Society. Hapgood was able to assure Rennell that in 5500 BC, plenty of water existed in what is now the Sahara Desert. For several thousand years after the last pole displacement, which occurred around 10,000 BC, the Sahara desert was green and had many lakes. Some of the Saharan rock carvings from that time depict cattle and herdsmen.

The observations of Rennell and Dolphin fit very comfortably with the conclusions Hapgood was reaching through his study of the portolans. If man was building ocean-going vessels in 5000 BC, then he possessed a civilization capable of that level of expertise and could also easily have designed other sophisticated technological products.

Besides, Hapgood had himself seen a necklace of pure gold, although it had come from Mexico, not Egypt. And Captain Arlington Mallery, who had taken part in the Georgetown panel broadcast of 1956 (mentioned earlier in this book) about the Piri Reis map, had also made some astonishing claims. Mallery had excavated a number of furnaces in Ohio and Virginia and, as a result, was certain that iron-smelting techniques were in use before 4000 BC. And the ancient Egyptians, Mallery declared, were using tremendously high temperatures, which they obtained "by the same processes that made the atom bomb possible."[3] Mallery was convinced that 5000 years ago, the Egyptians were using the same fission process that scientists have thought was a new discovery in the twentieth century.

But Hapgood was skeptical about the atomic power theory. He had heard about an unknown people whose civilization was now under the sea off the coast of Ecuador, who knew all about optics, and had made lenses and prisms to focus the sun's rays. Concave mirrors can be used to concentrate the sun's rays; Archimedes devised huge metal mirrors to set alight the Roman galleys besieging Syracuse in 211 BC. (Robert Temple would devote a book entitled *The Crystal Sun* to the subject of ancient lenses, made long before man was supposed to have discovered them.)

So it was Hapgood's view that the ancients may well have learned the secret of creating very high temperatures—but using lenses, not atomic energy.

An interesting footnote to this curious story has since been provided by Dr. Farouk El-Baz, of Boston University. Dr. El-Baz had traveled in Egypt's western desert, 300 miles to the west of Cairo, and had been fascinated by its strange natural pyramids, dozens of great triangular rocks rising from the flat desert plain. It struck him that these natural pyramids might well have inspired the pyramids of dynastic Egypt.

He noted that the winds in the western desert blow from the north, the Mediterranean. So the desert sand could not have been carried there by wind. Since it was made of sandstone, it must have come from the south. How? It had to be by water—rivers. But where were the rivers in this great dry waste?

Now it happened that Dr. El-Baz had been the Director of Lunar Planning on the Apollo Space Program between 1967 and 1972, so he was able to call NASA to his aid. In 1994, he arranged for the orbiting space shuttle to use radar to penetrate the sea of sand. The resulting photographs amazed him. They showed that the area had been covered with a vast network of rivers that dated back fifty million years, some of them twelve miles wide. Here was proof that this great desert had once been green and lush.

Research by the University of Rome geologist Fekri Hassan around a dry lake bed revealed evidence of primitive human dwellings dating back ten thousand years, to the end of the last ice age.

We know that at this time, there was plenty of rain all the years round. Two thousand years later (c. 6000 BC) the rain fell only in summer. Three thousand years after that, at about the time that dynastic Egypt came into being, the great drought began—El-Baz thinks it was due to some variation in the sun's energy. But when the Great Pyramid was built, the Giza plateau was still green.

What we do not know, of course, is what degree of civilization was achieved by these dwellers around the lake in what is now the western desert. But at least we know that the conditions for civilization existed thousands of years before dynastic Egypt. They even set up standing stones for astronomical purposes, thousands of years before Stonehenge.

Does this explain the paradox noted by John West in *Serpent in the Sky*—that the science, medicine, and mathematics of Khufu's Egypt had achieved a level of sophistication that seems inexplicable for a culture that was little more than 500 years old?

A few weeks before Joy and I had set out on our trip down the Nile, I had come across yet another possible solution to the mystery of the Libyan desert glass. I was in Toronto, at the Waterfront Literary Festival, where I met an acquaintance of Rand's named Shawn Montgomery, who was obsessed by scientific anomalies.

Shawn had heard about an even simpler method of producing very high temperatures. This had been discovered by a Bulgarian who called himself Yull Brown, and who had spent his last years in California, where Shawn had been to visit him.

Brown had invented a kind of welding torch, which burned a mixture of hydrogen and oxygen, which could vaporize metals. Shawn had seen one in action. It belonged to a professor named Andrew Michrowski in Ottawa.

Michrowski lit the flame, which came from a small nozzle, with a spark. Brown had told Shawn that the flame could instantly poke a hole in wood or metal. Montgomery held out a wooden spoon; there was a hiss of yellow flame, and a small, clean hole appeared through half an inch of wood.

Michrowski handed Shawn the welding torch and told him to feel the temperature of the nozzle. Nervously, Shawn touched it an inch from the flame. To his surprise, it was merely warm.

Shawn picked up a rod of welder's tungsten and applied the flame to it. The tungsten burned like a piece of magnesium ribbon. It should have become too hot to hold, yet even when the white flame was within an inch of Shawn's fingers, there was no heat.

When Shawn tried playing the flame on his forearm, moving it back and forth, again it felt merely warm. It would burn tungsten at 6000 degrees Celsius but did little harm to flesh.

Michrowski showed Montgomery what the generator was capable of. Played on a piece of brick, the flame caused it to glaze, then begin to melt. They welded a piece of glass to a piece of copper, then cut holes in a fire brick—designed to withstand high temperatures—and welded copper to it. They turned a fistful of sand into a glass ball, welded together various dissimilar metals, and turned metals into molten pools.

But how did it work? Michrowski admitted he did not know and said that neither did anyone else. And this was why scientists had ignored Brown's Gas—the name the inventor gave to his mixture of hydrogen and oxygen.

Back in Toronto, Shawn and a friend ordered a Brown's gas generator from China, the only country that manufactured them. It was the largest they could afford—the same size as Michrowski's—and the flame was only as big as the tip of a pencil. But it was obvious that it worked—even if it did seem to contradict the laws of nature.

Who was the magician who had created this extraordinary machine? Bulgarian Yull Brown's real name was Ilya Velbov; he was born at Easter in 1922. Intended for the priesthood, he had become a student in a seminary. Reading the Second Epistle of St. Peter, he had been struck by the warning that one day the earth would be consumed by fire, and he found himself wondering how a planet whose surface is mostly water could be consumed by fire.

Not long after that, reading Jules Verne's *The Mysterious Island*, he was fascinated by the remark that in the future, the energy needs of the human race will be met by splitting hydrogen and oxygen in water. "Water will be the coal of the future."[4]

During the war, Velbov was in the army and ended in Moscow. Denounced by his wife for his hatred of communism, he spent six years in a "hard regime" concentration camp. When he escaped into Turkey he was again arrested and spent the next five years in a Turkish jail.

He was released with the aid of a U.S. Intelligence officer called Brown, and he changed his own name to Brown in his honor. He called himself Yull because he admired Yul Brynner. And he went to Sydney, Australia, qualified as an electrical engineer, and became head of testing in an instruments company. After ten years he tired of being an employee and set up on his own as an inventor.

He gave his full attention to the idea of turning water into fuel. It was dangerous, because when hydrogen and oxygen are mixed, they become highly explosive; he wrecked his laboratory and came close to losing his life.

It is, of course, easy enough to separate hydrogen and oxygen in water by electrolysis; but it takes more electricity to do this division than can be regained by recombining the two gases in an explosion.

Brown's major insight came when he realized that if hydrogen and oxygen are allowed to mix in exactly the same proportion as in water, they are, so to speak, glad to recombine and do so without an explosion.

This discovery was the secret of Brown's welder. The two gases implode instead of explode. They do so with almost no heat. The result is a welding flame that burns at a temperature a little more than boiling water.

How can a flame of that temperature cause a tungsten rod to burn? We can only guess that the hydrogen-oxygen flame somehow enters into a chemical combination with the tungsten. The atoms of the hydrogen and oxygen are in their original state, as single atoms, not combined into molecules of O_2 and H_2. But it is not clear why single atoms rather than molecules should make a substance like tungsten behave so unaccountably. In another later discovery, Brown showed that Brown's Gas will completely detoxify nuclear waste.

Two American businessmen, Bob Dzalkich and David Ennis, were excited by Brown's demonstrations. As far as the men could see, there was no reason why Brown's Gas should not create an energy revolution. They thought it would be easy to design a car engine that ran on Brown's Gas instead of on gasoline or diesel fuel, a considerably cheaper method than using oil-based fuels. Yet Dzalkich and Ennis were unable to raise the hundred million dollars required to exploit the energy possibilities of Brown's Gas. For a while, the United States military showed some interest but withdrew when Brown said that, as a pacifist, he was not interested in its military applications.

When it began to look as if Brown's discoveries were destined to be ignored, the Chinese People's Republic made him an offer.

The Chinese saw the most useful application of Brown's Gas to be its implosive properties. When ignited, its volume reduced by the proportion of 1860-to-1 and, as a result, the implosion could create an instantaneous vacuum. This fact, in turn, meant that the technique could be used to turn seawater into fresh water, because when warm seawater is placed in a total vacuum, it turns into steam, and its salt and other chemicals are left behind. The steam can then be drawn off with an extractor fan and condensed to make pure drinking water.

In the late 1980s, Brown went to Beijing and was invited to take up residence in the research city of Baotou, in Inner Mongolia, where he was provided with a laboratory. Brown set up shop at a complex known as Institute 52, with a staff of twenty specialists. Shortly after that, the Northern Industrial Company began to manufacture Brown's Gas Generators.

Even in China, Brown was still anxious to make his invention accessible to Americans. After lengthy bargaining with the Chinese political authorities, Brown secured an agreement to allow an American company to distribute Brown's Gas Generators throughout the world. The Americans and the Chinese were to pay an investment cost of a million dollars between them. But the deal fell through, because although the Chinese advanced their share, the Americans failed to keep their part of the bargain.

In spite of the breakdown of the agreement, and the suspicion it raised in the minds of the Chinese, Brown continued working at Baotou. The result was that Chinese submarines began to go out to sea with Brown's Gas Generators instead of huge tanks of fresh water, and Chinese scientists began disposing of their nuclear waste.

Brown returned to the United States in 1992, still hoping to persuade the Americans—whom he now regarded as his fellow countrymen—to invest in his ideas. Why he was unable to do so was incomprehensible to those who went to his laboratory to see his demonstrations, for the idea of using water as fuel seemed as commercial as any other great inventions, from the steam engine to television. But then, these inventions had also met with obstacles.

Shawn Montgomery began to understand some of these obstacles when he went to meet Yull Brown in California in April 1996. He drove down from Vancouver, took a hotel room in Los Angeles, and telephoned Brown, as he had been instructed to do. To his surprise, Montgomery was met with a tirade of broken English and incomprehensible anger. Finally, Brown's girlfriend Terri York got on the phone, and, although equally indignant, she spoke English well enough to understand Montgomery when he said he had nothing to do with some person doing experiments in Toronto, the man who turned out to be the real focus of Brown's anger. (The experimenter had been using a plastic container as the "implosion chamber," contrary to all Brown's instructions. It seemed that hydrogen atoms could leak through the plastic walls, and in doing so, upset the precise mixture and rendered it potentially lethal.)

Once this problem was sorted out, Shawn drove to a Los Angeles suburb, where he finally met Yull Brown. The door was answered by an attractive, well-groomed woman of about seventy, and behind her came Brown, bald, bespectacled, short (about five feet four), and portly. Shortly after, while seated in a comfortable, middle-class sitting room, Montgomery listened to his host describe his invention.

Brown's words were not easy to follow, since his accent was a mixture of Bulgarian consonants and Australian vowels. He talked quietly and often mumbled. But it was clear that he loved to explain his ideas, and that he was a teacher at heart. Soon, the two men were bent over the table in their shirtsleeves, a growing pile of notes and diagrams between them, while Brown chain-smoked furiously.

In the kitchen afterwards, as Terri York made tea, she told Shawn about some of the problems that had made life with the professor so stressful. "I learned," Montgomery said later, "that Brown is a very frustrated man. Unfortunately (and as usual in cases like his) he is his own worst enemy."[5]

Terri described how Brown had finally received the offer he had been waiting for, from a large American corporation that could market his invention and make him wealthy. They both expected it to fall through, as similar American offers had in the past. Again and again, there had been lively interest in his work, until it reached a certain level within the hierarchy of a company, when it would be quite abruptly cut off. Both Brown and Terri expected this to happen again.

But it didn't. On the contrary, the company provided what the Chinese had provided, a laboratory and an industrial facility to develop the gas. Brown's problems seemed to be over at last.

On the day Brown moved in as Chief of Research, the company held a celebration in his honor, after which the staff went to the laboratory to show him what they had created for him. As they approached the door of the laboratory, everyone became aware of the billowing smoke of Brown's eternal cigar. Everyone looked embarrassed. No one wanted to be the first to tell this great inventor that there were strict smoking laws that applied especially to areas like this, and that insurance and the fire code demanded complete compliance. To everyone's relief, Brown squeezed it out and crushed it beneath his shoe.

They entered the lab. Everyone was eager for his reaction, for it was, so to speak, an inventor's paradise. But as soon as they were inside, Brown took out another cigar and lit up. Finally, with deep embarrassment, someone had to tell him that smoking was not allowed.

Brown looked incredulous. The boss was not allowed to smoke in his own laboratory? They explained awkwardly that this was not a company rule but the law of the land. But, said Brown, he had to smoke. He could not work without smoking.

Desperately, they suggested that he should step outside for a smoke. He replied that with him there was no such thing as a smoking break, because he chain smoked all the time he was awake. He could not think clearly without smoking, and without cigars or cigarettes, he would be useless to the staff.

It was an impasse. No one could believe that, within sight of the objective he had struggled for years to achieve, Brown would refuse to compromise. They did not know Yull Brown. He turned and walked out. That moment was the end of his dream.

Shawn Montgomery's theory is that Brown's extreme stubbornness, his refusal to yield an inch, was due to his years as a prisoner of the Russians and the Turks. He had determined that, once he was free, he would never again obey an order unless he wanted to. Possibly the fact that prison guards had stubbed out cigarettes on his skin made him particularly stubborn about cigarettes.

At all events, his tobacco habit—what a friend called his "arrogant addiction," was one of the reasons that when he died in March 1998, the general public had still never heard of Yull Brown.

Montgomery's reaction to Brown's experiments was that he was witnessing something akin to alchemy. We can see why. If a flame that burns at around 135 degrees centigrade can punch holes in a firebrick and vaporize tungsten, then the laws of nature are, at the very least, not as straightforward as we assumed. It looks as if the Brown's Gas flame can somehow take into account the substance it is heating. And that sensitivity sounds more like medieval alchemy than the chemistry we were taught at school.

The same might be said of the gas's ability to detoxify nuclear waste, which Brown demonstrated repeatedly. Brown would melt a piece of radioactive Americanum 241 on a brick, with small pieces of steel and aluminum. "After a couple of minutes under the flame," says Christopher Bird, "the molten metals sent up an instant flash, in what Brown said is the reaction that destroys the radioactivity."[6]

The Americanum, which had originally measured 16,000 curies of radiation per minute, now showed only 100 curies per minute, or about the same harmless low-level radiation as the background.

How is it possible that Brown's Gas flame produces a chemical reaction? An ordinary flame burns by heating the substance until its elements dissociate. This reaction is what happens when you apply a match to a piece of paper. On the other hand, if you mix sulfur and iron filings, then heat them over a flame in a metal tray, the sulfur will melt and turn brown, then will begin to fizz and bubble. You can remove the heat, and the reaction will continue until, instead of sulfur and iron, you have a solid lump of iron sulfide.

Again, if sulfur dioxide and oxygen are passed over heated platinized asbestos, they combine to form sulfur trioxide, which, when dissolved in water, makes sulfuric acid. The platinized asbestos is a catalyst—that is, it is not changed by the reaction. Again, this sounds like alchemy, certainly the kind of alchemy that takes place when tungsten vaporizes when heated with a mere 135-degree flame.

In other words, Brown's Gas may simply cause tungsten, firebrick, gold ore, radioactive waste, or other substances to react like the sulfur and iron filings, combining in an essentially chemical reaction, as straightforward as dropping a piece of zinc into hydrochloric acid and watching it dissolve. If so, then the essence of Brown's Gas is simply that it causes chemical reactions. This would explain why it is possible to hold one end of a piece of tungsten as it "burns."

This discovery makes it altogether more believable that the ancients knew the secret of Brown's Gas. Much evidence points in this direction. In June 1936, a German archaeologist named William König, from the Iraq Museum in Baghdad, was opening a Parthian grave when he came upon a clay vase containing a copper cylinder. The cylinder, held in place by asphalt and molten lead, was an iron rod. It looked to König like a primitive battery.

Fellow archaeologists disputed his findings, since the grave was dated to about 250 BC. But Dr. Arne Eggebrecht constructed a duplicate of the primitive battery and poured fruit juice into it. The result was a half-volt current that lasted for eighteen days, with which Eggebrecht was able to coat a silver figurine in gold in half an hour. He did this because he had observed that on many gold-covered Egyptian statues, the gold seemed to be too fine to have been glued or beaten on. Eggebrecht became convinced that the ancient Egyptians knew the secret of electroplating.

A century earlier, in 1837, when Colonel Howard-Vyse was exploring the Great Pyramid, he instructed one of his assistants, J. R. Hill, to use gunpowder to unblock the end of the southern airshaft from the King's chamber. The result was that Hill found an iron plate, a foot long, four inches wide and an eighth of an inch thick, embedded in the masonry at the far end of the air shaft.

When scientists at the Mineral Resources Department of Imperial College in London examined the plate in 1989, they found that the plate's iron had been smelted at a temperature of over 1000 degrees centigrade. In spite of the claims of Captain Arlington Mallery, the ancient Egyptians were not supposed to know about smelting iron; all the iron they possessed supposedly came from meteorites. But the plate was not meteoric iron; it contained too much nickel. So it would seem that the Egyptians knew about smelting iron ore two thousand years before the Iron Age.

Oddly enough, Hill found traces of gold on one side of the iron plate, indicating that it had been gold-plated. The gold may, of course, have been beaten onto the plate. But if Eggebrecht was correct about his statues, the iron may have been electroplated.

No one has ever explained how the walls of Egyptian tombs were illuminated as they were decorated. No sign of lampblack exists on the ceilings. Perhaps the artists went to the trouble of cleaning off any carbon. On the other hand, engravings that look oddly like electric lights and insulators are present on the walls of the temple at Dendera.

Now if the Egyptians had possessed a technology even as rudimentary as the Baghdad battery, they would have been able to dissociate the hydrogen and oxygen in water by electrolysis and would have possessed the basic tool to create Brown's Gas.

When Shawn Montgomery interviewed Yull Brown in April 1996, Brown told him that the Aztecs had a means of producing Brown's Gas. According to Brown, Aztecs had a particular mixture of wet wood and dry wood, which they set alight. The fire caused a high temperature that caused the imprisoned steam to dissociate and become Brown's Gas. It would, of course, implode in the fire. But, according to Brown, this implosion could cause gold ore—presumably also trapped in the burning wood—to yield ten times as much gold as in the normal separation process.

According to Brown, "They were producing a lot of gold. A lot of gold. But they couldn't have produced that much gold from the amount of ore that they were producing. I was experimenting with this matter, and I found out why. Now with Brown's Gas you can produce ten times more gold with the same amount of ore."[7]

Montgomery asked if Brown has done this experiment himself, and Brown replied, "Oh yes. There are even some Mayans who use this in the production of gold. They have examined it, and done the lab work, and conclude that this (technique) works. Not only (for making) gold, but platinum, silver and so on."[8]

When we recall Lord Rennell's pure gold necklace, and the pure gold Mexican necklace seen by Hapgood, it is natural to wonder whether these items might have been products of Brown's Gas.

Shawn asked if there would be any way of using Brown's Gas to make tektites. Brown said, yes, the idea was possible. "I have already sent two Brown's Gas machines to Texas Instruments to purify silica to make silicon chips," Brown said. "If you put any gas that has a hydrocarbon product to melt the silica, carbon contaminates and destroys the pure crystalline structure of the chip. . . . But with Brown's Gas it melts the silica and leaves only water, which is near to the crystallization and creates only an ideal crystal. This gives a superior high-speed chip and also a good solar cell."[9]

Shawn found himself speculating on the notion of a huge sheet of purified silicon in a sunny environment—perhaps the Libyan desert—and of using it to produce vast quantities of cheap electricity. But silicon, of course, is not quite the same thing as Libyan desert glass that looks as if it has been made in an atomic explosion.

There are other clues.

In the spring of 1997, I was in Mexico, making the television documentary based on *From Atlantis to the Sphinx*. We spent a day at the ancient site of Tula (once called Tollan), fifty miles north of Mexico City. This was once the capital of the Toltecs, the predecessors of the Aztecs, whose empire flourished from about 700 to 900 AD (although they date from the pre-Christian era).

The significance of Tollan is that it is, according to legend, the site of the final battle between two gods, Quetzalcoatl and Tezcatlipoca, usually identified as the forces of good and evil (although the Toltecs would have felt that is an oversimplification). Quetzalcoatl, who is identified with Viracocha, Kon Tiki, Votan, and other gods of Central and South America, is the white god who came from the east at some remote epoch.

In my book I had cited the views of the nineteenth-century Mayan scholar Brasseur de Bourberg, who believed that Quetzalcoatl was an Atlantis survivor who brought with him the arts of civilization.

According to legend, he was finally defeated by Tezcatlipoca, the "Lord of the Smoking Mirror" (which, like some magic crystal, conferred vision of distant places) and sailed away on a raft with a promise that he would one day return.

This explains why I was so interested in Tula, where this final battle took place. I had also been greatly intrigued by a passage in Graham

Hancock's *Fingerprints of the Gods*, which speaks of the curious objects held by the four great statues of Tula. These stone figures, sixteen feet tall, stand on a platform at the top of a truncated pyramid, the Temple of the Morning Star, and once supported the temple's wooden roof.

In 1880, the discoverer of the sacred site, the French explorer Desiré Charnay, found some blocks of black basalt that he thought to be the feet of giant statues, which he called Atlanteans (Atlantes), from which we can deduce that he also accepted the legend of Atlantean origin. The four great statues of Tula were discovered sixty years later, and the name was transferred to them.

The odd thing about these statues is the objects they hold in their hands, which are pressed flat against their sides. No one has ever worked out what these are supposed to be. The object on the right hand side looks at first like a western gunfighter's six-shooter in its holster, with the barrel sticking out of the bottom of the holster. But the handle by which the object is held (by two fingers) looks more like the handle of some power tool. In the left hand there is something that scholars have described as a bunch of arrows and an incense bag; but since the parallel strands are curved, they cannot possibly be arrows. Graham Hancock remarks that he got the feeling that the original devices were made out of metal.

I was so intrigued by these that I got Joy to take photographs of them. When examined back at home they still failed to yield any clue as to their purpose. It was certainly impossible to see how they might have been used as atl-atls, or spear-throwers, as many of the guidebooks state.

Later, Shawn Montgomery drew my attention to a passage about Tula in a book by Zecharia Sitchin, *The Lost Realms*, the fourth volume of his *Earth Chronicles* series. Among respectable scholars, Sitchin's is not a name to conjure with, for he is often associated with Erich von Däniken as someone who believes that the earth was once colonized by visitors from outer space. Sitchin argues, on the basis of Sumerian texts, that these visitors (whom he calls Anunnaki) came to earth from a twelfth planet of the solar system, Niburu, nearly half a million years ago, and created human beings as their servants.

But Sitchin differs from Däniken in an important respect: the sound basis of his scholarship. Whether or not we find his theories tenable, he is an endless mine of scholarly information. And in *The Lost Realms* he discusses the statues of Tollan and points out that one of the pilasters has a peculiar carving of a man wearing a segmented suit, with what looks like a kind of backpack. In his hands he is holding the same tool—the one that resembles a pistol in its holster—and is pointing it at the rock face in front of him; a surging flame is bursting out of the barrel of the "pistol." Sitchin says: "He uses it as a flamethrower to shape stone."[10] He points out that "thermo-jet torches" were used to carve the monument of Georgia's Stone Mountain.

Whether or not thermo-jet torches can be used to carve stone, there is no doubt whatever that Brown's Gas could be used for this purpose. And whether or not we dismiss this possibility as too far-fetched, the fact remains that the strange objects held by the gods of Tollan are devices from which curving tongues of flame issue forth. It would seem that the Toltecs must either have possessed some technology, or at least known enough about it to ascribe it to their gods. Most gods in world mythology can hurl thunderbolts, but I can think of no other who is depicted holding some kind of flame-spitting welding torch in his hands.

Sitchin has even more interesting things to say about Tollan. It seems that the pyramid was again excavated in the 1940s by the archaeologist Jorge Acosta, who also excavated Teotihuacan. It was Acosta who found a deep trench inside the pyramid, with the sixteen-foot "Atlanteans" in it. There were also four columns, which had once stood in the corners of the roof.

An earlier pyramid lay under this Temple of the Morning Star. There were the remains of inner chambers and passages, which have still not been explored. And there was a carved stone pipe, in sections that fit together, with a diameter of about eighteen inches. It was at the same angle as the pyramid and ran throughout its whole height.

Acosta assumed it had been intended to drain water. But, as Sitchin asks, why carve an elaborate stone pipe when a clay pipe would do just as well? The stone pipe was obviously part of the structure of the pyramid, and a part of its purpose. Sitchin says: "The fact that the remains of the adjoining multichambered and multistoried buildings suggest some industrial processing, and also the fact that in antiquity, water from the Tula river was channelled to flow by these buildings, raise the possibility that at this site, as at Teotihuacan, some kind of purification and refining process had taken place at a very early period."[11]

Such notions bring to mind the speculations of John Dolphin and Lord Rennell about the possibility that the Libyan desert glass was a by-product of some industrial process.

Sitchin goes even further:

"Was the enigmatic tool a tool not to engrave stones, but to break up stones for their ores? Was it, in other words, a sophisticated mining tool?

"And was gold the mineral sought after?"[12]

Why gold? Because Sitchin argues that the purpose of the space-visitors was to mine earth for precious minerals, the most important being gold—which they needed for scientific purposes. He quotes reports of the Anglo-American Corporation, who engaged archaeologists to study ancient mines, to the effect that "Mining technology was used in southern Africa during much of the period subsequent to 100,000 BC."[13] And he points out that although, in Peru and Mexico, gold was obtained by panning in streams, "this could in no way account for the immense treasures of these countries."[14]

He quotes a Spanish chronicler to the effect that the Spaniards extracted from the Incas alone six million ounces of gold and twenty million ounces of silver annually. He believes, as does Yull Brown, that they had some far more efficient method of extracting precious metals from the ore.

He goes on to point out that the four "Atlanteans" holding up the roof of the Temple of the Morning Star bring to mind the ancient Egyptian belief that the four sons of Horus hold up the sky at four cardinal points. And these same four gods would accompany the deceased pharaoh up a "Stairway to Heaven," depicted in hieroglyphs as a kind of step pyramid. This same step pyramid symbol, which decorates the walls around the Tollan pyramid, also became a major symbol for the Aztecs, the conquerors who came after the Toltecs.

Sitchin also suggests a connection between the "feathered serpent," Quetzalcoatl and the winged serpent of the Egyptians that helps transport the deceased pharaoh heavenward. One of Sitchin's basic theses is that there is a close connection between the gods of ancient Egypt and the gods of Mexico.

I was offered another clue to a possible connection between Egypt and Mexico when making the same television program. We drove from La Paz, Bolivia, across the immense plain called the Altiplano, to the ancient city of Tiahuanaco, in the Andes. The sacred ruins are two and a half miles above sea level; but Tiahuanaco was once a port on nearby Lake Titicaca, before some geological upheaval tilted the ground and caused the lake to move a dozen miles away.

Lake Titicaca is still full of marine creatures, like sea horses, which make it clear that it was once at sea level. Geologists speculate that this was about a hundred million years ago. But whatever cataclysm tilted the land and caused Tiahuanaco to cease to be a port must obviously have happened during the history of Tiahuanaco, not in prehistory.

Little remains of the great port now except the ruins of the port area, the Puma Punku (Puma Gate), where giant blocks lay scattered like ninepins; one of these blocks has a long incision cut by a saw blade that seems to have been made with a diamond-tipped saw.

A few hundred yards away are the remains of a vast temple enclosure called the Kalasasaya. In the northwestern corner of this enclosure stands the most famous feature of Tiahuanaco, the Gateway of the Sun, which looks like a miniature Arc de Triomphe. The lintel of the gateway has a crack that runs down to the "doorway" in its center. But until the twentieth century it was more than just a crack; photographs in Professor Arthur Posnansky's classic work *Tiahuanacu: The Cradle of American Man* show it literally torn in two, quite obviously by some convulsion of the earth.

As I wandered around the ruins of Tiahuanaco, I was struck by the precision of the workmanship. Massive blocks of stone, many weighing more than a 100 tons, were carved with such exactitude that a razor blade could not be inserted between the blocks. But where blocks had been separated, as in the Puma Punku, it could be seen that they were often joined by metal clamps, obviously to prevent them coming apart in an earthquake. The archaeoastronomer Professor Neil Steede, who was in the same TV program, examined one of these clamps, roughly six inches long and shaped like a capital, and remarked that the builders must have possessed some kind of portable forge—examination under a microscope has shown that the metal was poured in hot.

No signs of any such portable forge have ever been found. Yet an open fire would obviously not be hot enough to melt the metal for these clamps. And there are few trees on the Altiplano to provide the fuel.

When I came to read Shawn Montgomery's account of the Brown's Gas flame creating a pool of molten metal within seconds, I remembered the metal clamps of Tiahuanaco and found myself wondering whether they had been melted in a "portable forge," as Steede suggested, or by some device more like the "blow torch" seen on the pilaster at Tula.

The next sequence of the program found me in Egypt, at the Giza site. Fifty yards from the Menkaura pyramid I was filmed examining a wall of precisely carved blocks, and pointing out that in Egypt also, such blocks have been found to be joined by metal clamps. And, as Graham Hancock has pointed out, they can also be found in Angkor Wat, in Cambodia.

Tiahuanaco has one more feature that raises some of the same questions as Tula: a pyramid known as the Akapana. This was once a vast step pyramid with seven terraces and a flat top, that must have looked rather like some industrial complex, or perhaps a modernistic building designed to house Common Market bureaucrats.

It had once dominated the temple area, but 90 percent of its flat facing stones have been removed over the years by builders, so that what remains looks at first glance like a natural hill. Anyone who clambers to the top finds that it contains a kind of lake.

But it was not a hill. Inside, as in the Tollan pyramid, there are tunnels, and a chamber of unknown purpose, which one Bolivian archaeologist, Oswaldo Rivera, has referred to as its "King's Chamber." There had been jointed stone channels to water, and it had been surrounded by a moat. The large quantities of water that would have fallen on top of the pyramid ran into the central court—what now looks like a lake—then into a drainage system that probably ran around all four sides of the first terrace, to be allowed to emerge into the open. It was then conducted back inside again, then out, all the way to the moat. The top was covered with green pebbles looking like the water of the "lake." So the whole building was a monument to water.

We are reminded of Sitchin's words about Tula, and "the remains of the adjoining multichambered and multistoried buildings," which suggest some industrial processing, and . . . raise the possibility that at this site, as at Teotihuacan, some kind of purification and refining process had taken place at a very early period."[15]

As I stood on top of the Akapana pyramid, looking south toward the Quimsachata mountains, then at the vast plain that extended all around me, I found myself trying to imagine what this place had looked like when Tiahuanaco was at the height of its prosperity. It was virtually impossible to conjure up a huge city, with a port area constructed of massive blocks, some weighing nearly two hundred tons. How did they get them up here? And what was a city doing in the middle of this rather soggy plain? It was obvious that it must have all been quite different, with dozens of small, prosperous villages, and plenty of manpower.

Then what had happened to it?—for it was obvious that some great catastrophe had turned in into this barrren plain.

Above all, when?

According to the museum opposite the Kalasasaya, and to Alan L. Kolata's book *The Tiawanaku*, Tiahuanaco rose to power around 100 AD, reached its peak around 500 AD, then went into steady decline until about 1000 AD. Yet this raises an obvious question. What, in that case, was the tremendous cataclysm that snapped the Gateway of the Sun in two, and hurled the huge stones of the port all over the place? It was obviously more than a local earthquake. Yet there is simply no record of such a cataclysm around 500 AD.

Professor Arthur Posnansky, who spent his life studying the ruins, concluded, around the turn of the twentieth century, that Tiahuanaco was founded about 15,000 BC. His reasoning was based on two observation points in the Kalasasaya, which marked the summer and winter solstices (the solstice is the point when the sun is directly overhead, either the Tropic of Cancer or the Tropic of Capricorn, and is about to turn back and go the other way). At the moment, the two tropics are 23 degrees 30 seconds on either side of the equator. But when the Kalasasaya was built, the tropics were slightly closer to the equator—to be exact, 23 degrees, 8 minutes, and 48 seconds. This change in the width of the tropics is due to a slight rolling motion of the earth known as the obliquity of the ecliptic, and this enabled Posnansky to calculate when the Kalasasaya was built. He concluded, as we have seen, that it was around 15,000 BC.

Posnansky's dating upset scholars, who felt it was thousands of years too early. But between 1927 and 1930, a team of German scientists, led by Dr. Hans Ludendorff of Potsdam, checked Posnansky's results and were inclined to agree with him. However, the academic furor led them to revise their figure downward, and they ended by suggesting that perhaps Tiahuanaco might date from 9300 BC. But even this struck archaeologists and historians as nine thousand years too early. And this view, as we have seen, still prevails today.

Yet not entirely. The meso-American archaeologist Professor Niel Steede, who studied Tiahuanaco for many years, concluded the sacred city was built about twelve thousand years ago. And, more surprisingly, so does Dr. Oswaldo Rivera, the Director of the Bolivian National Institute of Archaeology, who excavated at Tiahuanaco for twenty-one years.

This is surprising because in a television program called *The Mysterious Origins of Man*, made in 1996, Rivera went on record as disagreeing with Steede's estimate. His own view was that the builders of Tiahuanaco had simply made a slight mistake—after all, we are only speaking of about 21 seconds of a degree. Steede disagreed; he felt that builders as accurate as the founders of Tiahuanaco would not have made even a minor error.

During the remainder of 1996, Rivera went on to observe the sunsets over Tiahuanaco, which obviously involves taking the measurements from the other end of the Kalasasaya, facing west. And his measurement finally convinced him that Steede was right. There was no "minor error." The measurements of the sunsets gave precisely the same reading as the sunrises. Rivera came to agree that the Kalasasaya was built twelve thousand years ago.

In a 1998 interview with Graham Hancock (included in the television series *Heaven's Mirror*) Rivera even admitted that Tiahuanaco must have been built by a lost civilization, and that this civilization "could be Atlantis, more or less."[16]

It would seem that the ideas that Hapgood proposed in 1959, and which geologists ignored or dismissed, were slowly beginning to make headway.

FOUR

THE FLOOD

I found something oddly haunting about Tiahuanaco. It seemed obvious to me that the academics were simply trying to play down the significance of one of the most puzzling sites on earth. To date its beginning, as Kolata did, to 100 BC seemed laughable. How could anyone accept that the original people were Indians called the Wankerani, in whose villages one would find "a combination of subsistence agriculture (primarily of potato and quinoa and camelid pastoralism)."[1] How did these simple Indians move the giant stone blocks?

On my return from South America I found a copy of Arthur Posnansky's *Tiahunanacu: The Cradle of American Man* on the web.[2] The first thing I saw when I opened it was a plate showing the Gate of the Sun in 1904, before it was repaired. It was split in two, with the two halves leaning crazily against one another. It was obvious that some giant convulsion had torn it in half. This was plainly the consequence of the same earthquake that had tossed around those immense blocks of the harbor (Puma Punku).

What had happened was obvious. At some time in the remote past, an immense harbor had been built, fronting on Lake Titicaca, the highest lake in the world, 12,500 feet above sea level and covering more than three thousand square miles.

Here the alert reader will instantly say: "Wait a moment. Why on earth are these people building a harbor two and a half miles up in the air? Are they mad?"

The explanation—that this is not a sea harbor but a lake harbor—fails to satisfy. For surely, a harbor is a place where ships from over the sea bring their goods for trade and exchange? How many other harbors are there on Lake Titicaca?

When the answer emerges: "None," the whole thing begins to seem absurd—particularly when we learn that the only people to sail on Lake Titicaca are Indians in reed boats. This port has obviously been built in the wrong place.

Then we learn that Lake Titicaca is full of sea creatures who have adapted to fresh water, and the obvious explanation begins to dawn. It must have been on sea level when some great convulsion raised the Andes 12,500 feet in the air.

And when was that? Well clearly, it must have been in historical times, not a million or so years ago, because human beings built the harbor.

In fact, Posnansky suggests the date when the catastrophe happened: around the 11th millennium BC. Say, 11,000.

That date struck a chord. Not long before, I had been in the George C. Page Museum in Los Angeles, filming in a hall full of the bones of dead dinosaurs. In the grounds of the museum, the "Tar Trap of La Brea" still bubbles ominously. Over tens of thousands of years, thousands of animals died as they waded into the oily water to drink, then found themselves slowly engulfed in mud.

But around 10,000 BC—I was told by John Harris, curator of the museum—there was a more violent catastrophe. A great earth tremor wiped out twenty-five species in a few years, including mastodons and saber-tooth tigers.

Is it too much to assume that the same earth tremor split the great gate of Tiahuanaco, some four thousand miles to the southeast, as it raised the Andes two and a half miles above sea level? If this sounds unlikely, bear in mind that according to Hapgood, this same convulsion caused the face of the earth to slip two thousand miles and devastated the continent Plato calls Atlantis.

We should note that this is not the only great flood. According to the *Critias*, there had been three floods "before that of Deucalion."[3] Deucalion's legendary flood, which Zeus sent to punish the men of the Bronze Age, must have been some time after 2500 BC.

The first, I would suggest, was Hapgood's crust-shift that caused the devastation of La Brea.

A similar scenario is recorded in myths all over the world. For days before it happens, the sky is red and there are earth tremors. Then one day the sky turns black, the earth convulses and seems to lurch; a muddy rain falls in torrents, accompanied by deafening crashes of thunder and blinding sheet lightning.

The Flem-Aths, recording the legends of Native Americans—the Ute, the Kutenai, the Okamagan, the A'a'tem, the Cahto, and the Cherokee, down to the Araucanians of Peru—heard almost identical tales of "when the sky fell."

The most famous of all such catastrophes originated in the land of the Bible—not Palestine, but Mesopotamia, the "Land of the Two Rivers."

Early nineteenth-century travelers who visited Mesopotamia must have been disappointed to find it so bare and unromantic: no pyramids or temples or obelisks: just an arid country of desert and dust storms, with odd-looking mounds that rose out of the brown plain like miniature volcanoes. Yet this was the land of Babylon and Nineveh and Ur—the latter the birthplace of Abraham.

Europe was indifferent to such places until 1815, when a book called *Memoir on the Ruins of Babylon* caused widespread excitement, and made its brilliant young author famous.

His name was Claudius Rich, and his adventures had started when he was sixteen; he had been shipwrecked on his way to Egypt, where he was about take up a job with the East India Company. He finally arrived at Smyrna (in Turkey) by way of Malta and Italy. Disguised as a Turk, and speaking fluent Arabic, he then journeyed through Egypt, Syria, and Palestine and even succeeded in entering the Great Mosque in Damascus.

In 1807, at the age of twenty, he was posted to Bombay; but the East India Company soon realized it was a waste to keep a man who spoke half a dozen Arabic languages in India. Which is how he came to find himself in Baghdad.

One day when in nearby Mosul, on the banks of the Tigris, he heard about some interesting sculptures that had been found in a mound across the river. But the local Muslim priest had ordered them to be destroyed as works of the devil, and not a trace remained. This is what provoked Rich to start searching among those volcano-like mounds, for he was convinced that one of them concealed the ruins of Nineveh. Unfortunately, he was not sure which.

At least he thought he knew where to look for the ruins of ancient Babylon. This was at a place called Birs Nimrud, where the ruins of the Tower of Babel were still to be seen, towering 235 feet above the plain. Rich studied these and wrote his *Memoir on the Ruins of Babylon*, which came out in 1815 and made him famous. Suddenly, all Europe became excited about ancient ruins.

Rich had little time to enjoy his fame, for he caught cholera in Shiraz, and died in 1820 at the age of thirty-three. He never knew that the place he thought was Babylon was actually the ancient city of Borsippa.

But Rich was correct about one thing: the whereabouts of Nineveh. Twenty years later, the French consul at Mosul was a doctor named Paul Emile Botta. He was a linguist and a scholar and took a lively interest in those academic and philosophical disputes, which, then as now, divided French intellectuals into warring camps.

Ever since Napoleon had taken archaeologists with him to Egypt to study its pyramids and temples, the French had been archaeology-mad—particularly since a young genius named Champollion had succeeded in deciphering Egyptian hieroglyphics by means of the Rosetta Stone.

Botta had recently been following a dispute about the whereabouts of Nineveh, the capital of the Assyrians, where Sennacherib and Assurbanipal had struck terror into the hearts of their neighbors. Amazingly, it seemed to have vanished without a trace. But one suggestion was that it had been in the region of Mosul.

Botta found his consular duties less than absorbing, and Mosul itself a typical Arab city, full of dust and noise. He began to make a habit of riding out at evening, to enjoy the breeze along the river, and the desert with its mysterious mounds. He also bought pieces of ancient pottery and inscribed fragments of clay tablets from local Arabs. And one day he decided to start digging at a village called Kuyunjik, where there was a promising-looking mound.

As month after month went by without any find more significant than broken pottery and clay tablets, Botta began to suspect he was wasting his time and money. The local Turkish pasha—Mesopotamia was then ruled by the Turks—also made life difficult by spying on the excavation and intimidating the workmen, convinced that the French consul was in search of treasure.

Botta was about to abandon archaeology when a persuasive Arab told him that he ought to try his village, where he would find plenty of ancient bricks and pottery. Botta needed little persuasion to take his workmen to a village called Khorsabad, seven miles to the north. There they sunk a shaft, and soon came upon a wall lined with slabs of stone, on which there were drawings of animals.

Botta had no doubt that he had found Nineveh. Actually, he was wrong—he had discovered the palace of a king named Sargon II, who ruled around 700 BC.

The palace proved to be immense, with about two hundred rooms, and friezes of bearded men, warriors on horseback, and winged animals. Botta might not have discovered Nineveh, but he had discovered ancient Assyria.

And why did they need to be rediscovered? Because for three centuries, from 911 BC until 610 BC, the Assyrians had hacked and slaughtered their way to power with such ferocity that their enemies finally banded against them and killed them like vermin, reducing their cities to charred rubble.

Two centuries later, the Greek mercenaries of King Cyrus passed the vast ruins of Nineveh and Nimrud—the story is told by the historian Xenophon—and marveled at these gigantic empty ruins. But the local inhabitants could tell them nothing about the devastated cities—even the memory of the Assyrians had been destroyed.

In 1842, Botta met a young Englishman named Henry Layard, who had been dreaming about the Middle East ever since he read the *Arabian Nights* as a boy. The two often shared a pipe together—sometimes of opium. And when Botta showed him the mound of Kuyunjik, Layard seems to have been bitten by the bug of archaeological research, which has something in common with the gambler's love of backing long odds.

Layard had no money, but he had a persuasive tongue and, three years later, succeeded in inducing the British Ambassador in Constantinople to give him £60. With that he began excavating yet another mysterious mound, that of Nimrud (Calah), and unearthed finds even more spectacular than Botta's—huge winged lions and bulls that were soon on their way back to the British Museum.

Now famous, and financed (parsimoniously) by the British treasury, Layard turned his attention to Kuyunjik, which had defeated Botta a few years earlier. And within hours, he realized how close the Frenchman had come to making one of the most momentous finds in the history of archaeology. For this indeed was Nineveh, the great city of the Bible, and Layard was soon digging into the burnt out palace of Assurbanipal (669–626 BC), one of its mightiest and most ruthless kings.

By now, the French were back in the race, and the mound of Kuyunjik was divided between them. But one day in 1852, when the French were absent, Layard's assistant Hormuzd Rassam decided to do a little poaching and ordered his workmen to tunnel into the French territory on the other side of the dividing line. The God of Archeology was with him, and he cut through a wall and found himself in the library of Assurbanipal, full of clay tablets inscribed with wedgelike cuneiform. On one of these was the fifteen-digit number that would so excite Maurice Chatelain more than a century later.

Now it so happened that Assurbanipal, in spite of being one of the cruelest tyrants in history, was an enthusiastic collector of written records. Whenever he conquered a city, he had its library transported to Nineveh. As a result, he had collected some thirty thousand clay tablets, mostly concerned with magic, exorcism, and divination. Layard had them sent back to the British Museum.

At the time, no one could read cuneiform writing, although a British officer named Henry Rawlinson had made an important start by copying an inscription on a cliff near Behistun, in Persia; it had been carved there by the Persian king Darius and was in Old Persian, Elamite, and Babylonian (which was more-or-less Assyrian).

And in 1857, Rawlinson published his first translations from the Assyrian language. By this time he had returned to England and was working for the British Museum. And a young man named George Smith, a banknote engraver who was interested in archaeology, came to work for him.

It was in 1872, while George Smith was pondering over the vast pile of clay tablets sent by Hormuzd Rassam, that he suddenly realized that he had something rather more important than some old treatise on reading entrails. He came upon the statement that a ship came to rest on the mountains of Nizir, followed by an account of how a dove was sent out in search of dry land. It was obviously a fragment of the story of the Flood.

As Smith continued piecing together the fragments of eleven tablets that seemed to belong together, it dawned on him that he had stumbled on a major literary work, an epic about a hero named Gilgamesh. And what was so exciting was that this was much earlier than any known work in the history of world literature—at least a thousand years older than the Bible or the works of Homer.

As he continued piecing together this story of Gilgamesh, it became clear to him that it was incomplete. He was missing an important part of the Flood story, and the conclusion of the narrative.

Smith's announcement that he had discovered a version of the Flood that was even older than the Bible account caused widespread excitement. Soon the *Daily Telegraph* offered £1000 to anyone who could find the missing fragment, and Smith took up the offer.

What followed is one of the most famous stories in archaeology. Smith went to the mound of Kuyunjik, and his workmen began digging. Even confining his search to the library, there seemed as little chance of finding it as a needle in a haystack. Every day his workmen found plenty of broken fragments of terracotta with cuneiform inscriptions—but not what he was looking for.

Then on the fifth day he brushed the earth off a fragment, and instantly recognized that it contained seventeen lines that had been missing from the Flood story. He telegraphed his success to the newspaper and returned to England in triumph.

Soon, the British were able to read the story of a hero whose deeds had first been recounted in the Sumerian language before the building of the Great Pyramid.

This epic in twelve tablets told the story of the young hero Gilgamesh, king of Uruk (Erech, the capital of Sumeria, also called Sumer), who behaved like a juvenile delinquent. "His lust leaves no virgin to her lover, neither the warrior's daughter nor the wife of the noble; yet this man is supposed to be the shepherd of the city, wise, comely and resolute."[4]

The gods themselves complained to Aruru, the goddess of creation, and begged her to make a hero who would be as savage and untameable as Gilgamesh. She obliged by creating a wild man named Enkidu, who lived in the wilderness with the cattle and ate grass.

One day, a trapper saw Enkidu at the water hole and was frozen with terror. But when he told his father, the old man was delighted. This sounded like the kind of man who could subdue Gilgamesh. So he told the trapper to go and fetch a harlot from the temple of love and take her to the water hole. And next time Enkidu came to drink with the animals, the trapper told her, "Bare your breasts and go and seduce him."[5] And, nothing loath, she stripped off her clothes and was soon teaching Enkidu the arts of love. After seven days he was so sexually exhausted that he had lost his swiftness. Now the harlot invited him to come with her to Uruk.

Soon they encountered a man who was complaining that Gilgamesh had forced his way into an assembly where a bride was being chosen, and insisted on being the first to take her virginity.

That night, as the bride was lying in bed waiting for her husband, Gilgamesh entered the house. At that moment, Enkidu stuck out his foot and tripped him up. The two heroes hurled themselves at one another like raging bulls, and the house shook. But eventually, Gilgamesh threw Enkidu, who sat up from the ground and said: "There is not another like you in the world."[6] Whereupon the two embraced and became sworn friends.

The next chapter of the epic described how they went off together in search of adventure and slew the giant Humbaba, demon guardian of the forest. On their return, the goddess Ishtar (the Babylonian Venus) falls in love with Gilgamesh; unwisely, he rejects her, declaring that she will turn against him as she has turned against all her lovers. In a bitter rage, she goes to her father Anu, chief of the gods, and asks him to make her a bull. This animal is so formidable that it can kill hundreds of men with a single snort; but together, Enkidu and Gilgamesh slay it.

This angers Anu, who says that one of the two heroes must be destroyed. Enkidu is stricken with sickness and dies. Gilgamesh becomes almost insane with grief. And when he recovers, he sets out in quest of immortality—for although his mother is a goddess, he has inherited mortality from his father, who is a priest.

After a long journey he finds Uta Napishtim, the Babylonian Noah, to whom the gods have granted eternal life. And it is then, in the eleventh tablet, that Uta Napishtim tells him the story of the Flood—of how the gods decided to destroy mankind, but chose Uta Napishtim to survive, because he was virtuous. Like Noah, he was told to build a ship that is six stories high, and to make it waterproof with pitch, then to take aboard all his family and servants, as well as each of the beasts of the field.

Then the rains began, and all the rest of mankind was drowned. After seven days and nights, the flood subsided. The ship came to rest on a mountaintop, and Uta Napishtim sent out first a dove, then a swallow, then a raven, in search of dry land. When the raven failed to return, Uta Napishtim knew the flood had subsided.

In gratitude, Uta Napishtim offered incense to the gods. They, in turn, granted him immortality.

In the final part of the epic, Gilgamesh dives under the sea and finds the plant of eternal life. But while he is bathing in a well of cool water, a serpent steals the flower of immortality—echoing the Garden of Eden story—and Gilgamesh, weary and worn out with labor, finally dies.

Although this story of Gilgamesh was probably sung by minstrels before 3000 BC—long before it was written down—it was translated into many middle eastern languages and is known in several versions.

The Gilgamesh epic made George Smith famous—a celebrity that would be cut short three years later when he died of a virus contracted in Aleppo on his way to Mesopotamia. By that time he had discovered more tablets in Assurbanipal's library with an account of the creation of the world, whose similarities to the story in Genesis were as striking as those of the Flood story.

For this was what created the worldwide interest: the notion that the Bible stories might simply be a later version of Sumerian originals. The believers could feel that these stories brought the truth of the Bible closer to the Victorian sitting room, while the skeptics (or, as they preferred to call themselves in the Victorian age, agnostics) could classify the Bible and *The Epic of Gilgamesh* together as ancient fictions. Smith made everybody happy.

The discoveries of Botta, Layard, and Rawlinson had started a landslide of interest in ancient Mesopotamia. One obvious candidate for exploration was another typical desert mound at a spot about twenty miles north of the port of Basra. The Arabs called it Tell al Muqayyar, meaning the Mound of Pitch. It stands in a bare, flat region with little shelter from sandstorms. And in 1854, two years after Rassam had found the library of Assurbanipal, a British civil servant named J. E. Taylor was sent by the British Foreign Office to look at the mound on behalf of the British Museum.

Taylor was not an archaeologist and was totally inexperienced in judging historical constructions. As far as he could see, it was a kind of square building, which might have been a palace, with three more square structures stuck on top so it rose like a step pyramid. (When news of it reached civilization, there would be speculation that this was the original Tower of Babel.)

Taylor crawled up and down it, disturbing the owls that had been nesting there for centuries, studied the base carefully, looking for some kind of access, then finally smashed his way into its center, and found that it was solid. After that, he decided to start at the top.

It was a stupid and disastrous decision, whose effect could only have been completely destructive. It was as if some future archaeologist decided to excavate St. Paul's cathedral by smashing in the dome. The top layers of the mound were simply torn apart as if by a wrecking-crew. And the only discoveries that came to light were a few clay cylinders covered with wedgelike cuneiform.

Taylor was disgruntled and disappointed—unaware that he was looking at some of the first writing in human history. For the mound at al Muqayyar was, in fact, Ur of the Chaldees, the legendary home of the patriarch Abraham, and the capital city of the Sumerians, who had founded the first great civilization in the Middle East some time around 4000 BC.

Who were these Sumerians, who invented writing nearly six thousand years ago? No one knows—their origin is a complete mystery. Their language is unlike any other language in the Middle East, neither Indo-European nor Semitic. One authority—as we shall see later—believes they came from a land drowned by floods, not far from China. We only know that when historians talk about the beginning of civilization, they speak of the land of Shinar, or Sumer. One archeologist, Samuel Kramer, even wrote a remarkable book called *History Begins at Sumer*.

Taylor continued vandalizing Ur for two more years, then went home, blissfully unaware that future generations of archaeologists would curse his memory. For Taylor had not merely despoiled and mutilated one of the most important sites in ancient history; he had also cleared the way for crowds of Arabs who came to al Muqayyar to take the hard-baked bricks for their own buildings—it was fortunate that their transport consisted of mules and camels rather than tractors and trailers. During the next three quarters of a century, the zigurrat of Ur ceased to look like a step-pyramid and became merely a truncated tower.

This was all quite inexcusable, because in the days of George Smith, Henry Rawlinson had translated some of the clay cylinders sent back by

Taylor and had learned that the tower had been built by someone named Ur-Nammu. That first syllable aroused his interest. *The Book of Genesis* mentions that the father of Abraham took his family away from a city called Ur of the Chaldees. Could this battered tower be part of the Biblical Ur? And indeed, time would reveal that it was just that.

Appropriately, it was a clergyman's son who was appointed by the British Museum to go and excavate in 1922. Before the First World War, Leonard Woolley had dug at Carchemish, in Syria, with an assistant named T. E. Lawrence, who would soon become famous as Lawrence of Arabia.

To the untrained eye, the site of al Muqayyar looked utterly unpromising, when the joint British and American expeditions arrived there in 1923. Around the half-ruined tower stretched the flat, biscuit-colored desert broken by a number of mounds. But Woolley was an archaeological detective whose powers of deduction rivaled Sherlock Holmes, and he knew he was looking at the ruins of a fortified city that had been surrounded by fields of corn and barley, intersected by canals that glittered in the blinding sun.

The problem was to uncover the temples and palaces and houses that had once been the center of this prosperous region in the days when the Middle East had been green.

The first step was to dig trenches. Even in December, at the coolest time of year, this raised clouds of dust that drifted like the smoke of bonfires. (The head of the Persian Gulf has one of the hottest summer climates in the world.) First they uncovered pottery, then the remains of buildings—five temples grouped in a semicircle around the zigurrat. There were the remains of fountains in the courtyards, and water troughs coated with bitumen. The sheer number of buildings buried under the sandy soil made it clear that this excavation would go on for many years.

Just outside the temple area there was an ancient graveyard, probably dating to 3000 BC. The bodies had been buried with some of their possessions—bowls, jugs, and tools, revealing that these people believed they would find use for their possessions in the afterlife.

Below the graves were tombs that were obviously of nobles, and here the finds were more sinister. Outside one stone vault they found two ox-drawn carts, with the skeletons of the oxen still in the shafts. Inside the carts were the bones of the drivers, and by the skulls of the oxen lay the bones of the grooms. Inside the tomb lay the skeletons of soldiers with copper helmets and spears beside them.

In another tomb, identified as that of Queen Shubad, they found skeletons of the court, lying in two parallel rows, and the skeleton of a harpist whose harp had been broken. By the wooden bier of the queen crouched the skeletons of two ladies in waiting. It seemed that in ancient Ur, kings and queens (or nobles and their wives) expected to be escorted into the other world by their servants. And since there was no sign of struggle Woolley had to assume that the servants went willingly, perhaps taking some kind of drug before they were left to suffocate.

The queen's tomb was full of rich gifts, including two model boats, one of silver and one of copper, each two feet long. There was also a headdress, a wig decorated with lapis lazuli, carnelian, and with gold rings, beach leaves, and flowers. Woolley's wife Kate, a talented if domineering lady, whose temperament probably had much in common with Queen Shubad's, modeled and painted a clay head of the queen, which rivals the bust of Nefertiti in the Cairo Musem.

Three years into the dig, Woolley and his co-workers could look down on the old city of Ur, with its narrow alleyways, and two-story houses that revealed the prosperity of its citizens. (Most houses of the period had only one story.) Arched doorways were common, although they were not known in Europe until after the time of Alexander the Great. It looked as if Ur had been a city of the well-off middle classes, who lived in spacious villas with many rooms.

The team had excavated a huge pit, two hundred feet wide and forty feet deep. The soil was mostly rubbish, and ashes from old fires. A refuse pit forty feet deep suggested that its contents had accumulated over a very long period, perhaps centuries. Apparently the inhabitants had thrown their household waste from the top of the town wall.

But rubbish is mostly undateable; so in 1929, in the sixth year of the dig, Woolley decided to sink a number of shafts to see if he could find something he could date. He soon came upon a discovery that electrified him.

"Suddenly the character of the soil changed. Instead of the stratified pottery and rubbish we were in perfectly clean clay, uniform throughout, the texture of which showed that it had been laid there by water. The workmen thought we had come to the bottom of everything, to the river silt of which the original delta was formed. . . ."[7]

But they were wrong. For after almost nine feet of clean clay, they were back in layers of rubbish—but this time, full of stone implements. It was obvious that they were now in a more primitive age—an age that had been brought to an end by a great flood. Yet the presence of a fire-baked brick showed that they were not looking at evidence of some early village of mud brick. What had been submerged by the flood was a town.

Woolley's announcement that he had discovered evidence of the Biblical Flood made headlines all over the world. And the book he dashed off in a few months—*Ur of the Chaldees*—and published that December, sold more than any archaeological book in history. That was not because people were interested in archaeology. It was because Woolley was telling them that the Bible was true.

Twenty years later, an eccentric scholar named Immanuel Velikovsky created the same effect with *Worlds in Collision*, in which he claimed that a comet torn out of Jupiter had swept past the earth, and caused the collapse of the walls of Jericho and the parting of the Red Sea. And in 1956, Werner Keller's *The Bible as History* had the same worldwide success as it surveyed the scientific evidence for stories from the fall of Sodom and Gomorrah to the star of Bethlehem.

But was Woolley's flood the Flood of Genesis?

There are reasons for thinking not. To begin with, there were similarities between the culture found above the clay level and the culture found below it—like the baked brick. So this flood had not wiped out civilization. Even though Woolley estimated that it covered an area 400 by 200 miles, extending from the Persian Gulf to the north of modern Baghdad, it was still basically a local flood.

The archaeologist Max Mallowen (the husband of Agatha Christie) had excavated at Nineveh in 1931 and '32 and again found evidence of a flood. He estimated that this had taken place round about 3500 BC, and was probably the flood talked about in *The Epic of Gilgamesh*—which George Smith assumed to be the Flood of the Bible. But Nineveh fell within the area covered by Woolley's flood. So again, it looked like some local flood rather than the great Biblical inundation.

Then, in the mid-1990s, two American scientists, Bill Ryan and Walter Pitman, startled the world of archaeology by advancing a wholly new candidate for the great flood: the Black Sea. Before we speak of this, it is necessary to explain that the Mediterranean has not always existed. A mere twenty million years ago, Africa and Europe had not yet joined together, and Africa was an island. Then Africa began to move northwards, until, seven million years ago, it collided with Europe, trapping the Mediterranean between the tectonic plates. And since there were not enough rivers flowing into it, the sun gradually evaporated the water until it virtually disappeared. The Mediterranean became a sun-dried basin full of cracked mud and sand.

About five and a half million years ago, the Atlantic began to break through at the point we now call Gibraltar, where Spain and North Africa face one another. It must have been one of the greatest waterfalls in the world's history, about fifty times higher than Niagara, and the volume of water that poured down was a thousand times greater. In a few years, the Straits of Gibraltar had appeared.

Oddly enough, no one suspected how recently the Mediterranean had appeared until 1970. Bill Ryan was on board a research vessel called the *Glomar Challenger*, which was studying core samples from the sea bottom for evidence of reversals in the earth's magnetic field. And they began bringing up samples that were pure salt—long tubes of hard-packed sea salt. These left no doubt that the Mediterranean had once dried out, leaving "salt flats." Then the sea had suddenly poured in. Scientists at first found this hard to accept; but the evidence was overwhelming.

A year later, Ryan was sitting with Walter Pitman, an oceanographer, and a young English researcher named John Dewey. And when

Ryan told him about the great Mediterranean Niagara, Dewey remarked unthinkingly that perhaps this might explain the flood legends—until it struck him that all this took place long before man's appearance on earth. But as Ryan went on talking about the flood, Dewey—half jokingly— challenged him to try and find the evidence. This was the start of Ryan and Pitman's investigation.

Both Ryan and Pitman had studied *The Epic of Gilgamesh* at college, and this was an obvious starting point. When they looked at it again, they noted that when Gilgamesh goes in search of Uta Napishtim, he walks in the direction of the setting sun.

Now if Gilgamesh lived in Uruk, which was then much closer to the seashore of the Persian Gulf, then we might suppose that he would go south to look for evidence of the Flood, not west. Woolley's flood was confined to the land of the two rivers, which run north-south, or at least, northwest to southeast.

What Ryan and Pitman were looking for was a repetition of what happened when the Atlantic broke through at Gibraltar, but far more recent in date. It required a bottleneck, like the Straits of Gibraltar, which had been sealed, then was washed open by the sea.

There was only one obvious candidate in the Mediterranean area— the Black Sea, which lies north of Turkey. This is separated from the Mediterranean by the narrow stretch of water called the Bosphorus. And this is where Ryan and Pitman felt it would be worth looking for their answer to Dewey's challenge.

The Black Sea is shaped like a mile-deep salad bowl. The fresh water that flows into it from rivers like the Danube, the Dniester, and the Dnieper flows over its top layer on its way to the Mediterranean. At the bottom of the salad bowl lies heavy and concentrated salt water, rather like that of the Dead Sea.

This prevents the sea from "breathing" and explains why it is a dark green color, compared with the azure of the Mediterranean: it is relatively lifeless—which also explains why it is sometimes known as the Sea of Death.

And it was the fact that Gilgamesh is also recorded as going off in search of the Sea of Death that strengthened Ryan and Pitman's conviction that they were on the right track.

As long ago as 1680, an Italian scientist named Luigi Marsilli had discovered that the Black Sea has two currents, one on the surface and one far below. Ryan and Pitman repeated his experiment. This consisted in lowering a basket of stones into the water on a very long rope, with a float, which would prevent it from sinking to the bottom. And at a certain point, as the basket encountered the undersea current flowing the other way, the float began to move north instead of south. If Ryan and Pitman were right, this northward current had started to flow about nine thousand years ago, when the Black Sea—then a fresh water lake—was invaded by a waterfall from the rising Mediterranean.

Some of their colleagues were skeptical about the waterfall theory. They were willing enough to believe that the Black Sea had been "topped up" by the Mediterranean, but they believed it had probably been a very gradual process, perhaps taking centuries.

There was a minor problem about researching the flood theory: the Russians. The Black Sea was full of their ships and naval equipment, and they were understandably concerned in case scientific expeditions funded by the Americans were also intent on spying. Things began to improve with the end of the Cold War in 1990. But it was not until March 19, 1993, that Ryan and Pitman had their first real breakthrough.

It was in the form of a letter from a Bulgarian named Petko Dimitrov, and it informed them that he had convincing evidence that 9750 years ago, the Black Sea level was about a 100 meters lower than it is today. Investigating the Black Sea in a submersible—a miniature submarine—Dimitrov had discovered an ancient beach 110 meters below the surface. The fact that it was fossilized proved that it had been submerged by a flood. If the sea rise had been gradual, the lapping waves would have eaten away the beach.

Soon after, a second piece of luck came their way: an invitation to join an expedition to the Black Sea, mounted by the Shirsov Institute of Oceanology in Moscow. They wanted to know whether the explosion at the Chernobyl nuclear power plant in the Ukraine had contaminated the Black Sea.

The Russians had made another interesting discovery. North of the Black Sea, on the other side of a four-mile-wide strait, there is the Sea of Azov, sticking out of the Black Sea like a misshapen bubble. The Russians had planned to build a railway bridge across the strait and had drilled down under the water to test the depth of the bedrock.

But below the sediment on the bottom, they found a chasm that plunged another two hundred feet. This undersea gorge must have been cut by a river, probably the Don, which now flows into the north of the Sea of Azov. What this meant was that the Sea of Azov had once been dry land, with the Don flowing across it, into the small ice-age lake that is now the Black Sea.

So Ryan and Pitman set sail on a Russian ship called the *Aquanaut* and had a chance at last to study the bottom of the Black Sea. What worried them basically was the view held among Russian specialists that there had been no flood as such—that what had happened was simply that the Black Sea had risen gradually due to meltwater from the north, while the Mediterranean had also risen because of the melting ice of the last ice age, so that when the two finally mingled, there was no gigantic waterfall, but merely a slow rise above the "dam" that separated them.

Their Black Sea cruise gradually made this seem less and less likely. The highly sophisticated Russian equipment showed them the old beaches, and riverbeds that were now drowned under salt water. And cores from the bottom showed a very clear distinction between hard mud that had been dried out by the sun, and the soft black mud on top of it—the old mud actually looked dried out. And at the junction of the two were Mediterranean crustacea that had been carried in by a waterfall. Former lagoons and swamps still released trapped gas from decaying vegetation.

So there could be no doubt—there had been a sudden flood, just like the one that had turned the dry Mediterranean into a sea five or six million years ago. Pitman's computations showed that it had been equal to about 250 Niagaras and that the current had been flowing from the Mediterranean at a swift and dangerous sixty miles an hour.

A television program Ryan and Pitman made for the BBC presented it all with graphic impact—how local inhabitants at the side of the Black Sea freshwater lake might have been wandering along the intervening land barrier, and one day noticed a trickle of water splashing down the cliff. When they tried drinking it they found it was salty. By the following year the flow was twice as strong. Then it turned into a gushing stream, which made the barrier crumble fast, and caused a rise in the water level of perhaps a foot a day. They would have had to move quickly northward at a rate of a mile a day to keep ahead of the rising flood. And finally, on high ground, they would turn to look back on a drowned land.

These facts have been established beyond doubt by Ryan and Pitman. There was a great flood that turned a small Ice Age lake into the Black Sea. But when? Dimitrov had estimated that it had happened about 9750 years ago, based on the carbon dating of mollusk shells. But when the shells were carbon dated in an American laboratory, Ryan and Pitman were in for a shock—Ryan especially, since he had already given a lecture proposing a date somewhere in excess of 9000 years ago—say 7000 BC. But the carbon dating showed he was about 1500 years out. This flood had taken place around 5450 BC.

This date confused everybody—including myself, when I first watched the BBC program. I had been hoping that the flood would be dated about 12,000 years ago, around the date of Plato's Atlantis. To discover that it came about 5000 years later was puzzling.

For Ryan and Pitman the result had its consolations. At that date, it could be the flood described in Gilgamesh and Genesis. Admittedly, Woolley and Mallowan had placed it much later. But men have long memories, and perhaps this flood had been preserved in the songs of minstrels long before writing existed. . . .

Ryan and Pitman even suggested that perhaps the Sumerians were the survivors of the Black Sea flood, who had brought their knowledge of irrigation channels with them from the days when the Black Sea was a freshwater lake that steadily shrank in size.

Most of their colleagues, inevitably, thought that was going too far.

Surely the natural place for survivors to flee would be northward, not south to Mesopotamia? In reply, Ryan pointed out that when, in *The Epic of Gilgamesh*, Gilgamesh travels to the Sea of Death in search of Uta-Napishtim, he is transported over the sea by a boatman who lowers a basket of stones into the water—precisely as Ryan had done on the Black Sea to contact the underlying current.

In the BBC program, Stephanie Dalley, an expert on Mesopotamian myth and on *The Epic of Gilgamesh*, dismissed this as pure fantasy, declaring that Gilgamesh is so full of amazing stories that it is impossible to use it as a guidebook to modern Mesopotamia. She also points out that the Black Sea flood happened about two thousand years before the Sumerians began building Ur, some time after 4000 BC.

Yet a piece of research conducted in the 1980s seems to indicate that Ryan and Pitman were basically correct, whether or not the author of Gilgamesh was talking about the Black Sea flood or a flood further south.

In the Caribbean, near Barbados, it had been noticed that the coral—which is normally only a few yards below the surface—was tens of yards below. That meant that the sea level had been rising steadily since the reef was laid down several thousand years ago.

In 1988, Rick Fairbanks, of the Lamont-Docherty Geological Observatory, began to take core samples from these coral reefs. The first cores came to the surface just before Thanksgiving, 1988. These showed that that there had been not one flood, but three.

FIVE

MORE CATASTROPHES

Eighteen thousand years ago, when the last Ice Age (which began about 130,000 years ago) was particularly severe, the sea level was 120 meters lower than it is today. Then, slowly, the ice began to melt.

About 14,500 years ago, after another temporary freeze (called the Older Dryas), the melting suddenly accelerated. At that time, the ice cap of the North Pole still stretched down as far as the British Isles. Suddenly, an altogether swifter meltdown began. Icebergs flaked off the ice sheet and drifted into the Atlantic. About 12,000 BC (i.e., 14,000 years ago), a vast lake in North America, Lake Livingstone, collapsed and released such a huge pocket of water into the sea—84,000 cubic kilometers—that the world's sea levels immediately rose by nine inches, causing the first great flood.

Then, erratically, the cold came back. We still do not know the reason for these swings in climate, although meteorologists often credit something called the Milankovitch cycle. Around 11,000 BC, the world froze again (a freeze known as the Younger Dryas) and temperatures dropped even lower than during the Older Dryas. Then, around 9500 BC, another sudden melting took place, and within fifty years, the world was drowned again.

Another great ice lake, this time in northeast Canada, released its floodwaters. If Charles Hapgood is correct, this flood was the "Atlantis flood" referred to by Plato. Its date corresponds exactly.

But a third flood was still to come. Sometime around 6400 BC another freeze took place and lasted about 400 years. Then once again, warm weather returned, and around 6000 BC, caused one of the greatest floods so far. Hudson Bay was mainly responsible for this latest flood, when a huge ice plug melted and released millions of tons of freezing water into the sea. Other parts of the great Canadian ice sheet followed the same route. The result was a dramatic rise in sea levels of possibly eighty feet, to their present level.

It was this rise in sea levels that finally flooded the Black Sea, or the freshwater lake that then occupied its place in about 5750 BC. (Ryan and Pitman date it to 5600 BC, but in these matters, precise dating is virtually impossible.) The waterfall that came in from the Mediterranean was about 350 feet high, and Pitman, as we have seen, estimates its volume as equal to the water in 250 Niagara Falls.

It would seem that Noah's flood (presumably also known as the flood of Gilgamesh) occurred around 6000 BC, between two and three thousand years before the early Sumerian version of *The Epic of Gilgamesh* was written.

This time frame sounds astonishing. I can understand Stephanie Dalley's skepticism when she argued that the Gilgamesh flood was far too late to be the flood confirmed by Ryan and Pitman. But apart from local floods, which would seem to include Woolley's ten feet of sediment at Ur, no Great Flood occurred after about 5500 BC (although there were plenty of smaller ones). As a result, I have to assume that human memory, aided by bards and minstrels, preserved the Great Flood story for 3000 years.

When we look at *Gilgamesh* or *Genesis*, one thing seems clear. This flood was not accompanied by earthquakes, erupting volcanoes, and the erratic movement of the sun in the sky that are chronicled in *When the Sky Fell*. Uta-Napishtim describes darkness and tempest, but not earth tremors. It therefore seems unlikely that this flood was the one described in so many Indian legends, from Canada to Peru, a flood in which the sun was said to have moved in the sky.

And that legend was apparently why Indians of Mexico and Peru were terrified of an eclipse of the sun, and performed sacrifices to avert it. Graham Hancock devoted many pages in *Fingerprints of the Gods* to those legends of the sun wandering from its course and the sky falling.

We know the sun cannot wander from its course. But if the earth's crust moved, as Hapgood suggested, the sun would appear to have changed its course.

What proof do we have that the earth's crust actually moved? One interesting piece of evidence can be found in the BBC book *Earth Story*[1] in a map that shows the earth as it was 18,000 years ago.

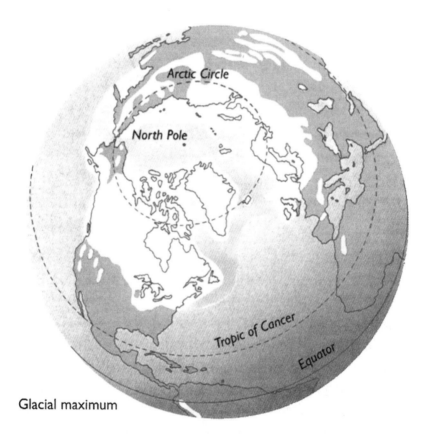

A map of the ice sheet in America during the last Ice Age.

This map clearly shows that at the height of the last Ice Age, the ice sheet in America extended south of the Great Lakes. A different map showed it extending south of New York. Yet in the British Isles, the ice does not even extend as far south as Cornwall, whose latitude is roughly the same as Newfoundland's, 700 miles north of New York.

If this ancient ice sheet were to extend around the world at a uniform distance from the present North Pole, it would have to reach as far south as central Spain. In fact—as Hapgood had explained more than forty years earlier—to account for this lopsided distribution of ice, the North Pole would have to be somewhere in the area of Hudson Bay. At some point since 18,000 years ago, the North Pole must have moved further north. Or, rather, that part of the earth must have moved south.

And so the findings of earth science in the 1990s tell us of three great floods since the end of the last ice age, the first around 12,000 BC, the second around 9500, and the third around 6000 BC. And from its dating, the second of these floods is clearly the one that interested Charles Hapgood, the "Atlantis" flood.

Now as we have seen, the major difference between the Atlantis flood and the Black Sea (Gilgamesh) flood seems to have been that the Atlantis catastrophe was accompanied by earthquakes and volcanic eruptions. What happened at the time of Plato's Atlantis was sudden and violent—just as Plato described it. But what actually did happen?

In 1993, Professor Alexander Tollmann, a geologist at the Institute of Geology at the University of Vienna, and his wife Edith Tollmann, published a study in which they set out to answer that question.[2] Their answer was that the earth had been struck by a giant comet made of ice—they had even worked out the date—September 23, 7545 BC. (A Middle Eastern tradition that the event happened on the day of the autumn equinox provided the date for the Tollmanns.) The comet's arrival caused an enormous tidal wave and filled the earth's atmosphere with dust, the Tollmanns said, resulting in the extinction of such species as the mammoth and the saber-tooth cat.

The Tollmanns were convinced that this catastrophe was the cause of not only Plato's great flood but also Noah's flood in the Bible. They disagree with Ryan and Pitman that the Black Sea flood was the flood described in Genesis. But I believe strong evidence exists that the Tollmanns were wrong on both counts.

Their study was based on the discovery of an immense concentration of tektites that were laid down in sediment all over the world, in 7600 BC. The tektites, the Tollmanns suggested, indicated the presence of a comet or large meteor. They also believed that there was evidence that the comet split into seven smaller bodies. They quoted the apocryphal *Book of Enoch* that speaks of seven stars, like seven burning mountains, falling to earth. (A similar break-up occurred in July 1994 before the comet Shoemaker-Levy struck Jupiter at more than 130,000 miles an hour, with a force estimated at fifty times the nuclear arsenal of earth.) The Tollmanns also found evidence in radioactive carbon-14 in the trees of that date. This carbon, they claimed, was due to the destruction of the earth's ozone layer by the comet, which had exposed earth to more radioactivity from space.

The Tollmanns backed their theory with myths from many parts of the world: the Middle East, China, India, and the American continent. They said that the flood that struck the west coast of America swept so far inland that it created the Great Salt Lake on which Salt Lake City stands. They also noted that several of these myths described the earth being threatened by seven burning suns. The location of the seven impacts can be seen from the map. The Tollmanns added: "This all makes it extremely difficult nowadays to maintain convincing arguments against the existence of Atlantis."[3]

One of the comet fragments fell—as can be seen from the map—in the China sea, an observation, as we shall see, of some significance.

An eighth, smaller impact occurred in the Otz Valley, in Austria, where the comet fragment formed the Kofels crater. This impact has been dated to about 8000 BC.

The Tollmanns' claims were supported, in principle, by an Oxford astrophysicist, Victor Clube, who summarized twenty years of research into cometary impacts in a book called *The Cosmic Winter*, which he coauthored with astronomer Bill Napier.

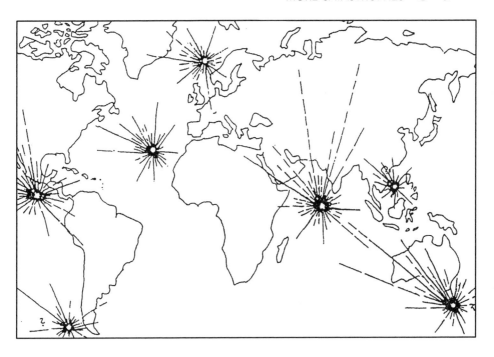

The probable impact locations of the seven main fragments of the comet that collided with the planet Earth about 9,545 years ago and caused the Flood.

Since the 1950s, scientists have believed that comets are not visitors from some remote region of outer space, but are instead fragments left over from the time when our solar system condensed from a cloud of whirling gas. In 1950, the Dutch astronomer Jan H. Oort suggested that the material of comets resides in a cloud of freezing gas in orbit somewhere outside of our solar system.

Periodically, a passing star or a molecular cloud would dislodge some of it, Oort said, and send it falling toward the sun. And the fragment would continue to travel in a huge elliptic orbit at regular intervals of, perhaps 77 years (like Halley's comet), until it disintegrated. Most comets are a dozen or so miles wide and are believed to be made of fairly light matter, often gas. But clearly this was not true of Shoemaker-Levy.

Comets tend to break down over time, until they form a huge cloud of debris. When the earth goes through such clouds, the result is a spectacular display of "shooting stars." Most of these, of course, burn up in the earth's atmosphere; but some are large enough to reach earth—as was the case with the object from the Taurid meteor stream that exploded over Tunguska, Siberia, on June 30, 1908, flattening and burning trees in an 18-mile radius circle. The meteors apparently failed to make a crater, vaporizing a few miles above the earth.

We were fortunate, in 1908, for we now know that impacts from space have changed the history of our earth, and brought a sudden and violent end to geological ages.

Sixty million years ago, the earth was struck by a giant comet or meteor. It fell into the sea at Chicxulub, off the coast of Mexico, and filled the earth's atmosphere with a dust that eventually cut off the sunlight and killed off plant life, and the dinosaurs that lived on it.

Something similar has happened more frequently than we would like to contemplate. The comet that killed the dinosaurs is only one of five comets or asteroids that have caused major extinctions in the earth's history: one at the Triassic-Jurassic boundary (213 million years ago), one at the Permian-Triassic boundary (248 million years ago), one at the Devonian-Carboniferous boundary (308 million years ago), and one at the Ordovician and Silurian boundary (438 million years ago). It looks as if each new geological era, up to 60 million years ago, has been caused by a comet impact. Chesapeake Bay, southeast of Washington DC, was created by a giant meteor 35 million years ago. But since the earth's crust, unlike that of the moon, is constantly changing, the craters tend to heal.

In their book, Victor Clube and Bill Napier argue that streams of comets tumble out of the Oort cloud every three to five million years, due to the earth's passage through molecular clouds, as well as the earth's passage close to a spiral arm of our galaxy (the Milky Way). The two astronomers state that our solar system is due for another bombardment about now. We can see that such a notion is compatible with Tollmann's belief that some giant body from space caused a widespread catastrophe around 7600 BC.

Further support for Clube and Napier's theory came from Queen's University, Belfast, where in 1997, studies of ancient tree rings revealed that the earth had suddenly cooled in the nine years between 2354 BC and 2345 BC. The temperature shift is believed by Napier to be evidence of yet another cometary impact. Archaeological digs in northern Syria revealed signs of a catastrophic event at the same time that caused mud-brick buildings to disintegrate. The event was almost certainly caused by the impact of a single comet or asteroid in the Mediterranean.

Napier has pointed out that three major civilizations went into decline at this period: Egypt, Sumer, and the Harrapin Kingdom of the Indus Valley in India. He further said that forty cities around the world were destroyed during the same period.

The bombardment from outer space seems to have continued. French researchers in the Middle East have found layers of a mineral called calcite, which is normally found only in rocks from space, and which is estimated to date from 2200 BC. All this evidence suggests that around this period, earth was struck by an asteroid or comet that cut off sunlight and caused crop failures.

In case the reader is becoming confused by the sheer number of floods and catastrophes, let us attempt to bring a little order into the narrative.

The first great flood, which marked the end of the Ice Age, occurred around 12,000 BC, and may be ignored here, since it seems to have left no mark in myth or literature, or even racial memory. The reason is obvious: it was due to melting ice and involved a mere nine-inch rise in sea level.

The second, of 9500 BC, is Hapgood's flood, the flood that destroyed Atlantis. This is almost certainly the "first flood" referred to by Critias, who learned of it from his uncle Solon, who heard it from the priests of Sais in Egypt.

The "second flood" mentioned by Critias must therefore be Tollmann's flood of 7545 BC, caused by the impact of a comet or aster-oid. The "third flood" is the Black Sea Flood, the flood of *Gilgamesh*.

The fourth flood, as the *Critias* noted, is Deucalion's Flood, which occurred in the Bronze Age around 2200 BC. This also seems to have been due to the impact of a body from space.

Which leaves us with the problem that troubled Hapgood so much, and started him on his quest for Atlantis: what actually caused the "Atlantis flood"?

The answer has to be: an asteroid or cometary impact. And this is the conclusion that is argued, brilliantly and conclusively, in a book called *When the Earth Nearly Died, Compelling Evidence of a Cosmic Catastrophe of 9500 BC*, by D. S. Allan and J. B. Delair, the first a paleogeographer, the second an anthropologist who is Curator of the Museum of Geology at the University of Southampton.

They argue that the day when the earth was almost destroyed occurred at the time of the destruction of Plato's Atlantis. With painstaking thoroughness, the author's present in chapter after chapter (the book is so massive that the publisher had to print it in double columns) the geological and mythological evidence that some great cataclysm shook the earth around 9500 BC. And it is not until about halfway through that they outline their own theory: that some cosmic body, either a giant meteor or a fragment of an exploding nova, hurtled through our solar system 11,500 years ago, leaving a trail of wreckage.

The authors suggest that it tilted Uranus on its side and tore away a moon, which went spinning through space until it ended as the outermost planet Pluto, ripped a satellite away from Saturn, then demolished a planet between Jupiter and Mars, which became the asteroids. As it passed the earth, it increased the tilt of the axis and produced those catastrophic effects that Charles Hapgood had noted, and ascribed to the slipping of the earth's crust. This "additional tilt," which has now "worn off," explains what the astronomer Norman Lockyer called "the obliquity of the ecliptic," the slight tilting back and forward of the earth's axis (although this is now being questioned).

Particularly fascinating is their account of the destruction of Tiahuanaco—for Allan and Delair have no doubt that it was this chunk of space debris (which they call Phaeton) that caused the upheaval. They produce evidence that not only was Tiahuanaco devastated but that the Andes suddenly became considerably higher in 9500 BC. For example, there are many stonewalls and agricultural terraces in the Andes that are well above the present level of perpetual snow, and demonstrate that they must have been upraised in historical times.

Again, Lake Titicaca is full of sea creatures and was obviously once at sea level. And there is an ancient strand-line on mountains nearby, with a white band of calcareous deposits of algae. This is more than two miles above sea level. Geologists have always assumed that this elevation occurred many millions of years ago. Allan and Delair present us with clear evidence that it happened when some giant meteor struck the earth in 9600 BC.

Significantly, Tiahuanaco also has its flood myth. The god Viracocha was the creator of the earth, and lived in Tiahuanaco, but when human beings became disobedient, he destroyed them in a great flood that engulfed the earth. Only two people survived: a man and a woman, who had taken refuge in a box, and the subsiding floodwaters left them at Tiahuanaco. Then Viracocha recreated the peoples of the earth, and gave each one his own language and songs.

There is an obvious parallel here with the Biblical flood, although the man and woman sound more like Adam and Eve. But after Noah's flood in Genesis, all human beings speak the same language until God gives them different languages (to make them incapable of building another Tower of Babel) and scatters them over the earth.

In *When the Sky Fell*, Rand and Rose Flem-Ath had discussed many flood legends, particularly those of American and Canadian Indians, and had pointed out the similarities between the flood stories of the Haida Indians, of the Queen Charlotte Islands, off the northwest coast of Canada, and the Flood story of Sumeria—not *The Epic of Gilgamesh*, but an earlier version, discovered in Nippur at the end of the nineteenth century, about a priest named Ziusudra, who seems to be identical with Uta-Napishtim.[4]

Both stories state that men of long ago lived in a golden age when life was carefree. The Sumerians say that their ancestors lived in an island called Dilmun; the Haida that their forefathers lived in "the world's largest village." The gods decided to destroy them—various reasons are given, from the sinfulness of mankind to the complaint that they made too much noise. In the Haida myth survivors escaped in large canoes, which took them to a new land where they landed on a mountain. In the Sumerian story Ziusudra builds an ark and eventually lands on a mountaintop. Rand Flem-Ath notes that the Haida speak a language called Na-Dene; this is, in fact, a whole group of Native American languages, of which the Haida version is the oldest.

And, incredibly, investigation in the 1980s by the Russian linguistic expert Merritt Ruhlen indicated that this might well be related to the Sumerian language.[5] If so, there could hardly be more remarkable proof of the existence of Hapgood's worldwide maritime civilization.

It is worth bearing in mind that Hapgood's interest in the problem of Atlantis started in 1949, when a student named Henry Warrington asked him about the lost continent of Mu that, according to legend, also sank beneath the waves at the same time as Atlantis. Hapgood told him to go away and research Mu—and then added, as an afterthought, that he might as well examine the evidence of Atlantis at the same time.

Warrington would have discovered that Mu—or Lemuria—has a respectable scientific provenance. In the 1850s, an English zoologist named P. L. Sclater observed a curious similarity between animals and plants as far apart as India and Australia and speculated that there might have been a sunken continent connecting them. This, he thought, existed about 55 million years ago, during the Eocene. He called it Lemuria because his missing continent connected places where lemurs—a primitive species of monkey—were common.

In the 1880s, a brilliant but erratic scholar named Augustus Le Plongeon claimed to be able to read texts of the ancient Maya of Mexico, and announced that he had found references to a continent called Mu, that had vanished beneath the Pacific after a tremendous earthquake. The mention of earthquakes suggests that we could be speaking either about the Atlantis catastrophe, or about Tollmann's comet strike of 7500 BC.

In a remarkable book called *Eden in the East: The Drowned Continent of Southeast Asia*, Professor Stephen Oppenheimer argues that the Sumerians were descendents of survivors of a great flood, which also drowned the coast of China, and a pacific continent that lay in the region he calls "Sundaland."

What Oppenheimer is suggesting bears some resemblance to the British zoologist P. L. Sclater's suggestion about the land bridge between India and Australia. But Sclater thought that "Lemuria" existed 55 million years ago in the Eocene. Oppenheimer thinks the land bridge was finally submerged as recently as the time of the great flood of 6000 BC.

Oppenheimer discusses Hapgood and the Piri Reis map, and Graham Hancock's belief that there was a "lost founder-civilization" in Antarctica. But his own candidate for the lost founder-civilization is the submerged continent of Southeast Asia, which he calls Sundaland. This, he believes, not only preceded Sumeria and Egypt, but was the source of both.

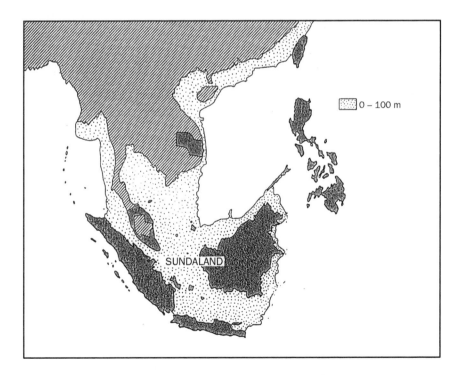

The lost founder-civilization of Sundaland (after Stephen Oppenheimer).

Oppenheimer's account pointed out that, according to Genesis, the Garden of Eden was located in the east. In the Bible's words, "As men migrated from the east, they found a plain in the land of Shinar and settled there."[6] The land of Shinar is, of course, the Biblical name for Sumeria, the "first civilization."

Oppenheimer pointed out that the Sumerian language, like the language of the region's neighbors, the Elamites, was unique among Semitic languages. (Babylonian, or Akkadian, which replaced it, and in which *The Epic of Gilgamesh* was written, is a more typical Semitic language.) In some respects, Sumerian was more like Finnish or Hungarian. No one quite knows its origin.

Unfortunately, Oppenheimer seemed unaware of one vital piece of information: Tollmann's comet impact of 7545 BC. The sheer magnitude of the catastrophe Oppenheimer described makes it unlikely that the massive flood was due to melting ice. On the other hand, two of Tollmann's cometary fragments struck in the Indian Ocean and in the South China Sea, while two more landed near the west coast of South America. These four would have been enough to submerge Sundaland.

Tollmann's comet certainly makes a better candidate for Oppenheimer's catastrophe than the Black Sea Flood. In fact, Tollmann himself wrote, "In Asia, mankind reached the then ice-free mammoth steppes of Siberia 15,000 years ago. The islands of South-East Asia were also accessible over the then-dry continental shelf, and the latest research indicates that man got as far as Australia between 50,000 and 40,000 years ago after traversing the Timor Sea by boat."[7] This area was devastated by the flood of 7545 BC.

Tollmann owns a Chinese woodcut with a dragon motif that symbolizes the flood. The woodcut reveals a huge tidal wave and a funnel of ejected water with the characteristic tulip form. Tollmann described the woodcut as "undoubtedly based on a transmitted eye-witness account of the geologically authenticated impact in the South-China Sea, which has been confirmed by rock-vitrificion products in Vietnam. Otherwise the details of such an impact, which have only recently been scientifically confirmed, could never have been so accurately depicted."[8]

Oppenheimer suggested in *Eden in the East* that after the flood, refugees from Sundaland went in all four directions of the compass. Some carried rice-growing skills into India, probably to the Indus valley. Some headed to southwest China, Burma, and Tibet, taking their art with them. Others went south to Australia and east to Micronesia. All these lands, Oppenheimer claimed, show the linguistic and genetic traces of the nomads who had been flooded out of their homes. From India, according to Oppenheimer, others went to Egypt and Sumer and founded new civilizations. In a book called *Historical Metrology* author A. E. Berriman points out that what he calls the Indus inch is precisely twice a Sumerian measure called the shusi while many of the ancient Polynesians called their sun god Ra, as in ancient Egypt.

"In their dispersal," wrote Oppenheimer, "the Southeast Asian explorers fertilized the Neolithic cultures of China, India, Mesopotamia, Egypt and Crete."[9] In short, they were the true founders of Western culture.

Oppenheimer could well be correct. But if Charles Hapgood is also correct, then a worldwide culture already existed before the Sundaland catastrophe. Even while Hapgood was still alive, new pieces of evidence kept surfacing for his ancient seafarers. One of the most intriguing is the story of the cocaine mummies.

In September 1976, the mummy of Rameses II, the last of the great Egyptian pharaohs, who died in 1213 BC, arrived in Paris, to form the centerpiece of an exhibition at the Museum of Mankind. Rameses had spent much of his life battling the Hittites, and the great hall of columns in the temple at Karnak is perhaps his greatest memorial. But when his mummy was examined, it was found to be deteriorating. Scientists were asked to repair the damage. One of these scientists was Dr. Michelle Lescot, of the Natural History Museum.

Lescot examined a piece of mummy bandage under an electron microscope. To her astonishment, she recognized grains of tobacco, a finding that seemed absurd, for tobacco first came to Europe from South America in the time of Christopher Columbus.

The announcement of her find caused a storm. Egyptologists

declared that the tobacco grains must have come from the pipe of some modern scientist who was smoking as he studied the mummy. So Lescot took samples from deep inside the mummy, and again found tobacco grains. Still other experts refused to accept the presence of tobacco. They said the grains probably came from some other plant, such as henbane, which was a member of the tobacco family. Lescot knew they weren't but decided not to press her point.

Fifteen years passed. Then, in 1992, German researchers at the Munich Museum began studying the materials used by the ancient Egyptians in mummification. Since they wanted to find out whether any drugs were present, they turned to a forensic scientist whose expertise had often been called upon by the police in cases of suspicious deaths. She was Dr. Svetlana Balabanova, of the Institute of Forensic Medicine in Ulm.

Dr. Balabanova was not asked to study the mummy of anybody as distinguished as a great pharaoh. She was given the remains of a mere priestess named Henut Taui, who had died around 1000 BC in Thebes. Taui's tomb had been plundered by robbers in the nineteenth century, and the mummy was then sold to Ludwig I, Bavaria's art-loving monarch, who gave it to the museum in Munich.

Dr. Balabanova tested the mummy, utilizing an antibody-reaction. She also analyzed the molecular weights of some of the body's substances and graphed the results. Both approaches showed that the mummy contained both nicotine and cocaine, which had been used as preservatives.

Her findings were even more startling than Lescot's. If Balabanova was correct, then the ancient Egyptians had not only been in contact with the Native Americans of the east coast of the Americas but had also been to the opposite coast as well. The ancient Peruvians also mummified their dead.

Cocaine is native to the Andes. When a tired traveler arrives at a hotel in La Paz or Cuzco, he is given a cup of tea made from coca leaves, which instantly relieves the dizziness due to the high altitude. Balabanova's findings make it look as if the Egyptians knew about cocaine's preservative properties more than three thousand years ago.

The reception of Balabanova's analyses was even stormier than in the case of Lescot. Balabanova received abusive and insulting letters, accusing her of being a fantasist. Her response was to publish her figures and graphs. In response, the archaeological establishment fell back on its second line of defense and suggested that the mummy was contaminated. To those accusations, Balabanova said that, as a forensic scientist, contamination was the very first thing she had ruled out. Then her critics suggested that the mummy was a "forgery," a fake concocted by Arab racketeers. Additional tests, including carbon dating, proved that accusation to be untrue.

Embarrassed by this publicity, museum officials concerned were inclined to disregard the whole thing. But Balabanova went on testing mummies, regularly finding tobacco and cocaine in them. The skeptics continued to insist that it must be some other type of tobacco, native to Europe and long extinct. But their suggestion still failed to explain the presence of cocaine.

Someone recalled that in 1975, Roman jars had been found off the coast of Brazil in a bay known as the Bay of Jars, a place where jars had been turning up for centuries. The Roman jars were almost certainly from a sunken Roman galley. Since Roman historians would probably have mentioned if they had known about transatlantic voyages, we can probably assume that the galley was swept out to sea by storms and carried across the Atlantic by the same westward currents that in 1969 would carry Thor Heyerdahl's ship *Ra*. But in the case of the Egyptians, the sheer quantity of mummies with cocaine traces ruled out this explanation.

Now since Egyptologists have found no other signs of tobacco or cocaine in ancient Egypt, we can probably assume that no regular trade existed in these two commodities. The drugs must have been brought to Egypt at great expense and used to preserve the mummies of kings and queens, guaranteeing their immortality. But we are left with the unavoidable conclusion that the Egyptian priests knew about the great continent across three thousand miles of ocean, and knew that it could be reached by taking advantage of the currents. Unless those explorers trekked across forests and prairies and mountains to reach Peru, we must also assume they sailed around the Cape of Storms (unless they took the even longer Pacific route). There could hardly be stronger evidence for Hapgood's ancient ocean-going civilization.

Hapgood's map (below) from *Maps of the Ancient Sea Kings*, and his account of the map of Hadji Ahmad, is also relevant to this discussion.

As we look at this map, which appeared in Turkey in 1559, we note that the drawing of Europe is not particularly accurate. The Mediterranean, for example, is entirely the wrong shape, and it is not clear whether the body of water running south from it is the Red Sea or the Persian Gulf. According to Hapgood, the coast of Africa does not compare in accuracy with the Piri Reis map of nearly half a century earlier.

On the other hand, the American continent is so accurate that we could easily mistake it for a modern map. It seems unbelievable that Columbus had arrived a mere 67 years earlier. How had the mapmaker gained such accurate knowledge, when the continent was still mostly a vast wilderness? Above all, how had the Pacific coast been drawn with such precision? Pizzaro and his conquistadores had landed on the coast of Peru as recently as 1532, a mere 27 years earlier. There was simply no time for this knowledge of detail to have been developed.

There can be only one solution. The European part of the map must have been based on one of the old, inaccurate maps, probably Ptolemy. But the American part must have been based on an ancient portolan made by someone who knew both coasts from personal experience.

This might, of course, have been ancient Egyptians in search of cocaine and tobacco. But there is evidence that whoever made the portolan came far earlier than Rameses.

For there is another oddity about this Hadji Ahmad map. Looking down on the North Pole, as it were, it shows Asia and Alaska joined together. It does not, admittedly, show Beringia, the land bridge across the Bering Strait, which was submerged by the sea at the end of the last Ice Age. But if the two continents had been separate, as they are today, it would have been easy enough to indicate this with a narrow

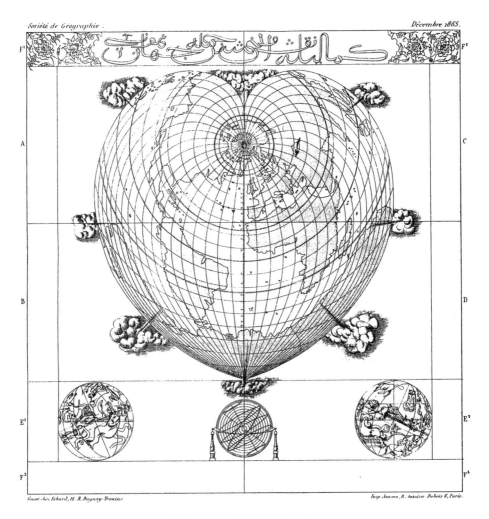

The map of Hadji Ahmad.

gap between them. As it is, they are simply joined, as if by a land bridge a thousand miles wide.

Hapgood quotes an Oxford scientist, Derek S. Allan, who pointed out that what is now the island of Novya Zemlya is shown as being joined to the Siberian coast, and that what are now the New Siberian Islands are shown as an area of dry land.

In other words, the mapmaker showed the world as it was about 14,000 years ago.

But who was around 14,000 years ago to make maps?

The answer is probably: plenty of people. To begin with, the forebears of the "Atlanteans," as well as the Sundalanders, the early Australians and the builders of Tiahuanaco—which Posnansky dates to 15,000 BC, at which time it would still have been at sea level.

But a major problem remains unanswered: what turned our ancestors into "sea kings"? With a little imagination, we can put ourselves in the place of our Cro-Magnon forebears at the end of the Ice Age, realizing that the ice is melting, that the summers are becoming warmer, that game is more plentiful, and that they can venture further and further from the shore in search of fish. But who was the original Columbus to cross the Atlantic, the first Balboa to cross the Pacific?

And what gave them the courage to attempt anything so terrifying?

These questions were answered, almost accidentally, by a young Costa Rican professor named Ivar Zapp. And he started by trying to solve one of the world's greatest mysteries: the stone balls of Costa Rica.

They were discovered in the early 1930s when the United Fruit Company began clearing jungles of southwest Costa Rica, in Central America, to make a banana plantation in the area called the Diquis Delta. The workers hacking and burning their way through jungle began to find huge stone hemispheres sticking up out of the earth, and some hard digging revealed that they were spheres, like giant beachballs—except that they were made of granite. The largest was over nine feet in diameter, the smallest the size of a tennis ball.

It was obvious that the spheres had once formed part of various religious sites. They had been supported on top of mounds and were surrounded by stelae and statues. What was so astonishing was the perfect workmanship; many were exact spheres, and the surface was as smooth as paper.

But while giant stone balls are certainly an oddity, there is something about them, which quickly exhausts one's curiosity. Some of the wealthier inhabitants of San Jose and Limon, Costa Rica's major cities, had them transported on to their front lawns and learned in the process that the largest weighed twenty tons. A few archaeologists looked at them, shook their heads, and opined that they probably represented either the sun or the moon, or perhaps both, and turned their attention elsewhere.

Ten years or so later, an American archaeologist named Samuel K. Lothrop was taking a brief vacation in the Diquis area with his pretty wife when he saw one of the balls on a lawn in Palmar Sur; he was told that there were hundreds of them, and that no one had any idea of what they were. Here was a puzzle worth solving. And since Lothrop happened to have time on his hands—bandits were making it difficult to continue his current task of excavating the pottery of the Chortega Indians—he decided to devote some time to this intriguing problem.

He made little headway, for a smooth stone ball is devoid of clues. But at least he went and looked at some of the balls that had been left in situ and noted that they often seemed to occur in threes, in the form of a triangle. Others occurred in straight lines consisting of as many as forty-five spheres. But the triangles were oddly irregular and were often made of balls of differing sizes.

That suggested that there was some special purpose in their arrangement, some hidden code. But that purpose was impossible to fathom. Lothrop wrote a paper on the stone balls, which was published under the auspices of the Peabody Institute at Harvard, and returned to less impenetrable mysteries. No other archaeologist pursued the mystery, for Lothrop seemed to have exhausted it in his brief paper.

Three decades passed, and the stone spheres seemed to have been forgotten. Then, in 1981, Ivar Zapp, the young Professor of Architecture at the University of Costa Rica, thought he saw a new approach. His inspiration came from the work of an English scholar named John Michell, whose name had become associated with "ley lines"—long, straight tracks that run like canals across the English countryside. Zapp recalled the long, straight lines of stone spheres in the Diquis Delta, and began to speculate. . . .

To follow Zapp's reasoning, it is necessary to explain what he knew of John Michell and ley lines.

The lines had been "discovered" in 1921, by an English business-man named Alfred Watkins, who was riding his horse across the hills near Bredwardine, in Herefordshire, when he noticed that some ancient footpaths ran straight as an arrow for mile after mile, often toward hill-tops. And it suddenly struck him that England seems to be criss-crossed with hundreds of these "old straight tracks." He called them "leys" or "leas" and concluded that they were ancient trade routes used by the earliest inhabitants of Britain.

When John Michell came to the problem in the mid-1960s, it was largely because he was fascinated by the mystery of flying saucers. Michell noted the curious fact that many reports of flying saucers placed them close to ley lines, which are obviously more easily seen from the air than the ground, and especially at the crossing points of several leys.

Learning that the Chinese have similar lines called lung mei, or dragon paths, which are designed to channel the "magic energies of heaven and earth," Michell speculated that ley lines may be lines that mark some current of "earth force." He learned that dowsers, for example, can detect ley lines by the response of their dowsing rods or pendulums. Michell noted that ley lines often pass through "holy" sites, such as burial mounds, old churches, and ancient monuments like Stonehenge.

Ivar Zapp could see that the stone balls of the Diquis Delta seemed to pose some of the same questions as the megaliths of Stonehenge—or, for that matter, the huge stones of the Great Pyramid. How were they carved so perfectly? How were they moved? Some of them were even found high in the mountains along the coast of Costa Rica, and it was impossible to imagine even a large team of men rolling them uphill—it would be too difficult and dangerous.

Zapp took a party of his students to the Diquis Delta to try and fathom the mystery. They were baffled, but he began to see a gleam of light. Lothrop had left diagrams of what many of the original stones had looked like before they were moved to museums and front lawns. He noted two groups that seemed to be arranged on either side of a straight line. And the straight line pointed directly at the magnetic North Pole.

In that case, he wondered, was it possible that the other sides of the triangles pointed toward points on the earth?

When he tried out this theory on a map, extending the lines with a ruler, the result was disappointing. The lines seemed to point at nothing in particular. But then, of course, a map is a flat projection of the curved surface of the earth.

Zapp tried it again, this time with a tape measure and a globe, and knew immediately that it was not all self-delusion. One line, projected from Palmar Sur, where spheres had been found, went straight through Cocos Island, then through the Galapagos Islands, then to Easter Island. And he recalled that similar spheres have been discovered on Easter Island, although they were small compared to the giant balls of Costa Rica.

However, when he looked more closely at this "sight-line" from Palmar Sur to Easter Island, Zapp began to experience misgivings. The line actually missed Easter Island by 42 miles. Then he recalled something that reassured him. Polynesian sailors can detect the presence of an island up to 70 miles away by studying the waves and the clouds, for both are disturbed by the presence of land. Sailors also note the presence of land-based birds like the tern and the noddy. So a 7,000-mile long sight-line, via two other islands, which missed Easter Island by only 42 miles would be regarded a hit.

His doubts were set at rest as he began to study other sight-lines. Another side of the same triangle, extended across the Atlantic, led to the Straits of Gibraltar. In another group of stones the line led to the Great Pyramid. And in yet another, it not only pointed to southern England but ran right through Stonehenge. That could hardly be chance.

So it seemed that Ivar Zapp had discovered the purpose of the stone balls of Costa Rica. They were navigational aids. That explained why some were in straight lines on plains, and some were in the mountains overlooking the sea. It also explained why more of the stone balls had been found on the Island of Cano, off the south coast of Costa Rica, looking across the Pacific.

Lothrop had also noted that the balls were often found in association with Indian cemeteries, which led to the speculation that they might be some kind of homage to the dead. But if, in fact, they were direction-markers, you might expect them to be near cemeteries, since the sailors would hope for guidance from the spirits of dead navigators.

The question of when the spheres were carved remains a matter for debate. Archaeological finds in the Diquis Delta date from 12,000 BC to 500 AD. Some archaeologists (according to the Internet site on Costa Rica) date the stone balls to the most recent period, between a few centuries BC and 500 AD. But archaeologists tend to be intensely conservative, assuming that is the best way to avoid outraging their colleagues.

Extreme caution in dating a new find is a way of showing that you are a sober and respectable member of the academic community, not likely to leap to wild conclusions. But this can be a mistake. Zapp recalled that in the 1920s, when the MesoAmerican archaeologist Matthew W. Stirling found an immense negroid head at Tres Zapotes in Mexico, he suggested that the Olmec culture that carved them might be as early as 600 BC and was greeted with hoots of derision from his academic colleagues. But Stirling was, in fact, too conservative, and the Zapotec culture is now known to date from 1200 BC.

Zapp knew Hapgood's work and was perfectly aware of the possibility that the sailors who set up the stone balls were Hapgood's "ancient sea kings." And other evidence soon supported that hypothesis. A student named Humberto Carro noted that the story of Sinbad the Sailor in the *Arabian Nights* had a description of a steering device called a kamal. This consisted of a long knotted cord, with wooden squares at either end. The knots represented the latitudes of various ports. The Arab navigator would hold between his teeth a certain knot, and point the string at the Pole Star to determine the ship's position.

But Zapp had seen this knotted string before, on a small figure Lothrop had found near a group of stone balls. The figure was holding the ends of the string in either hand, and its center in his mouth, creating a V shape. Zapp had also seen similar figures from all over the world, from pottery designs in pre-Inca burial sites in Peru to depictions in the Indus Valley in India.

Costa Rica is, of course, a navigator's culture, since it is on one of the narrowest parts of Central America, with two vast oceans on either side. Humberto Carro came upon another interesting piece of evidence. He found an article by Thor Heyerdahl, which explained the techniques of sailing balsa rafts against the wind and current.

Thousands of years before the keel was invented, Peruvians used removable centerboards on their rafts, which served as keels and enabled them to tack. Pizzaro had encountered a whole flotilla of such rafts off the coast of Peru, of enormous size, which were moving toward them against the wind and current.

Pizzaro learned that they made journeys on these rafts along the whole coast of South America. Heyerdahl, of course, used a similar raft called *Kon Tiki* (one of the names of the god Quetzalcoatl), to prove that ancient mariners could have crossed the Pacific, and, later on, reinforced the point by crossing the Atlantic from Egypt to America.

When Christopher Columbus landed in Costa Rica in 1502, on his fourth voyage across the Atlantic, the explorers were received with great respect by the Native Americans, and taken on a two-hour walk to the grave of an important person, which was decorated with the prow of a ship.

The Costa Ricans were obviously introducing these great navigators from Spain to one of their own famous navigators. The stone lapidas, or funeral slabs, upon which the dead man was laid out looked like the centerboards of the Peruvian balsa rafts, and other figures—obviously priests and kings—were laid out on identical centerboards. The reason was obviously that the kings were being laid on stone replicas of the boards that played such an important part in their lives.

But could primitive navigators have sailed such enormous distances? It is true that Heyerdahl seemed to have proved the point. But would Costa Rican sailors of—let us say—5000 BC even have known of the existence of Easter Island? And even if they had, would they have dared to launch a balsawood raft into the vast and empty Pacific Ocean?

Then Zapp came upon a book that answered his question. It was called *We, The Navigators* by David Lewis, published in 1972, in which

Lewis described sailing with native islanders on native craft all over the Pacific, over 13,000 nautical miles. The islanders used the ocean-lore they had learned from their forefathers, and without any modern navigational equipment, never failed to reach their destination.

Zapp and his fellow author George Erickson had filled in the detail that Hapgood had been unable to supply and explained how ancient mariners had sailed the seven seas from China to North America.

All this, Zapp could see, might be used as confirmatory evidence to support the possibility of Hapgood's worldwide maritime civilization.

SIX

THE MYSTERY OF THE MAYA

After he had dinner with a Mayan specialist in Paris, Maurice Chatelain—the NASA scientist who investigated the "Nineveh number"—decided to look a little more closely at the Mayan people, who had appeared in Mexico about 300 BC, and vanished from history about 900 AD.

The Maya were a paradox. They had not even discovered the wheel, yet their calendar and knowledge of astronomy suggested that they were intellectual supermen. From Chatelain's point of view, one of the most impressive things about them was that they knew a version of the Nineveh number, with its fifteen digits.

Here again, as with the original Nineveh number, archaeologists had discovered immense numbers engraved on stone, in Mayan temples. Two of these numbers were found in one of the Maya's most sacred places, Quiriga, in Guatemala.

At the time these numbers were discovered, Europeans believed that the world had been created in 4004 BC, a date arrived at by Archbishop James Ussher by adding together all the dates in the Bible. No scholars paid any attention to such huge numbers, but when Chatelain looked at them—34,020 million, and 147,420 million—he was intrigued.

He guessed the numbers represented days, since the Mayans counted in days. This made the first about 93 million years, and the other a little more than 403 million years. Chatelain soon realized that the first is fifteen times the Nineveh number, while the other is sixty-five times. That meant, of course, that the Maya must have been familiar with the precession of the equinoxes.

Who were these amazing people?

Well, they had been discovered, or rather rediscovered, by a Spanish friar named Ramon de Ordonez, who lived in the town of Cuidad Real in Chiapas, southern Mexico, and who in 1773 was told about a city overgrown by the jungle, about seventy miles away. In the midst of the jungle, he discovered magnificent ruins, including a kind of pyramid, in a place that eventually became known as Palenque. Ordonez called it the City of the Serpents, because carvings of serpents had been reported there.

Ordonez had read something about the city's founder, a man named Votan, in a Maya book written in the Quiché language. The book had been discovered about 1690 in a temple and the local bishop, Nunes de la Vega, had quickly burned it. Fortunately, he had copied some of it before he burnt it, so Friar Ordonez was able to discover a little of its contents.

Votan was a tall, bearded man who had arrived in the New World many centuries earlier. His native city, in the Middle East, was called Valum Chivim. The manuscript described that during one of his four trips home, Votan had visited a city where the residents were attempting to build a tower that would reach to the sky. If this was the Tower of Babel, then the city would have been Babylon, and the date perhaps 2500 BC.

This link to Babylon, then, might possibly explain how the Maya, who accepted Votan as their ruler and teacher, came to know the Nineveh number. The Maya regarded Votan as a god. His symbol was the serpent. He also became known under other names: Viracocha, Kon Tiki, and Quetzalcoatl ("the plumed serpent").

In the "sunken temple," in front of the Kalasasiya in Tiahuanaco, is a statue of a tall, bearded European who is assumed to be the great teacher, Viracocha. He must have been European, since native Indians cannot grow beards. If the statue is indeed of Viracocha, and the town of Tiahuanaco dated from before 10,000 BC, then Votan probably arrived in the New World long before the building of Babylon. And since another legend states that the white god arrived from the east after some great natural catastrophe, it is even conceivable that we are talking about someone who escaped the Atlantis flood.

Of course, all this could be dismissed as speculation. But one thing is definitely not speculation: that the Maya knew a version of the Nineveh number, the precession number.

In 1841, the Mayan culture achieved the fame it deserved when a young American lawyer named John Lloyd Stephens decided to go to Mexico and see the famous ruins for himself. Stephens was already known for his travels in the Middle East, and his book *Incidents of Travel in South America* brought him overnight celebrity. The book's illustrations of jungle cities, by Stephen's friend James Catherwood, introduced the rest of the world to the architecture of the Maya.

These Mexican Indians, who developed a more precise calendar than anyone else—even more exact than the Romans whose Julian calendar was 365 days long—had a year that was 365.2420 days long. This kind of accuracy is astounding. How could the early Maya, the so-called "classic Maya"—who built cities in the jungle before they mysteriously abandoned them around 890 AD—want a calendar as accurate as that? Our own modern measurement of the year, based on the cesium clock, is 365.2422 days long, two ten-thousandths of a day longer.

Moreover, the Maya had invented a symbol for zero, which is regarded as a basic essential in mathematics, yet neither the Greeks nor the Romans had a zero. This may hardly seem important. But without the decimal system—counting in tens—it is impossible to arrange numbers in columns of ten, each column ten times the previous one. When the Romans wanted to write a figure like 1944, they had to write MCMXLIV.

Mayan astronomy is awe-inspiring. It is so complex and precise that some Martian scholar who had stumbled on it by chance might well conclude that the Maya were Earth's greatest scientists.

We calculate the year by the sun; so did the Maya. But they also calculated it by the planet Venus, as well as by Jupiter-Saturn cycles. As to our earthly year, they solved the problem that the Egyptians, the Greeks, and even the Romans had failed to solve by having no less than three distinct calendars: they had a sun calendar of 360 days, to which they added five supernumerary days (although, as already noted, they knew the exact length of the solar year), a lunar year of 354 days, and a special "sacred" calendar of 260 days called a tzolkin, used for magical and ritual purposes. This was divided into 13 months of 20 days each.

These three cycles ran concurrently. But since it is obvious that the tzolkin was well into its second year when the ordinary year had only just come to an end, their "century" was a total cycle in which the three lesser cycles had finally caught up with one another. This was 52 years long. The "Venus year" (584 days long) caught up with the other every two Mayan centuries (104 years).

There was still another calendar, called the Long Count, used to calculate long periods of time. Its unit, as we have noted, was 20 days. 360 days was a "tun." Twenty tuns was a "katun," and 20 katuns was a "baktun," which is 144,000 days. Thirteen baktuns equaled one "Great Cycle," or one "earth age," at the end of which everything would be destroyed and start all over again. The present earth cycle began in 3114 BC and will end in December 2012 AD.

The Maya also knew of the existence of Uranus and Neptune, although neither was discovered in Europe until the mid-nineteenth century. Robert Temple is inclined to believe they had some form of telescope.[1] (This also applies to the Sumerians, who represented Saturn with a ring round it, although it cannot be seen with the naked eye.)

The strange thing is that as civilization-builders, the Maya were not particularly remarkable. Professor Eric J. Thompson, the leading twentieth-century expert on the Maya, points out that this civilization, which had displayed such amazing astronomical knowledge, had still failed to invent the wheel or the curved arch, or even to weigh a sack of corn. Moreover, as many scholars have noted, the Maya simply failed to evolve or progress. Their late art and architecture looks much the same as the earlier.

But then, the Maya themselves claimed that their knowledge originally came from Votan, who arrived after some great catastrophe.

What happened to Votan—alias Viracocha, Kukulcan, Quetzalcoatl, and Kon Tiki? The legend says he was driven out again as a result of plots against him, and sailed away on a raft to the west, promising to return one day, and even specifying where he would land. And so when, by an incredible chance, the Spaniard Hernan Cortes and his small band of soldiers landed on that same beach at Vera Cruz in 1519, the Aztecs—the descendants of the Maya—assumed him to be the god-teacher and allowed themselves to be conquered and overthrown.

And this incredible, almost unbelievable coincidence, makes us aware of why the Indians of Central America were so obsessed by the stars. They had absolutely no doubt that the heavens foretold the future.

But there was another reason: irrational terror. They were terrified that one day they would wake up, and the sun would fail to appear over the horizon. Then the wind would rise and the rain would fall in torrents, and the earth would be drowned in a great flood, as it had been more than once before. It was this fear of a time "when the sky fell" that made them so fixated on the calendar, for the calendar dictated the time for religious observances, when the gods had to be propitiated.

And their method of bribing the gods was human sacrifice. The victim was held down on a stone slab, and the priest made an incision in the chest with a flint knife. Then a hand was plunged under the ribs, the beating heart was torn out and held aloft.

Which explains why the Spaniards who invaded Mexico—and later Peru—had so little compunction about torturing and killing these superstitious savages. They felt that anyone who habitually ripped out living hearts deserved whatever they got.

Just how bloodily and cruelly the Spaniards did this can be seen in William H. Prescott's *History of the Conquest of Mexico*, which takes an extremely strong stomach to read. We are inclined to feel sorry for the Aztecs—successors of the Maya—until we hear about how their eighth emperor, Ahuitzotl, ordered the sacrifice of eighty thousand prisoners to dedicate a temple, when the gutters ran with blood; the massacre took four days of nonstop killing. The priests then flayed the corpses and lubricated their own naked bodies with their fat before pulling on the skin like a wet suit. The slaughterers and their families followed this up with a cannibal feast. To say that all this was done in a spirit of religious piety is obviously absurd; any criminologist knows that sadistic murder becomes an addiction.

In his book *The Mayan Factor*, the artist and Maya specialist Jose Arguelles argues that such a description does not apply to the Maya, although he concedes that there are artistic representations of prisoners. But, he adds in their defense, "more important . . . than territoriality and making war was the needs to track the cycles of the planet Earth by means of a unique mathematical system."[2]

The problem with this is that the Maya did not work out the cycles of the planet for themselves; they learned it from some remarkable teacher—so they cannot really take credit for it. When the great Maya expert Sylvanus Griswold Morley calls them "the most brilliant aboriginal people on this planet," he is overpraising them for something they learned by rote.[3] And they preserved that knowledge out of fear of the end of the world.

Their failure to develop the wheel is surely a more accurate measure of their intellectual capacity? In a city with long avenues and immense plazas, you need to be fairly dim not to recognize that an ox cart will make life a great deal easier.

As to where the Maya learned their astronomy, as good a guess as any is the Olmecs. These aboriginal Mexicans, dating back to perhaps 2000 BC, were a late discovery. In 1884, archaeologist Alfredo Chavero discovered giant stone heads on the Gulf of Mexico, in a swampy area south of Veracruz. In the early 1930s, Matthew W. Stirling found the source of the heads at a place called La Venta, a wooded hill rising in the middle of a swamp. The undergrowth proved to conceal a cone-shaped pyramid almost a hundred feet high. Stirling also found huge altars, and more stone heads. These were of a powerful Negroid face with thick, sensual lips. Some archaeologists later suggested that they might be portraits of African slaves. But somehow, the heads had too much character to be slaves. Besides, who would commission a sixty-ton head of a slave? On the whole, it seemed more likely that these heads were intended as portraits of gods or men of importance.

Finally, La Venta was identified as the city of the Olmecs, a formerly unknown group of Mexican Indians; it seemed to date from about 1200 BC. They also worshipped Kukulcan, the feathered serpent, so presumably their ancestors had been taught by him. One of their main deities was a were-jaguar. Their white pyramid was an observatory, which had been re-aligned several times over the years, proving that Olmec astronomers recognized the celestial changes due to precession.

So it seems fairly certain that it was the Olmecs who passed on the knowledge of precession of the equinoxes to the Maya, and their knowledge of the calendar. Since we know that the Olmecs carried out human sacrifices, just like the Maya and the Aztecs, it seems that they shared the same fear of another great catastrophe. This is why they were so obsessed by the accuracy of their calendar.

One of the most impressive attempts to explain this obsession is made by a remarkable engineer named Maurice Cotterell. When in the merchant navy, Cotterell was fascinated to note how often his fellow mariners behaved in a manner you might expect from their astrological signs. In fact, most people who know a little about astrology have probably observed how often Tauruses are stubborn, Geminis changeable, Leos dominant, Libras charming, and so on.

But scientific studies have shown that this cannot be dismissed as superstition.

In 1946, radio engineer John Nelson set up a study of the influence of the sun on radio interference and finally established the astonishing fact that the planets and their positions were also involved. When two or more planets were spaced 120 degrees apart conditions were good, while 90 degrees and 180 degrees caused problems. Astrologers have always regarded "trines" (120 degrees) as favorable, while squares (90) and oppositions (180) are unfavorable.

In 1950, a statistician named Michel Gauquelin fed astrological data into his computer and discovered that while many astrological beliefs are nonsense, some have a sound factual basis. These included the notion that people born in the odd months (Aries, Gemini, Leo, etc.) are extraverts, while those born in the even months are introverts, and that a person's choice of profession is governed by their rising sign (the constellation coming up over the horizon when they are born). Gauquelin discovered that the first is statistically valid, and the second has some basis in fact—sportsmen tend to be born under Mars, actors under Jupiter, scientists and doctors under Saturn.

The psychologist H. J. Eysenck, a thoroughgoing materialist and behaviorist, accepted a challenge to check these results and was amazed to find them sound; he wrote a book: *Astrology: Science or Superstition?* with D. K. B. Nias in which he acknowledges this.

Why should people born under different signs of the zodiac have different characters? Is there some cosmic factor that changes from month to month? The "stars" cannot be responsible. They are so far away that they can have no possible influence. In effect, they are merely the figures around the face of the clock, merely there to help you tell the time.

The planets are closer, but their gravitational pull is minimal. For Cotterell, the obvious culprit was the sun, that roaring ball of energy, which sends out the equivalent of a gale-force wind. (This is why tails of comets stream behind them as they approach the sun.) And sunspots, the dark patches often observed toward the sun's equator, radiate a blast of magnetic particles, which cause radio interference and the Aurora Borealis.

Cotterell set out with the hypothesis that astrology "works" because the magnetic field of the sun can affect human embryos—particularly sunspot activity. Biologists know that the earth's weak magnetic field influences living cells and can affect the synthesis of DNA in the cells. So it seemed to Cotterell highly probable that changes in the sun's magnetic field affect babies at the moment of conception.

Astrologers to whom he explained his theory were dubious, for in astrology, it is the moment of birth that stamps us with our characters, not the moment of conception. But Cotterell was not actually contradicting this. He was saying that a baby conceived in, say, June is already stamped in that moment with the Pisces characteristics with which he will be born nine months later.

Because the sun is made of plasma—superheated gas—it does not rotate uniformly, like the earth; its equator rotates almost a third faster than its poles—26 days to a "turn" as compared to 37. So its lines of magnetism get twisted and sometimes stick out of the sun like bedsprings out of a broken mattress; these are "sunspots."

Cotterell was excited to learn that the sun not only changes the type of radiation emitted every month, but that there are four types of solar radiation that follow one another in sequence. So the sun's activities not only seem to correspond to the monthly astrological changes of "sun signs" but also to the four types of sign—fire, earth, air, water.

Because the earth is also revolving around the sun, a 26-day rotation of the sun takes 28 days as seen from earth. The earth receives a shower of alternating negative and positive particles every seven days.

When Cotterell was appointed to a job at the Cranfield Institute of Technology, he lost no time in feeding his data into its powerful computer. He wanted to plot the interaction of the sun's two magnetic fields (due to its different speeds of rotation at the poles and equator) and the earth's movement round the sun. What came out of the computer was a graph that showed a definite rhythmic cycle of eleven and a half years. Since astronomers compute the sunspot "cycle" at 11.1 years, it looked as if he was getting close.

The sun's two interacting magnetic fields come back to square one, so to speak, every 87.45 days, which Cotterell called a "bit." Looking at his graph, he saw that the sunspot cycle repeats itself and goes back to square one every 187 years. But there is a further complication called the sun's "neutral sheet"—the area around the equator where north and south balance out perfectly. This sheet is warped by the sun's magnetic field, so it shifts by one "bit" every 187 years, giving a total cycle—before it goes back to square one—of 18,139 years. And every 18,139 years, the sun's magnetic field reverses.

This period, Cotterell could see, broke down into 97 periods of 187 years, consisting of five major cycles, three of 19 times 187, and two of 20 times 187.

It was when Cotterell noticed that 20 times 187 years amounts to 1,366,040 days that he became excited. He had become interested in one of the Mayan astronomical documents known as the Dresden Codex, which the Maya used to work out eclipses, as well as with the cycles of the planet Venus, to which they attached tremendous importance. The Maya declared that Venus was "born" in the year 3114 BC, on 12 August. (This seems to have been the point when some passing meteor caused it to revolve anticlockwise.) They calculated using the period called a tzolkin—260 days—and according to them, a full cycle of the planet Venus amounted to 1,366,560 days. This, Cotterell noticed, was the same as his number 1,366,040, plus two tzolkins.

Was it possible, he wondered, that the Maya had somehow stumbled on his recognition about sunspot cycles, and that their highly complex calendar was based on it? And had they added the two extra "Venus cycles" to underline the importance of Venus as well as sunspots?

There was something else that made him feel he might be on the right track. He had noted a rather curious fact—that the sun's magnetic bombardment intensifies during periods of low activity in sunspot cycles. This seemed contradictory; surely you would expect it to be lower? The reason, he concluded, has to do with the belts of radiation around the earth known as the Van Allen belts, which were discovered by space scientist James Van Allen in 1958. These are due to the earth's magnetic field, and they trap solar radiation, which would otherwise destroy life on earth.

Cotterell's own explanation was that the Van Allen belt becomes supersaturated during periods of high sunspot activity, so preventing so much radiation reaching the surface. On the other hand, in periods of low activity, it all reaches the earth. And, he thought, this probably causes infertility and birth defects.

The earth was receiving maximum bombardment in AD 627, which was about the time the Maya began their slow decline. But AD 630 happened to be the end of the lesser Mayan cycle of 3,744 years, which began from the birth of Venus in 3114 BC. This was also the time the sun's magnetic cycle reversed.

According to Mayan experts, the end of the great Mayan cycle (of 13 baktuns) is on December 22, 2012, when the sun's magnetic field will again reverse, and we shall (possibly) face some catastrophe. However, the nervously inclined should note that a complete "sun cycle" (18,139 years) would, taken from a starting date of 3114 BC, actually come to an end in AD 4367. So we probably have more than two thousand years to go.

In *Maya Cosmogenesis 2012*, another Mayan expert, John Major Jenkins, has arrived at his own assessment of the date of 2012.

As we know, the daily path of the sun across the sky is known as the ecliptic, and the twelve constellations of the zodiac, from Aries to Pisces, are located along it. Our solar system is part of a constellation called the Milky Way, which is shaped like a giant magnifying glass. If we saw it from above, it would look roughly circular, like a whirlpool; but we see it from the side, so to speak, which is why it seems to contain such a dense concentration of stars.

The Milky Way crosses the ecliptic—not at right angles, but at 60 degrees—near the constellation of Sagittarius. When two planets in the sky pass one another in the lens of the astronomer's telescope, this is known as a conjunction. On December 21, 2012, the great Mayan cycle will end when the sun and the Milky Way achieve this conjunction. The center of the whirlpool is known as the Galactic Center, where a Black Hole seems to be located. This will be the part of the Milky Way's "edge" that will be conjunct with the sun on December 21, 2012.

Did the Maya know this when they worked out the end of their 13-baktun cycle? In view of their incredible calendar, and their mathematical skill, this seems highly likely. Jenkins certainly thinks so.

The reason for the earlier dating, Cotterell explains, is that the date given by the Maya themselves is Katun 13, Ahau (the equinox), which could bring us to December 21, 2012, or might simply mean the 7,200th day of cycle 13 ending in Ahau, which happens every 256 years, which could take us to 2048.

Cotterell explains that his own feeling is that the Maya were so much more clever than we are, they were probably correct about 2012. My own feeling is more skeptical. I find it hard to agree with Cotterell and Arguelles that the Maya were so much cleverer than we are, feeling that their failure to invent the wheel or the arch reveals an intellect that lacks vision and elasticity.

As to their astronomy, they called Venus "the twins" because they had failed to realize that the morning star and the evening star are the same. Moreover, I feel instinctively that their tendency to condone mass murder—for that is what human sacrifice amounts to—reveals an odd kind of moral obliquity that we see in the Nazi death camps. Do the gods really want streams of blood poured on their altars? I suspect that the forces behind evolution finally tired of these killers and decided to wipe them out before they did any more damage.

But Cotterell's own suggestion about the disappearance of the Maya sounds reasonable. He believes that, according to their own prediction, they began to decline in AD 627, as the sunspot bombardment caused an increasing number of birth defects and miscarriages. On the lid of the tomb of the Lord Pacal at Palenque, we see a female reclining backwards with her legs open. (Daniken and Chatelain both mistook her for an astronaut.) Below her are two stillborn children, while the sun god licks her with his tongue to try to restore her fertility.

Why the Maya were more affected than other American Indians is not clear; but Cotterell argues convincingly that they foresaw and predicted their own slow decline.

Jenkins sees the saga of MesoAmerican astronomy as a search for the unchanging galactic center, a cosmic axis, around which the rest of the universe turns. As with many primitive people, the first candidate was the North Pole, with its Pole Star. (It is often known as the Nail Star, or the Sky Nail, because it is believed to hold the world-axis in place.) The Olmec astronomers must have been dismayed to find that the Pole Star changed its position, and could not be relied upon. This may well be the reason the La Venta with its white pyramid was abandoned.

Eventually, it seems, they decided on the Galactic Center of the Milky

Way. But this in itself is a baffling mystery. Since we are seeing the Milky Way "edgeways," there is no way of knowing that it has a center. But here we must remember that the Maya priesthood must have included many "shamans," witch doctors, who are trained to learn the secrets of the universe in "cosmic flights," or out-of-the-body experiences. This is a central point to which we must return.

During the making of the television film *The Flood* I visited one of the most impressive Olmec sights, Monte Alban, overlooking Oaxaca (pronounced Hwa-haca). The Olmecs were the first to come there, about 500 BC, and they sliced off the top of the hill like a boiled egg to create a holy site. Without earth-moving equipment it is impossible to know how they did it. It is equally hard to imagine how the Zapotecs, the next tribe to occupy the site (from about AD 100), persuaded the Olmecs to give it up, and it seems more likely that they massacred them.

And there is certainly evidence of slaughter. There is a building faced with carved stone blocks, on which there are human figures in contorted postures. Some of these figures are Negroid, like the great heads of La Venta, while others are unmistakably white men, since they have beards. The figures are naked, and their sex organs have been cut off. The style is Olmec. But the glyphs on these slabs are Zapotec.

Then who were the bearded Europeans who were killed, and who were the Negroid males? Did the "white gods from the east" arrive with African servants who, since they served the whites, would be of superior rank to the ordinary Olmecs?

Perhaps the Zapotecs had decided to throw off their oppressors, and there was a massacre. This may also explain why the workmanship of the stone slabs is inferior to that of the Olmec heads found earlier; those who recorded the massacre were not as skilled as the Olmecs. And Monte Alban then became a Zapotec ceremonial site and observatory.

What happened at Teotihuacan, the great city founded by the Toltecs, once as large as ancient Rome, is equally obscure. This was the place that started Rand Flem-Ath's quest for Hapgood's old North Pole in Hudson Bay, when he guessed that the "Way of the Dead" would point at the middle of Hudson Bay. But extending this line proved him mistaken. On the curved surface of the globe, it missed its objective. But the error proved fruitful, since it led to a search for other geographical coordinates. It also led to the main discovery that if the line of 0 degrees longitude is extended through Giza, from the north to the south poles, it can be used as the basis of a remarkable grid on which an astonishing number of sacred sites fall at multiples of 10 degrees.

This I regarded as Flem-Ath's most interesting discovery, while rejecting from the start his theory that the sacred sites were originally "markers" set up by Atlantean scientists to measure how far the earth's crust had slipped, and which were later treated as sacred sites by the post-Atlantean scientists to measure how far the earth's crust had slipped, and which were later treated as sacred sites by the post-Atlanteans—that struck me as too fanciful. But what the 10-degree measure seemed to show beyond all doubt was that sacred sites were built according to some geographical pattern and revealed the existence of some remarkable "ur-civilization" that preceded any of those known to us.

From about 50 BC and for the first six centuries of the Christian era, this giant sacred city north of Tenochtitlan (now Mexico City) dominated the life of Mexico. The Aztecs called it "the city where the gods were made."

When Cortes came there in July 1520, he was fleeing from vengeful Aztecs, and in this ruined city they encountered still more of them. The Spaniards won the battle, in spite of odds of a hundred to one, by making for a man they perceived as the chief, and killing him; the rest fled.

Teotihuacan was a dead city, covered with giant heaps of earth. Cortes thought that the mounds were tombs and so called the central road "the Way of the Dead." In the 1880s, an archaeologist named Claude Joseph de Charnay made the interesting observation that the faces portrayed in its pottery included Caucasian, Greek, Chinese, Japanese, and Negro. There were even Semitic types. It seemed that Teotihuacan had once been a genuinely cosmopolitan center.

The story of how this great city became an earth-covered ruin has only just started to be understood by archaeologists.

Around the year AD 530, the earth was subjected to some devastating climatic catastrophe. "The sun became dark," wrote the eminent churchman John of Ephesus, "and its darkness lasted for 18 months. Each day it shone for about four hours, and still this light was only a feeble shadow. Everyone declared that the sun would never recover its full light again."[4] And a Roman civil servant named Cassiodorus Senator wrote: "The sun seems to have lost its wonted light, and appears of a bluish color. We marvel to see no shadows of our bodies at noon, to feel the mighty vigour of the sun's heat wasted into feebleness. . . ."[5]

What caused this immense catastrophe that, in effect, inaugurated the Dark Ages, we still do not know. It may have been a volcanic explosion, in which case Krakatoa in the Sunda Straits is the chief suspect. It would erupt at the end of August 1883, and the sea poured into the vortex of boiling lava, causing an explosion estimated to have been equal to a million H bombs. The detonation was heard three thousand miles away, and the ensuing tidal wave was over a hundred feet high and killed thirty-six thousand people. The dust cloud that spread all over the earth reduced the sun's radiation by 10 percent.

Yet its effects lasted only three years, not the three decades of the 532 AD event. So it seems more probable that the cause was an asteroid impact, like the one that destroyed the dinosaurs sixty-five million years ago.

The result was a drought that caused failure of the harvest for year after year. And for the rulers of Teotihuacan, this was a disaster, for it was their job, and that of their priests, to guarantee rainfall and a good harvest. None of these Central American civilizations were remotely democratic; all had an inflexible power structure, with the god-king at the top, then the nobles, then the priests. At the bottom were the workers, rigidly confined to their own place. Their feeling about their masters was one of respect mingled with fear; when they began to starve, fear turned to hatred.

When the revolt came, the mobs surged into the temples and palaces and hacked the priests and nobles to bits. They took pleasure in smashing their skulls, then dismembering the bodies and scattering the limbs in other rooms and courtyards. Then they set fire to the temples, built of wood and mud brick.

Even sacred statues were smashed. One two-foot high statue of a goddess was scattered over an 8,600 square foot area. These starving men were expressing contempt for the goddess who had failed to send rain. If these people had possessed the power, they would have torn the whole city to the ground; as it was, wrecking squads tore down walls, overthrew columns, and burned whatever would burn. Compared to this, the barbarian destruction of Rome was half-hearted.

We now know that this happened around 600 AD, not a century later, as historians have always assumed.

What we do not know is who covered the ruins with earth; it was probably the Aztec descendants of the Teotihuacanos, who continued to regard it as a sacred city, and lived among the ruins. Even the pyramid of the sun was turned into an enormous hill.

In 1884, an ex-soldier named Leopoldo Batres, brother-in-law of the infamous dictator Porfirio Diaz, persuaded Diaz to appoint him Inspector of Monuments and allow him to excavate the giant mounds. He was no archaeologist—merely a greedy adventurer hoping to find gold.

His biggest job was moving thousands of tons of earth. So Batres hired vast gangs of workmen at a few cents a day and even finally built a railroad to move earth. What began to emerge from the largest mound was a magnificent step pyramid, the Pyramid of the Sun. Its base was roughly the same as the Great Pyramid at Giza, although it was only half as high.

Toward the top of the pyramid Batres discovered an interesting mystery: two layers of mica, a glasslike substance used in insulation. This was a special mica brought 2,000 miles away, from Brazil. Did it serve some specific magical purpose? Whether it did or not, Batres lost no time in selling it. Fortunately, he did not locate the two sheets of mica under the floor in the nearby "Mica Temple."

Since the Pyramid of the Sun is made of a mixture of adobe and stones, Batres did an immense amount of damage, with the result that three of the four walls are several meters further in than they should be.

The excavations were due to be finished in 1910, for the dictator's "reelection," but by that time there was so much opposition to his rule that he decided against a celebration, and was thrown out in 1911, retiring abroad. Blessedly, his brother-in-law also vanished from history before he could wreck more ancient monuments.

In the corners of the pyramid, Batres had discovered the skeletons of young boys who had been entombed alive as offerings to the gods.

An engineer, Hugh Harleston, who surveyed Teotihuacan in the 1960s and '80s, suggested that it might be a model of the solar system, with the great pyramid as the sun, and the planets all represented at proportionally correct distances, even out to Neptune and Pluto. He also noted that, since the figure of 378 meters had been included so often, the basic unit used in Teotihuacan—1.059 meters, multiplied by 378 then by 100,000—gave an accurate measure of the polar radius of the earth. As with the Giza Pyramid, it suggests that the builders knew the exact size of the earth.

We have no idea of how Teotihuacan met its end, except that it must have been attacked and burned, then buried under rubble. Yet these millions of tons of rubble had apparently been placed there to preserve the ruins of the sacred city. Again, bearing in mind the effort it cost Batres to remove it all, we can only wonder again at the vast labors entailed.

We know that the world-view of these MesoAmerican Indians was unimaginably grim. They expected the gods to send tragedy and misery, and since there is probably no better way of inducing misfortune than confidently expecting it, that is what happened.

Maurice Cotterell's view of all this is rather strange. He is convinced that human history has been dominated by "super-gods" whom the Hindus called avatars, and that these included Krishna, Buddha, Jesus, and Lord Pacal (of Palenque). Oddly enough, he has since added Viracocha, whose tomb he believes to have been found at Sipan, in Peru, Tutankhamun, and the "great Lord of Ch'in," the Chinese emperor who built the Great Wall that cost a million or more lives, and was perhaps the most brutal ruler who ever lived.

So altogether, we know absurdly little about the amazing Maya civilization that flourished for two thousand years—far less, it seems, than the Greeks and Japanese and Semitics who visited it—presumably for purposes of trade—in the days when the Romans were conquering Europe.

Several thousands of miles away, on the west coast of South America, another civilization flourished and then declined.

In February 1987, a group of tomb robbers dug their way into a "pyramid" (which looked more like a heap of rubble) near a village called Sipan, in northern Peru. It was known as the Pyramid of the Moon. When the ringleader drove his crowbar into the ceiling of a tunnel, it collapsed, bringing a shower of gold; they had discovered one of the greatest treasures since Tutankhamen. The robbers staggered off with eleven sacks of gold, enough to make them all rich. But they quarreled about the division of the loot, one was shot to death, and another went to the police. The ringleader was killed as they tried to arrest him. Unfortunately, by then, much of the treasure had already been sold.

Whose tomb was it? Archaeologists decided to call the most important mummy in the Pyramid of the Moon "the Lord of Sipan." The Peruvians of the Lambayesque Valley, where the pyramids are situated, have an oral tradition of a king named Naymlap, who arrived from the west on a balsa wood raft, and led his followers inland for a mile, where he built a palace at a place called Chot.

Like Quetzalcoatl and Kon Tiki, he was worshipped as a god. And when he died, his followers buried him in a pyramid and announced that he had flown away. A Jesuit priest named Cabello, who recorded the ancient tradition, declared that Naymlap was succeeded by eleven generations of kings, who were also buried in pyramids.

This all came to an end when the last of the kings, Fempellec, was seduced by a demon in the guise of a beautiful woman. After that, the gods sent storms, followed by the Great Drought. To propitiate them, the king was tied up and thrown into the sea. But it was too late to avert catastrophe.

The explorer Thor Heyerdahl happened to be in Peru at the time of the tomb robbery. Heyerdahl, of course, had spent a lifetime investigating "ancient voyagers," and whether they could have sailed the world's great oceans. He was taken to the plundered tomb by the archaeologist Walter Alva, and shown a gold mask with bright blue eyes—obviously not a Peruvian. Was this intended as King Naymlap? If so, he was no oriental.

The pyramid was built by the Moche Indians, who flourished between AD 100 to AD 700, and who may be an offshoot of the Mexican Indians. They abruptly vanished. It was not until the 1990s that the mystery was solved, when it was discovered that there had been a forty-year drought in Peru in the sixth century AD, when the heavy rains caused by El Nino had ceased; the Moches had starved to death or simply left.

Alva told Heyerdahl of more pyramids 130 miles to the north, at a place called Tucume. There were seventeen of them, and the mud bricks were so worn that they looked like natural hills. These proved to contain no gold treasure like that of Sipan, but they contained something just as interesting: drawings on a wall showing a raft made of balsa wood. Here was evidence that the builders of the Tucume pyramids were seafarers who had used the same type of raft that Heyerdahl had used to carry him from Peru to Polynesia in 1947.

Like the Mexican Indians, the Moche had practiced human sacrifice, as the discovery of a hundred hacked skeletons in a pyramid called the Huaca del Luna indicated. Oddly enough, these were clearly not prisoners of war, but Moche warriors who had lost in single combat and therefore been selected for sacrifice to the ancestors. Clay portraits were made of them before they were despatched with a tremendous blow of a club that scattered their brains, and then hurled down a mountainside for good measure. This raises an interesting possibility: that the victims found portrayed on slabs at Monte Alban may also have been sacrificial victims chosen by "combat" in the ball court.

The Incas who finally became the conquerors of Peru also had a custom of appointing a child as a "messenger to the gods," and sealing him in a mountain cave, to freeze to death.

In 1998, the year following the Tucume investigation, Heyerdahl followed another strange trail that suggested prehistoric voyagers had used the natural currents of the Atlantic Ocean. For a long time, he had been fascinated by an ancient people called the Guanches, who were tall and blond, and had built black stone pyramids at Tenerife, in the Canaries. One authority, Dr. Arysio Nonos dos Santos, has pointed out that their language is related to the Dravidian family of languages from India and speculated that, since they were sheep farmers who disliked the sea, they must have arrived on the Canaries on rafts, complete with families and herds, possibly fleeing from Atlantis, which Santos places somewhere in the region of Indonesia. We are probably safe in speculating that he has the wrong catastrophe in mind, and that it is more likely that the Guanches were fleeing from the Sundaland catastrophe caused by Tollmann's comet.

When Heyerdahl was told about black stone pyramids in the Canary Islands, 700 miles off the coast of Spain, he lost no time in going to see for himself.

The pyramids had not been recognized as such because they were step pyramids, like those of Mexico; one was even in the center of Tenerife but had not been recognized because it had six terraces and a flat top. Heyerdahl was able to persuade a Norwegian businessman to buy the pyramids and set up a museum.

As to the "Tutankhamen" tomb found in the Sipan pyramid, Maurice Cotterell had an interesting speculation. Noting that one of the figures found in the tomb was a two-foot-high "crab-man" made of gold, he points out that the crab is a creature that lives between sea and land, where the waves break and create foam, and that the name Viracocha means "foam of the sea."

This tomb, he argues, should be regarded as "the lost tomb of Viracocha" (in a book of that title). This, he speculates, is the Viracocha of Tiahuanaco. Many kings in Mexico called themselves Quetzalcoatl, and there was even a king Viracocha. But the Lord of Sipan is clearly more than a king; from his tomb ornaments, this one was regarded as a god, a reincarnation of Viracocha.

Cotterell's first insight into Viracocha had come in the mid-1980s, on a visit to Mexico in pursuit of his increasing conviction that the Maya had worked out the sun cycles and their influence on human beings. For Cotterell, the tomb of Pacal at Palenque was the greatest revelation.

The Temple of the Inscriptions had been discovered by Father Ramon de Ordonez in 1773. In 1952, the Mexican archaeologist Alberto Ruz noticed four pairs of circular holes in the floor and was able to insert hooks and lift the slab. He found a rubble-filled stairway that led down to the heart of the pyramid. On the other side of a wall, he found a small square chamber, which was almost entirely filled by a huge sarcophagus with a lid. This was a massive and elaborately carved limestone slab, at the center of which was the figure that was later taken by Daniken and Chatelain to be an astronaut. Inside was the mummy of Pacal, with a beautiful jade mask over his face. He had died in AD 683.

Cotterell bought a scaled-down replica of the lid. Back in England he settled down to study it. He started from the insight that his own investigations had revealed: that 260, the number of days in the Mayan sacred year, was the number of days it took for the sun's polar and equatorial magnetic fields to complete their cycle of interaction. It seemed possible that this was the explanation of the Mayan sacred year.

This is not, of course, to assume that the Maya had some means of counting sun-cycles. They must simply have felt them instinctively.

Cotterell soon discovered that if he wanted to identify various Mayan gods on the lid he had to turn it upside down. This was logical—after all, on a coffin lid, symbols had to be packed, as into a suitcase. Moreover, it was obvious that the borders were also jammed with symbols: bats and jaguars, humans and gods, day and night, birth and death. Moreover, the lid was missing its two top corners, which had to be some kind of clue.

It was an x-shaped cross that gave him the next clue. This was truncated by part of the missing corner. Cotterell now had a eureka moment. If you imagined an upright mirror along the right edge, "doubling" the lid, so speak, the "x" would then be completed by its reflection.

Cotterell now made photographs of the lid in transparent acetate. And sliding them around, he found he could not only complete the "x" but that all the other symbols down the edge were also completed by their photographic mirror-images.

The same happened with the opposite edge. Half-figures turned into full figures.

Another symbol on the border was a human face. But down its nose, from the forehead to the tip, there was a kind of long lozenge with pointed ends. When faced with its own transparency, the "lozenge" disappeared and simply became the usual space between the two noses. Above the faces was the image of a hovering bat, which would have been indistinguishable as a mere half-bat. Moreover, if the two transparencies were laid on top of one another at an angle, a face with two eyes was suddenly staring out at the viewer.

By sliding the two transparencies around at various angles, many more shapes and faces, birds and animals, emerged.

There could be no doubt: whoever had devised the lid—probably Pacal himself—had filled it with visual codes. And the two missing corners were intended to give the viewer the first clue.

But this hardly seemed to make sense. Unless someone had invented photographic transparencies back in the seventh century AD, how could a baffled viewer be expected to stumble on this odd visual code?

Cotterell decided to try out his discoveries on the experts. However, they felt from the beginning that he was a crank and were dismissive. They made the same objection as stated above: that Pacal could not have intended such a code because he did not have photographic transparencies.

Cotterell replied that probably Pacal did not need transparencies; he could probably see the whole thing in "his mind's eye."

Now psychologists know about such a faculty: they call it eidetic vision. (Eidos is Greek for "essence.") Some people possess it naturally. As we have seen, mathematical prodigies who can tell instantly if a large number is a prime (not divisible by any other number) seem to be able to take a kind of bird's eye view of the number field. And the inventor Nicola Tesla is said to have built his first alternating-current dynamo in his head. Pacal must have possessed this ability with visual images.

In fact, perhaps ancient man, with his mind uncluttered with intellectual considerations, was born like it. That would explain how he noticed precession of the equinoxes; his mind, so to speak, "photographed" a particular configuration of stars and noticed fifty years later that two of them had altered their positions. . . .

And the *Popol Vuh*, the sacred book of the Maya, seemed to confirm that. It says of these ancient people: "They saw, and could see instantly far, they succeeded in knowing all there is in the World. When they looked, instantly they saw all around them and they contemplated in turn the arch of the heaven and the round face of the earth. The thing hidden (in the distance) they saw all, without first having to move; at once they saw the world . . . great was their wisdom."[6]

But then, says the *Popol Vuh*, the Creator began to have second thoughts. He recognized that what man gets too easily he does not value. So he instituted a change:

"Let their sight reach only that which is near; let them see only a little of the face of the earth."[7]

So man was made "short sighted," blinded by "the triviality of everydayness," trapped in a "worm's-eye view."

"Their eyes were covered and they could see only that which is close."[8]

Whatever we think about these MesoAmericans and their unfortunate tendency to human sacrifice, we have to agree that they saw straight to the heart of the human condition.

SEVEN

THE SHAMANIC VISION

Ross Salmon is a radio and TV broadcaster who became fascinated by the lost world of the Incas, and who set out, like the remarkable Colonel Percy Fawcett, to try to find a forgotten city.

Ross worked for BBC Television, in Plymouth, and since I also worked for them occasionally as a presenter, I got to know him well.

The legend of a lost city in South America dates back to a manuscript labeled No. 512, in the National Library in Rio de Janeiro, which came into its possession in the 1760s. This sounds like an adventure story by Conan Doyle—indeed, Fawcett's explorations provided Conan Doyle with material for *The Lost World*—but it is actually an account of ten years of wandering by a band of Portugese treasure hunters in central Brazil.

The manuscript claims that they discovered a deserted city built of huge blocks of stone. They decided to send a message for reinforcements back to civilization, and an account of their discovery was sent to the viceroy in Bahia by a native runner. But nothing was done about it, and the manuscript has been in the library ever since. Peter Fleming, the brother of novelist Ian Fleming, read it there before he set out on the expedition he describes in *Brazilian Adventure*. It has also been printed in full in *Mysteries of Ancient South America* by Harold Wilkins.

Colonel Percy Fawcett, a distinguished traveler and adventurer, had read the manuscript and set out to find the "lost city" in January 1925. He vanished in the Brazilian Matto Grosso in May 1925, almost certainly murdered by natives. There have been many attempts to follow his trail, none of them successful.

However, Ross Salmon's interest in lost cities (which he describes in *My Quest for El Dorado*) owed nothing to Fawcett. After spending the Second World War in the army, he dreamed of a life of adventure and found himself a job on a cattle ranch in Venezuela. Then he was placed in charge of a ranch in neighboring Columbia; it was there he began to read about the Spanish Conquistadores and the tribes they conquered.

An inquiry directed toward Indians who lived in the mountains elicited the information that a people called the "Injka" had been driven to live in remote jungles by the "Blue Eyes" (white men) but would one day return to slaughter the invaders. "Injka" sounded as if it might mean Inca, and so the quest began.

An assignment working for the BBC making travel films brought Ross to Bolivia, in search of an Inca city once known as Cochabamba. Slogging over mountains and along dry riverbeds, he and another Englishman were guided by an Indian youth to the remains of a city, now overgrown by vegetation. Old artifacts they found there convinced them they were the first to find the city—the local Indians were too terrified of the ghosts of ancestors to venture there. But Ross's companion almost died of a fever, and their hope of leading an expedition to Cochabamba had to be postponed.

So it was years later when Ross again took up the search in Bolivia. He was not expecting to find a fortune in gold—only evidence of ancient civilization.

Making a documentary film in the area called Beni, to the east of the Bolivian Andes, he came upon a great plain that was covered with canals, and with hill-like mounds. These, it seemed, were all the remains of a civilization that had now vanished. Every year, the plain had flooded to a depth of about a meter, and the Indians had built the mounds to live there until the flood went away again. An American student named Bill Denevan had discovered these mounds from an airplane in 1962 but had had immense trouble persuading any academic organization to investigate. Satellite pictures have showed around four thousand of the mounds, all untouched by archaeologists.

Dr. Victor Bustos, an expert on early Inca sites, told Ross that the evidence indicated that this "mound civilization" had been finally driven to abandon the mounds by a great flood. Ross asked if he was speaking of the Biblical Flood. "Yes, indeed," said Bustos, "There is overwhelming evidence from all over the world that this planet was engulfed in floods, following phenomenal rains, about ten thousand years ago."[1] It was not a sudden catastrophe, Bustos thought, but a slow inundation that took many decades.

Ross asked: "Was the mound culture founded by then?" and Bustos admitted: "Maybe there was a culture here that far back in history. It could be they were driven up into the Andes by great floods, and that they founded the first Andean culture thousands of years ago."[2]

Another archaeologist, Dr. Carlos Ponce Sangines, told Ross that the empire of the Aymara Indians had reached its peak about AD 900 in the area of Tiahuanaco. It was probably larger than the Greek or Roman empires before it began to disintegrate.

I was interested in the Aymara because of comments Rand Flem-Ath had made in *When the Sky Fell*. More than two and a half million people still speak the Aymara language. He had made the interesting comment that "In 1984 Ivan Guzman de Rojas, a Bolivian mathematician, scored a notable first in the development of computer software in showing that [the Aymara language] could be used as an intermediate language for simultaneously translating English into several other languages."

It seems that the Aymara language has a rigorous and simple structure, "which means that its syntactical rules always apply, and can be written out concisely in the sort of algebraic shorthand that computers understand. Indeed, such is its purity that some historians think it did not just evolve, like other languages, but was actually constructed from scratch."[3]

Had he come across it, Maurice Chatelain would certainly have read into that statement a hint that the Aymara language may have been constructed by extraterrestrials as a computer language.

Ross Salmon found a curious piece of evidence that might be read as pointing in the same direction. At an old Inca fortress called Pukarilla, which looked like a great natural pyramid, he found two curious objects. One was a gold Inca surgeons' knife, with a flat blade like a crescent moon. The other was a thin breastplate about the size of the cover of a paperback book. Incised into one side was a design covering sixteen squares, almost like a game of noughts and crosses. The angular symbols are each placed in a square.

A young Quechua Indian named Wanaku, who was acting as Ross's guide, told him: "It is the language of my ancestors. This is how they sent messages to other cities."[4]

Looking at it, Ross became convinced that it was a written language, even though scholars say that the Incas had no written language. He later appealed on television for anyone who might be able to interpret the symbols, and a Cornishman named Noel Billings, of Portreath, was convinced that the answer had come to him in a dream. It was, he said, a mathematical language, created by brilliant mathematicians, surveyors and builders. . . .

Ross had no further luck in his attempts to decipher it. But it is worth bearing in mind that the Quechua family of languages, one of which was spoken by the Incas, is closely related to Aymara. And if indeed the symbols are the method by which Wanaku's ancestors communicated, then Ross may have stumbled on some sign that Bolivian Indians of the remote past may have possessed a scientific culture beyond anything we attribute to them.

The strangest story in Ross's book *My Quest for El Dorado* concerns a girl name Wakchu, a member of the Callawaya tribe to the north of Lake Titicaca. Her husband, the shaman, had gone to the city to earn money for the tribe, and Wakchu was suspected of having been unfaithful. A council of elders and local women were undecided about her guilt, so the priests announced that they would "call the condor" to settle the matter. The Callawaya believe that human beings are reincarnated as condors, and that a particularly "great condor" is a reincarnation of a famous Inca leader who conquered that part of the world.

Ross, who had been invited to film the ceremony, watched as Wakchu was stripped to her loincloth and tied to a stake on the plateau at the top of the cliff. Then the ritual began, a discordant racket of drums, flutes, and tin whistles. The sound reverberated off the surrounding mountains.

Ross was quite convinced that nothing would happen; he had never even seen a condor at close quarters. After a while, the chanting died down, and Ross began to suspect that they felt that his presence was bringing them bad luck.

Then there was a shout of triumph, and against the opposite mountain top, the dark shapes of three condors appeared. With a twelve-foot wingspan, they dived down toward the Callawayas. There were two black females, and the leader, a larger black condor with his white collar gleaming in the frosty sunlight.

The music was renewed, and Wakchu struggled against her bonds. Then silence fell as the male condor landed. Ross looked with awe at this great bird only a few feet away, as it strutted around like a gladiator. Then, with wings outstretched, it ran toward Wakchu, its beak pointing at her throat. Ross's assistant ran toward the bird and shooed it away. It sprinted down the slope, then launched itself into the air. The elders cried: "Guilty—she must take her own life."[5]

Ten days later, Wakchu did just that, flinging herself from the top of the cliff.

I saw Ross's film on BBC television, with Ross's commentary. And when *My Quest for El Dorado* apppeared in 1979, I lost no time in buying a copy.

To my astonishment and bafflement, the version of the Wakchu story was quite different. Ross explains that Wakchu had been selected as a "sacrifice"—he does not explain to what—and Ross's Quechu assistant Gerardo tells him that the amautas (priests) have decided to reenact the condor ceremony so he can film it.[6]

Wakchu's infidelity is not even mentioned. Neither is the exclamation: "She must take her own life." And the story ends abruptly as the condors fly away. There is no mention of Wakchu's suicide. The whole story becomes quite pointless, for there is no further mention of Wakchu being a sacrifice. Ross concludes: "Assuming that the Callawayas do not possess any magical powers to persuade a wild condor to land at their feet, one must look for the reason"—and suggests that it must have been a tame condor.[7]

The next time I bumped into Ross at the BBC in Plymouth, I asked him what on earth had happened. He explained that some "experts" who had seen his film had been convinced that he must have been taken in—perhaps the Callawaya had been paid to deceive him. I pointed out that nothing was less likely, and Ross looked slightly shamefaced and said he agreed. . . .

It was sad that he allowed himself to be convinced. What his film visibly demonstrated is that there was some kind of telepathic relation between the condors and the amautas.

Ross's mentor, Colonel Fawcett, was less of a doubter. In *Exploration Fawcett,* he tells how the novelist Rider Haggard gave him a ten-inch high statuette carved from black basalt, which came from Brazil. It was of a man with a plaque on his chest, which was covered with unknown characters. All who held this figure, says Fawcett, felt as if "an electric current were flowing up one's arm," so that some people had to put it down.[8]

Experts in the British Museum declared that it was not a fake but was "quite beyond their experience."[9] Fakes are intended to be sold as antiquities, and this was nothing like any known antiquity.

So Fawcett decided to try an odd and unconventional method of learning about the figure: psychometry. This is the ability that some people possess of "sensing" the history of an object by holding it in their hands. It sounds preposterous but was, in fact, subjected to thorough scientific investigation in the 1840s. It was labeled by its discoverer, Joseph Rodes Buchanan, "psychometry," which means "mind (or soul) measurement."[10]

The psychometist Fawcett consulted said that the statuette was of a priest, and that it had been kept in a temple with a large eye over the altar. There was much else about an island continent and its inhabitants, then of its destruction, when the sea rose "as in a hurricane."[11]

Fawcett went on to try his "idol" on other psychometrists, and received "impressions closely tallying with the above."[12] He now had no doubt that the statuette came from Atlantis. He writes: "However much romance may have colored the tales, the fact remains that the legendary existence of a highly civilized remnant of an ancient people persisted among the indigenes of the continent; and these traditions can be heard today from the Indians of remote places rarely visited by a white man. There is a remarkable similarity in the accounts, which makes it reasonable to conclude that there is a basis of truth in them."[13]

Fawcett states his belief—remarkable for that time—that "the curse of a great cataclysm" fell on South America and seems to accept that this was the catastrophe that destroyed Plato's Atlantis.[14]

There can be little doubt that a cataclysm of such dimensions produced tidal waves and minor catastrophes throughout the world. "It caused 'the rising of the Andes' (implying that this happened since the last Ice Age), and brought to South America 'a White Race' expert in the arts of civilization."[15] Fawcett's conclusions were remarkably similar to those reached by Charles Hapgood and Schwaller de Lubicz.

The survivors also built cities like the one discovered by the 1743 expedition.

"The existence of the old cities I do not for a moment doubt. How could I? I myself have seen a portion of one of them—and that is why I observed that it was imperative for me to go again. The remains seemed to be those of an outpost of one of the biggest cities. . . ."[16]

Why does he say "seemed to be"? The only answer can be: because the rest of the city was completely covered by the jungle, like the Mayan ruins discovered by Stephens and Catherwood in the 1830s. Which means, in turn, that Fawcett knew where to look for a lost city. It even emerges from his book that he thought there were many.

His objective on that last expedition was not apparently the deserted city of 1753. He had heard of "clothed natives of European appearance,"[17] who avoided all contact with the outside world.

"Our destination on the next expedition—I call it 'Z' for the sake of convenience—is a city reputed to be inhabited, possibly by some of these timid people. . . . "[18]

And so in January 1925 he left England once more for South America and vanished in its jungles. His book *Exploration Fawcett* was written before he set out.

Three hundred miles to the west of the home of the Callawaya Indians lies the desert plain of Nazca, whose surface is covered with drawings of giant birds and animals, and straight lines and geometrical shapes that stretch as far as the horizon.

First noticed by a Peruvian archaeologist named Xesspe in 1927, they remained unknown until Fawcett wrote an article about them in 1940. In June 1941, Dr. Paul Kosok, a historian at Long Island University, flew above Nazca looking for ancient canals (the lines had been likened to the canals of Mars) and saw the outline of a bird, then of a giant spider, on the red surface of the desert. There was also a condor, a lizard, a killer whale and a flower. And on a cliff-face there was a 900-foot high figure of a man with his arms outstretched as if in welcome.

Kosok studied the lines and drawings and was later joined by a German student, Maria Reiche, who would spend the rest of her life there. She admitted to being baffled by the purpose of the lines but thought they probably had some astronomical purpose, like a giant calendar. As to the images, her theory was that the Nazca Indians had divided into clans in the days of their economic prosperity, and that these figures were heraldic clan symbols.

The lines and drawings were created on the surface of the desert by carefully moving its red-brown stones, and since there was little wind on the pampa, they had remained undisturbed for a thousand years or so. There was, of course, no way of dating the stones, but artifacts such as pottery and grave goods indicated that the Nazca Indians were roughly contemporaneous with their northern neighbors, the Moche.

It took a long time for archaeologists to learn that in the years around 535 AD, some catastrophe had filled the earth's atmosphere with dust and blotted out the sun, and that a variety of catastrophes then followed for more than a century. No one knows what caused it, although in a book called *Catastrophe*, archaeological journalist David Keyes argues for a huge volcanic eruption in the area of the Sunda Strait, possibly Krakatoa—although another comet strike remains a possibility. Plague and drought spread worldwide.

The Moche were destroyed by the Great Drought, and we may infer that the same thing had happened to the Nazca, and that the giant surface markings—visible only from the air—were almost certainly a plea to the gods for rain.

In *Chariots of the Gods* Erich von Daniken inevitably suggested that the lines had been made by visitors from space. That he had failed to look at them at close quarters is revealed by his suggestion that the long-straight lines were intended as runways for alien spacecraft—the stones would guarantee a bumpy take-off. Even in his 1997 *Arrival of the Gods* he goes on referring to the lines as "runways."

Once we know about the Great Drought, the question about the purpose of the lines is solved. But a central problem remains. Unless the line-makers had invented the hot air balloon, how did they see their creation as it was intended to be seen?

Perhaps the answer is that they didn't need to. The drawings could have been "scaled up" from a smaller sketch made on sand, using simple tools like ropes and sticks.

But one of the most interesting clues is a drawing of a monkey on the pampa—a monkey that is unknown in the Nazca area, but is native to the rain forest to the east of the Peruvian Andes. For the rain forest—as we shall see presently—is the home of shamans who claim to be able to leave their bodies with the help of what we now call "psychedelic drugs."

One sign of such drugs is a copious nasal discharge; they also cause vomiting. And on one piece of Nazca pottery there is a picture that shows such a nasal discharge and vomiting. In the Nazca area, the hallucinogenic drug is the San Pedro cactus.

This interesting fact—which emerged on a BBC *Horizon* program—could explain the mystery of how the Nazca lines were seen from the air.

Space vehicles—or hot air balloons—are unnecessary. Hallucinogens are capable of creating a sense of flying which, all shamans assert, enables them to see things from above like a giant bird.

In his book *Shamanism: Archaic Techniques of Ecstasy*, the Rumanian scholar Mircea Eliade speaks of the widespread myth that shamans are hatched by a giant bird in the branches of the World Tree and remarks that "ability to turn into a bird is the common property of all kinds of shamanism."[19] The shaman has many animal helpers, from jaguars to mice, and even plants, and these are his teachers.

In *From Atlantis to the Sphinx* I attempted to show that this tradition posits a basic interaction between the shaman and nature. For example, *Wizard of the Upper Amazon* by F. Bruce Lamb describes how a Peruvian youth named Manuel Cordova, who was kidnapped by the Amahuaca Indians of Brazil—again, the Upper Amazon—was trained as a shaman. After drinking honi xuma, the "vision extract," the natives—including Cordova—experienced shared visions of snakes, birds, and animals that continued all night. The "boa chant" brought a giant boa constrictor, which glided through the clearing, followed by other snakes, then a long parade of birds, including a giant eagle, which spread its wings in front of them, flashed its yellow eyes, and snapped its beak. After that came many animals—Cordova explains that he can no longer recall much about it, "since the knowledge did not originate in my consciousness."[20]

On a later occasion, after a "shared vision" of jungle cats, Cordova suddenly remembered a black jaguar he had once encountered, and the jaguar immediately appeared, stalking through the middle of the group, causing a terrified shudder. Realizing that Cordova was responsible for the vision, the natives nicknamed him "black jaguar." In the process of becoming a shaman, Cordova learned to control these drug-induced visions by means of chants—again, we glimpse the deep significance of music.

Cordova described how the Amahuaca Indians were able to lure a herd of pigs into the hunter's trap by a ritual that involved burying a sow's head.

A Philadelphia explorer, Harry B. Wright, (in *Witness to Witchcraft*) has described witnessing the Leopard Dance of Dahomey, West Africa; as a naked girl performed the dance to the beating of a drum and the incantations of a priest, Wright's native companion asked; "Look, do you see the two leopards walking beside her?"[21] Wright saw nothing, but the other natives appeared to be following the leopards with their eyes. And then, in the midst of the ceremony, three leopards walked out of the jungle and across the clearing; Wright was convinced that these were real leopards—perhaps summoned by the "imaginary" leopards in the ritual.

Also in *From Atlantis to the Sphinx* I quoted the British colonial administrator Sir Arthur Grimble, who (in *Pattern of Islands*) was present when a shaman in the Gilbert Island entered into a trance, and somehow caused dozens of porpoises to swim ashore and ground themselves on the beach, to provide the natives with a feast. The shaman insisted that his spirit had left his body and had invited the porpoises to come ashore.

The drawings in Cro-Magnon caves showing shamans wearing bison skins used to be regarded as "primitive art" until anthropologists recognized that they were part of a shamanic ritual, whose aim was to ensure the success of the hunters. What our "civilized" mentality finds so hard to accept is that such rituals were almost certainly successful. In *Dawn Behind the Dawn* Geoffrey Ashe quotes the anthropologist Mirian Starhawk:

"Across the rich tundra, teeming with animal life, small groups of hunters followed the free-running reindeer and the thundering bison. They were armed with only the most primitive of weapons, but some among the clans were gifted, could "call" the herds to a cliff side or a pit, where a few beasts, in willing sacrifice, would let themselves be trapped. These gifted shamans could attune themselves to the spirits of the herds, and in so doing, they became aware of the pulsating rhythm that infuses all life, the dance of the double spiral, of whirling into being and whirling out again. . . ."[22]

Although this view of the animal as a willing participant in the hunt may sound bizarre, it is accepted by all shamans. They believe that the animal gives itself as a sacrifice to human beings—like Grimble's porpoises. And since the human beings feel the need to give something back, a vessel of the animal's blood is offered and spilled on an altar stone. Sometimes a whole animal is offered. The reasoning behind this is that the hunter who tries to take without giving will eventually starve.

The picture that begins to emerge is foreign to our western modes of thought; yet it can be found everywhere among primitive people who live close to the earth. It is the notion that nature is alive, that certain places are holy, and that the spirits that inhabit such sites need to be treated with respect if their displeasure is to be avoided.

We find the same basic insight in a story told by Jacquetta Hawkes in her book *Man and the Sun*. She points out: "The absence of any solar portrait or symbol in Palaeolithic art may not mean that the sun had absolutely no part in it. A rite practiced among the pygmies of the Congo warns against any such assumption. [The anthropologist Leo] Frobenius was travelling through the jungle with several of these skillful and brave little hunters when, toward evening, a need arose for fresh meat. The white man asked his companions if they could kill an antelope. They were astonished at the folly of the request, explaining that they could not hunt successfully that day because no proper preparation had been made; they promised to go hunting the next morning instead.

"Frobenius, curious to know what their preparations might be, got up before dawn and hid himself on the chosen hill-top. All the pygmies of the party appeared, three men and a woman, and presently they smoothed a patch of sand and drew an outline upon it. They waited; then, as the sun rose, one of the men fired an arrow into the drawing, while the woman raised her arms toward the sun and cried aloud. The men dashed off into the forest.

"When Frobenius approached the place, he found that the drawing was that of an antelope, and that the arrow stood in its neck. Later, when the hunting party had returned with a fine antelope shot through the neck, some of them took tufts of its hair and a calabash of blood, plastered them on the drawing and then wiped it out."[23]

Joseph Campbell comments: "The crucial point of the pygmy ceremony was that it should take place at dawn, the arrow flying into the antelope precisely when it was struck by a ray of the sun. . . . "[24]

In discussing this passage in *From Atlantis to the Sphinx* I commented: "It is easy to see that the Cro-Magnon hunter, using this kind of technique, would feel like a modern big game hunter using a high-powered rifle with a telescopic sight. By comparison, the older magic of Neanderthal man must have seemed as crude as a bow and arrow.

"This, I am inclined to believe, was the reason that Cro-Magnon man became the founder of civilization. His command of 'magic' gave him a sense of optimism, of purpose, of control, such as had been possessed by no animal before him."[25]

What seems absurd is that it was by the shamanic use of magic that Homo sapiens came to build civilization, for magic turned into science, and science made him the master of nature. In *From Atlantis to the Sphinx*, I argue that the shaman, because of his magical powers, became the priest-king, and was the founder of early civilizations like Sumer and Egypt.

The first westerner to note the existence of shamans was the Russian Archpriest Avvakum, one of the "Old Believers" who, in 1652, resisted the attempts of the new patriarch Nikon to bring Russia closer to the Greek Orthodox Church; they were excommunicated en masse in 1666. But five years earlier, in 1661, Avvakum was deported to Siberia, on the Tsar's orders, and there learned of the existence of shamans. On his return from Siberia in 1667, he spent fifteen years in prison, where he wrote his *Life*, which became the first classic of Russian literature.

Understandably, this dogmatic Old Believer regarded shamans as servants of the Devil. He describes how Paskov, the head of the expedition had decided to send his son Jeremy to make war on the Mongols, and went to consult the local shaman. "This villain of a magician," he says, sacrificed a ram and cut off its head, then began to "jump and dance and call the demons." Finally, with piercing screams, he collapsed on the ground and began to foam at the mouth. He then assured Paskov that the expedition would be a great victory and would bring tremendous wealth. Avvakum promptly began to pray to God: "May not one of them return. Send them evil!"[26]

And when, in due course, Jeremy returned with only one companion, telling how the rest had been massacred, Paskov understandably blamed Avvakum, and only the intervention of his son prevented him killing him on the spot.

Avvakum would be burned at the stake in 1682.

His attitude would persist among explorers for the next two and a half centuries. In their anthology *Shamans through Time* Jeremy Narby and Francis Huxley quote a number of eighteenth-century explorer and rationalists who are agreed that shamans are impostors and jugglers.

What becomes clear from this book is that in fact, shamans are basically healers. The term "witch doctor" to denote an African shaman is not a misnomer; a shaman is a doctor. But the main difference between shamans and western doctors lies in their training. The western doctor has to undergo a four-year course at medical school and absorb an updated version of the kind of knowledge accumulated by the Roman physician Galen. But the shaman has to undergo a discipline that is more like that of a medieval ascetic who flogs himself, starves himself, and spends his nights sleeping on a board. And he does not "choose" to become a shaman; he is chosen by the spirits and, if he refuses, may suffer death.

The torments he has to undergo can be horrific. He begins by losing his appetite for ordinary life and may become deeply unhappy, leaving home to become a wanderer. He becomes indifferent to his physical welfare. In his classic book *Shamanism: Archaic Techniques of Ecstasy*, Mircea Eliade quotes the daughter of an Araucanian fisherman of Chile as saying: "I was gathering shells from the reefs when I felt something like a blow on the breast, and a very clear voice inside me said: 'Become a machi! It is my will!' At the same time violent pains in my entrails made me lose consciousness. It was certainly the Ngenechen, the master of men, coming down into me."[27]

And Eliade goes on to speak of long fainting spells and lethargic sleep. There is a painful ceremony, which involves apparent death by dismemberment. The neophyte may starve until he seems on the point of death, or lie out in the cold until he is frozen. This period, says anthropologist Waldemar Bogoras, may be compared to a long and serious illness. If he recovers, then "inspiration" descends, and he learns the art of beating the drum and singing.[28]

Knud Rassmussen wrote in 1930 of an Eskimo shaman who told him: "When I was to be a shaman, I chose suffering through two things that are most dangerous to us humans, suffering through hunger and through cold. First I hungered five days and was then allowed to drink a mouthful of warm water. . . . Thereafter I went hungry another fifteen days, and was again given a mouthful of warm water. After that I hungered for ten days. . . .

"These days of 'seeking for knowledge;' are very tiring, for one must walk all the time, no matter what the weather is like, and only rest in short snatches."[29]

All this pain and torment, like the self-inflicted suffering of ascetics, is intended to cause the neophyte to shed the old self and all its habits, and to acquire what Gurdjieff calls "essence," a hard core of reality like tempered steel.

So shamanism takes the existence of spirits utterly for granted. In this its attitude differs from that of most westerners, who may or may not believe in the existence of "spirits" (i.e., ghosts), but certainly do not regard their belief as fundamental to their whole being. Shamans not only believe in spirits; they see them and talk to them. There is no reason to believe that they are self-deceivers who have allowed their imagination to run away with them. They would say that it is our western view of reality that needs revising.

What seems astonishing, as we study the development of western attitudes to shamanism in a collection like *Shamans through Time* is how dogmatic and suspicious early anthropologists could be. There is an extract from Everard F. Im Thurn, who in the late 1880s was living among the Macusi people of British Guiana. When a local shaman (called a peaiman) offered to cure a fever by magical means, Thurn accepted eagerly. After dark he went to the peaiman's house, which was large but had no walls or chimneys. A great crowd had come to witness the healing. Thurn lay down in his hammock in total darkness, a Macusi boy in the next hammock translating.

Then the shaman began with a series of "indescribable and terrible yells and roars and shouts, which filled the house, shaking walls and roof, sometimes rising rhythmically to a roar, sometimes sinking to a low distant-sounding growl, which never ceased for six hours. Questions seemed to be thundered out, and answers shouted back. . . ."

"Every now and then, through the mad din, there was a sound, at first low and indistinct, and then gathering in volume, as if some big winged thing came from far toward the house, passed through the roof, then settled heavily on the floor; and again, after an interval, as if the same winged thing rose and passed away as it had come. As each of these mysterious beings came and went, their air, as if displaced by wings, was driven oer my face. These were the kenaimas [evil spirits] coming and going.

"As each came, his yells were first indistinctly heard from far off, but grew louder and louder until, as he alighted on the floor of the house, they reached their height. The first thing each did was to lap up some of the tobacco-water, with an ostentatious noise, from the calabash on the floor. But while he lapped, the peaiman kept up the shouts, until the kenaima was ready to answer. When each kenaima had given an account of itself and promised not to trouble me, it flew rustling away. They came in the form of tigers, deer, monkeys, birds, turtles, snakes, and of Ackawoi and Arecuna Indians. . . ."

And then, incredibly, Thurn comments: "It was a clever piece of ventriloquism and acting. The whole terrific noise came from the throat of the peaiman; or perhaps a little of it from that of his wife. . . . The rustling of the wings of the kenaimas, and the thud which was heard as each alighted on the floor, were imitated, as I afterwards found, by skilfully shaking the leafy boughs and then dashing them against the ground. . . . Once, probably by accident, the boughs touched my face; and it was then that I discovered what they were, by seizing and holding some of the boughs with my teeth."[30]

Thurn passed into a semitrance and, when he woke up, still had the headache. He gave the shaman a fourpenny mirror for his services and remained convinced that it had all been a fraud. It is not clear how he thought the peaiman caused the voices to come from a distance, then through the roof. He seems to have thought that ventriloquism was the ability to "throw the voice," apparently unaware—as any stage ventriloquist could have told him—that ventriloquism requires daylight, so the audience will assume that the voice is issuing from the dummy's mouth.

A Pole who was exiled to Siberia in the 1870s, Wenceslas Sieroshevski, had no such doubts, and his description of Yakut shamans is wholly positive, describing them as "wild and free spirits."[31] And another Siberian exile, Waldemar Bogoras, also approached shamanism positively. He noted that if a young person was slow in obeying the "call" of the spirits, they were likely to appear in person to ask why. Young people, Bogoras says, are often deeply reluctant to obey. He goes on: "The parents of young persons 'doomed to inspiration,' act differently. . . . Sometimes they protest against the call coming to their child, and try to induce it to reject the 'spirits' and to keep to ordinary family life. This happens mostly in the case of only children, because of the danger pertaining to the shamanistic call, especially in the beginning. The protest of the parents is, however, of no avail, because the rejection of the 'spirits' is much more dangerous even than the acceptance of their call. A young man thwarted in his call to inspiration will either sicken and shortly die, or the spirits will induce him to renounce his home and go far away, where he may follow his vocation without hindrance."[32]

He adds that most of the shamans he knew claimed to have had no teachers, but developed their powers alone. Neither can shamanistic power be inherited. In this they differ from the powers of "witches," which may be inherited or taught. This is not to say, of course, that there are not families of shamans, where the son becomes a shaman like his father; but it is the spirits who become the teachers, not his father.

The drum is the most basic instrument of the shaman's calling; it seems to induce the state of mind in which contact with the spirits is possible. The Ogala Sioux shaman Black Elk told anthropologist John

G. Niehardt: "Four times I cried 'Hey-a-a-hey,' drumming as I cried to the Spirit of the World, and while I was doing this I could feel the power coming through me from my feet up, and I knew I could help the sick little boy."[33]

Willard Z. Park, an American anthropologist who lived among the Paviotso Indians of North Nevada emphasizes another important aspect of shamanism, the ability to charm game. After the herd has been located by a scout (or the shaman has located it through dreaming) a corral is built, then the "charming ceremony" is led by the shaman; they all join in the dance, which may last all night, and the shaman, under the guidance of the antelope spirit, goes into a trance and sings his antelope-song. Then the men, woman, and even children take part in the antelope drive, whose purpose is to funnel the animals into the corral.

Shamans through Time charts an interesting progression from total skepticism about shamans, through the detached observation of anthropologists like Park, to an altogether more involved attitude that would have struck early observers as unscientific. The wider public suddenly became aware of shamanism in 1957, when an American named R. Gordon Wasson described his experience of ingesting magic mushrooms with a Mexican shaman in *Life* magazine.

Wasson and a friend sat on a mat, watching the female shaman Maria Sabina through the smoke of resin incense as she prepared and handed out mushrooms to about twenty people. After they had eaten them, the visions began, "in vivid color, always harmonious. They began with art motifs, angular such as might decorate carpets or textiles or wallpaper. . . . Then they evolved into palaces with courts, arcades, gardens— resplendent palaces all laid out with semiprecious stones. Then I saw a mythological beast drawing a regal chariot. Later it was as though the walls of our house had dissolved, and my spirit had flown forth, and I was suspended in mid-air viewing the landscapes of mountains, with camel caravans advancing slowly across the slopes, the mountains rising tier above tier to the very heavens." And he comments: "I felt that I was now seeing plain whereas ordinary vision gives us an imperfect view; I was seeing the archetypes, the Platonic ideas, that underlie the imperfect images of everyday life. The thought crossed my mind: could the divine mushrooms be the secret that lay behind the ancient Mysteries? Could the miraculous ability I was now enjoying be the explanation for the flying witches that plays so important a part in the folklore and fairy tales of northern Europe?"[34]

The article provoked a rush of American tourists to Mexico, all anxious to escape the boredom of everyday life and replace it with Rimbaud's "reasoned derangement of the senses."[35]

Maria Sabina realized she had become a celebrity when Americans began arriving at her door explaining that they wanted to find God. In an interview with a Mexican journalist she says plaintively: "Before Wasson, nobody took the mushrooms simply to find God. One had always taken them to heal the sick."[36]

But there was no escape from her celebrity, and the local mayor ordered her to put herself at the disposal of a group of foreigners. The problem was that the young groupies who sought her out took the sacred mushroom at any time and any place, not at night, as they were intended to. And she found that these foreigners sucked away some of her own power.

But the magic mushroom craze had been launched, and nothing could turn back the clock. Aldous Huxley had started the vogue in 1952 by speaking of the mushroom in his description of his mescalin experience, *The Doors of Perception* and two Harvard teachers, Timothy Leary and Richard Alpert, spread the word in the early sixties. It was Leary's friend Ralph Metzner who invented the word "psychedelic," meaning "consciousness-changing." Leary and Alpert soon left the academic profession, and Leary famously advised his younger contemporaries to "turn on, tune in, drop out."[37]

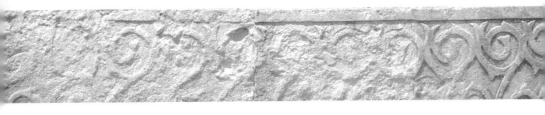

EIGHT

A MORE POWERFUL REALITY

It was as far back as 1951 that Mircea Eliade had devoted his substantial book *Shamanism: Archaic Techniques of Ecstasy* to the subject. Yet because Eliade was an authority on the history of religion, not an anthropologist, other scholars were inclined to be dismissive. Besides, at that time, anthropologists believed that shamans were tricksters or psychotics. "Briefly speaking," said anthropologist George Devereux in 1956, "we hold that the shaman is mentally deranged."[1]

Even so, the influence of Eliade's book continued to grow and was finally one of the major reasons that shamanism was taken seriously, and not dismissed as a mixture of superstition and "derangement."

It was also in 1956 that Michael Harner went to live on the eastern slopes of the Andes, to study that culture of the head-shrinking Jivaro Indians and—as mentioned in the Preface of this book—decided to try their drug ayahuasca. He encountered the "ancient ones," whom he described as dragonlike creatures, who claimed they had created all forms of life on earth so they could hide inside them. He noted the similarity of this idea to the DNA molecule discovered by Crick and Watson in 1953. And when he described to two missionaries his experience of a gigantic crocodile, from whose mouth gushed a torrent of water, they pointed out to him a passage in the *Book of Revelation* about a serpent who "cast water out of his mouth as in a flood."[2]

When he spoke of his experience to a blind Jivaro shaman and quoted the "dragons" as claiming that they were the masters of the earth, the shaman smiled and said: "Oh, they're always saying that. But they are only the Masters of Outer Darkness." Harner had not mentioned that he saw them coming from space.

In 1964 Harner returned to Ecuador, with the intention of studying shamanism first hand. He went to the northwestern part of the country, where the most powerful shamans were reputed to live, and flew to the remote village of Macas, under the active volcano called Sangay.

With a Jivaro guide, he spent all day walking to the house of a renowned shaman named Akachu, in the remote forest. In exchange for a shotgun, Akachu agreed to initiate him into the way of the shaman. The first step was to bathe in a sacred waterfall.

Their road took them upward into a misty forest. Harner was told to fast. "You must suffer, so that the grandfathers will take pity on you."[3] On the third night it began to rain, and they broke camp in the dark, too cold and hungry to sleep. Their only illumination came from flashes of lightning.

Harner soon lost sight of the other two in the forest, and his shouts brought no reply. He encountered many forks and had to choose again and again. After a day of staggering through the forest he was still alone and cut himself branches to make a lean-to shelter. The next morning he heard the boom of the shotgun and tried to run toward it. He found himself climbing down a precipitous canyon. Eventually, he found his companions standing beside an immense waterfall. He collapsed as he reached them.

After they had struggled through mist heavy with rain, Akachu led him into the sacred cave under the waterfall. This was the House of the Grandfathers. Here, in spite of being frozen to the bone, Harner experienced a sense of deep calm.

Finally, Akachu led him back along the cliff face, and they scaled the steep slope of slippery clay until they were overlooking the waterfall. There Akachu began to scrape stems of green bark into a gourd, then crushed them to squeeze out the juice. This was the liquid that Harner would drink. He was warned that if he saw something frightening, he should not flee. Harner knew of a number of Indians who had fled in panic after drinking the datura juice and died by drowning or falling from a cliff.

A few hours later, in total darkness, he drank the juice whose disagreeable taste reminded him of green tomatoes. He felt numb; then an immense terror swept through him. He was certain his companions meant to kill him. But they held him down, while he believed a horde of savages was restraining him. Then he became unconscious.

When he woke, lightning was flashing and the ground was trembling. He jumped to his feet, and a hurricane-like wind blew him down. Then he saw a great serpentine form writhing toward him. About to run away, he remembered the shaman's staff Akachu had made for him. It was not there but he found a stick. As the monster split into two intertwined serpents, he charged it with the stick. There was an earsplitting scream, and suddenly the forest was empty and silent. He experienced deep serenity, then lost his senses again.

When he woke up it was midday, and he ravenously ate some monkey meat and drank warmed beer. When he started to tell Akachu and the guide what he had seen, Akachu silenced him, warning him that if he spoke of it, he would lose all he had suffered for.

So he returned to Akachu's house and was taught how to acquire spirit helpers, or tsentsaks, to help him to cure the sick.

Later, Harner went on to study shamanism among several North American Indian groups and learned how shamanism could be practiced without ayahuasca or other drugs.

On his return, he published articles describing his experiences, which made his reputation. Then he spoilt it all by writing *The Way of the Shaman*, in which he went on to try to explain how others could practice shamanism. This "self-help" book caused a violent reaction among his academic colleagues, who felt he had joined the ranks of the Californian gurus. As far as academia was concerned, he became an outcast—in spite of which, the book has gone on to become a classic.

Harner's *Way of the Shaman* was one of the influences that led another anthropologist, Jeremy Narby, to go to the Pichis Valley in the Peruvian Amazon in 1985 to study the culture of the Ashaninca Indians.

The opening sentence of his book *The Cosmic Serpent* is: "The first time an Ashaninca man told me that he had learned the medicinal properties of plants by drinking a hallucinogenic brew, I thought he was joking."[4] In due course, Narby would learn to take such statements seriously. And he would be convinced that it was possible to learn a great many things from ayahuasca, including the properties of DNA.

The reason Narby asked the question about medicines was that there are around eighty-thousand species of plants in the rain forest, so to find a remedy by mixing them together would mean testing more than three thousand million different combinations. The nerve poison curare, for example, is made from a combination of plants, and the first stage is to boil them for three days—while staying well away from the boiling liquid, whose fumes are toxic. The final product, delivered by blow-gun, kills monkeys without poisoning their meat, at the same time causing them to relax their grip and fall to the ground, instead of clinging in a death spasm to the tree. How did they develop a substance with such remarkable properties?

The "hallucinogenic brew" ayahuasca is made up of two plants. One of them contains a hormone secreted in the human brain, called dimethyltryptamine, a powerful hallucinogen. But when swallowed, it is rendered harmless by a stomach enzyme. It has to be mixed with a substance obtained from a creeper, which prevents it from being broken down. Then it induces extraordinary visions.

Now in this part of Peru, shamans are known as ayahuasqeros, because they claim that their power of healing or prophesying the future are bestowed by the drug—or rather, by spirits who communicate when they are under the influence of the drug. Narby had been greatly impressed by the "polycultural" gardens "containing up to seventy-five different plants, mixed chaotically, but never innocently."[5] He asked a shaman named Ruperto: "How do you learn all this?" and was told that if he wanted to understand he must drink ayahuasca.[6]

The Columbian anthropologist Luis Eduardo Luna confirms this in an essay in *The Journal of Ethnopharmacology* included in *Shamans through Time*. He questioned four shamans in the Peruvian city of Iquitos, and all told him the same thing: "that the spirits of the plants taught them what they know." One of them, Don Celso, told him that this is why shamans were better than western doctors. Western doctors learn through books, but "we just take this liquid (ayahuasca), keep this diet, and then we learn."[7]

Two weeks later, Ruperto offered Narby a bottle of a reddish liquid, which Narby describes as tasting like acrid grapefruit juice. Narby vomited and was told to drink more of it.

"Suddenly I found myself surrounded by two gigantic boa constrictors that seemed fifty feet long. I was terrified . . . in the middle of these hazy thoughts, the snakes start talking to me without words. They explain that I am just a human being. I feel my mind crack, and in the fissures, I see the bottomless arrogance of my presuppositions. It is profoundly true that I am just a human being, and most of the time, I have the impression of understanding everything, whereas here I find myself in a more powerful reality that I do not understand at all and that, in my arrogance, I did not even suspect existed."[8]

At that point he had to go outside again to vomit, stepping over "fluorescent snakes."

This new sense of reality had its terrifying aspects: "language itself seemed inadequate. I tried to name what I was seeing, but mostly the words would not stick to the images. This was distressing, as if my last link to 'reality' had been severed. Reality itself seemed to be no more than a distant and one-dimensional memory."[9] He seemed to be vomiting colors and saw two beings on either side of him, one dark and one light.

Instructions seemed to come from outside him: time to stop vomiting, time to spit, to rinse his mouth. After hours of similar strange experiences, he fell asleep exhausted.

Two days later, an Indian friend remarked that he should have brought his camera and photographed the snakes. Narby said that the visions would not appear on film but was assured "Yes they would, because their colors are so bright."[10] He assumed his friend was talking nonsense. Later, he realized that nearly everything the Indian told him was true.

Not long afterward, another Indian told him that he could cure Narby's long-standing back pain with a vegetal tea drunk at the new moon. Again he was skeptical. In fact, the tea caused him to feel freezing cold, and his legs felt like rubber. But the back pain disappeared for good.

An even odder piece of information was imparted to him. His informant showed him a plant that could cure the bite of the deadly fer de lance snake. He noticed that the plant had tiny hooks resembling fangs and was told that "that is the sign that nature gives."[11] Again, he was skeptical, feeling that the plant's "fangs" must be coincidence, not a "sign" from nature.

He watched a shaman cure a sick baby by blowing tobacco smoke on it, then sucking at a spot on its belly and spitting. When he asked about this, he was told that tobacco was the mother of ayahuasca. And the mother of tobacco was a snake. He was also told that "souls" (maninkari) like tobacco. When he asked about these souls, he was told they are invisible, and fly through the air like radio waves—but that with tobacco or ayahuasca, they can be seen. All these things Narby dismissed as superstitions.

Back at home in Switzerland, he took his master's degree then began to write a book about what he had learned in Peru. "What if it were true that nature speaks in signs and that the secret to understanding its language consists in noticing similarities in shape or in form?"[12]

He began reading texts on shamanism and was struck by the comment: "You must de-focalise your gaze so as to perceive science and the indigenous vision at the same time."[13]

Narby's study began with the chemistry of hallucinogens. These operate by mimicking the important human hormone serotonin, which is produced in the pineal gland, in the middle of the brain—the so-called "third eye."

Serotonin is still something of a mystery. It seems to be connected with the evolution of intelligence. Men have more serotonin than animals. It looks as if its purpose may be to increase intelligence and inhibit sexual development. This may be why late developers tend to be more intelligent than early developers. Serotonin acts as a chemical messenger between brain cells. And it is speculated that serotonin and hallucinogens like mescalin and ayahuasca work like keys that fit a lock inside the brain. But what could that have to do with the enormous botanical knowledge of the Peruvian Indians?

Narby's first—and most important—assumption was that the Indians could be telling the truth when they said that they learned about plants from their ayahuasca visions.

Most scientists feel—reasonably—that the visions caused by hallucinogens are simply created by the unconscious mind, in the same manner as dreams. But Narby felt quite certain that the fluorescent snakes who had told him he was merely human were more than dreams. And this led him to consider the apparently insane hypothesis that the shaman's information about plants came from the plants themselves. Jung, after all, believed that he could converse with certain beings who inhabited his unconscious mind, and that these people were objectively real.[14]

For Narby, one of Michael Harner's most significant comments was that his visions were emanating from giant reptilian creatures *resting at the lowest depth of his brain* (my italics). And we may recall that in a footnote, Harner had remarked that the creatures "were like DNA."[15]

Narby was struck by the fact that the DNA molecule in fact looks like two intertwined serpents. Moreover, these serpents are joined by rungs, which make DNA look like a kind of spiral ladder.

From Eliade's book, he discovered that shamans the world over talk about ascending a ladder. Eliade adds that this is the earliest version of the idea of an "axis of the world."[16] (Another anthropologist, Barbara Myerhoff, who chewed peyote buttons under the guidance of Huichol shaman Ramon Medina in the 1970s, felt that she had been impaled on this axis, "an enormous tree with its roots buried far below the earth and its branches rising above sight toward the sky.")[17]

At this point in Narby's book, I recalled that Keith Critchlow had also mentioned the world axis and went back to *Time Stands Still*. Critchlow remarks that the idea seems to be bound up with the Pole Star, which, as noted earlier, is often called the Nail Star or the Sky Nail, and is said to hold the world axis in place. The houses of shamans are built with a central pillar that goes up through the roof, and which symbolizes the world axis that the shaman has to climb to reach "heaven"; this pillar has seven stories, just as the shaman's ladder has seven rungs. It enables him to ascend through the seven cosmic zones—which, of course, are reflected in our everyday speech when we say that some pleasure makes us feel as if we are "in the seventh heaven."

Moreover, the number seven runs throughout world mythology, magic, and religion. In Brewer's Dictionary of Phrase and Fable, seven is defined as "a mystic or sacred number." But why is it so universally associated with mysticism and magic? The British scholar Geoffrey Ashe once suggested that this is because there are seven stars in Ursa Major, the Great Bear; but this is in the northern hemisphere, while seven is revered as a magical number the world over. (He might also have noted that the Pleiades are known as the "seven sisters.")

I would suggest that the answer lies in shamanism, which, with its seven-runged ladder, is also the same all over the world. (It needs to be added that Eliade and Critchlow both point out that in shamanism, the number nine also occupies a central place, and that some shamanic roof-trees have nine notches.)

When Narby learned that Australian aborigines declare that the world was created by a rainbow-colored snake with the aid of a quartz crystal, and that the Desana Indians of the Columbian Amazon (who drink ayahuasca) also speak of a cosmic anaconda and a quartz crystal, he had no doubt that this was no coincidence.

In the four volumes of Joseph Campbell's work on world mythology, Narby found symbols of intertwined snakes "in most images representing sacred scenes."[18] And he found cosmic serpents who give birth to the universe in Amazonia, Mexico, Australia, Sumer, Egypt, Persia, India, the Pacific, Crete, Greece, and Scandinavia. And in the Levant, the serpent-creator had been revered for at least seven thousand years before the Book of Genesis.

Narby was soon convinced that the intertwined serpents were a symbol of DNA, and—most controversially—that shamans somehow communicate with DNA—or rather, the DNA communicates with the shamans. "In their visions shamans managed to take their consciousness down to the molecular level."[19] And he noted that Gerardo Reichel-Dolmatoff, another Amazonia anthropologist, described his own visions under ayahuasca as "like microphotographs of plants."[20] And so, "when they say the recipe for curare was given to them by the beings who created life, they are talking literally. When they say their knowledge comes from beings they see in their hallucinations, their words mean exactly what they say."[21]

Narby goes on: "I was staggered. It seemed that no one had noticed the possible links between the 'myths' of 'primitive peoples' and molecular biology. No one had seen that the double helix had symbolized the life principle for thousands of years around the world."[22]

Now if true, this is certainly astonishing. And if the DNA can act as the "teacher" of shamans, we must also admit that it introduces a concept that all scientists hate: the notion of "teleology" or purpose. Science is an attempt to study things under a microscope, and this works best if the things are inert. Then the universe, life, matter, can all be explained in mechanical terms that raise no awkward problems.

But Narby, like Francis Crick, the codiscoverer of DNA, feels that this view has major drawbacks. Crick has objected to the notion that living cells—or proteins—were an accident that evolved from the "primeval soup" by chance and calculated that the chance of a protein being built up from accidental collisions was 20 multiplied by itself 200 times, which is billions of times more then the number of atoms in the universe.

Narby also makes the important comment: "According to the shamans of the entire world, one establishes communication with spirits via music."[23] This is why shamans sing and dance. The central importance of music was recorded by the American ethnomusicologist Dale A. Olsen in the mid-1970s. Among the Warao Indians of the Orinoco Delta of Venezuela, he noted that music was more important than tobacco in achieving trance states. (They do not use mind-altering drugs.) "Music, combined with cultural conditioning, produces, I believe, a pure trance state, similar to the meditative trance state achieved by Buddhists while using music to reach enlightenment."[24] He remarks that Warao shamans do not become possessed, but sink into deep meditation during which they achieve contact with their supernatural helping spirits.

The Warao shaman agreed to sing a "bewitching song" taught to him by his supernatural teacher, explaining first that it would destroy the tape recorders, both the expensive recorder on loan from UCLA, and the cheap one owned by Olsen. The shaman ended his lengthy song by speaking about the "great scissors of the spirit world"[25] that would destroy the machines of the foreigner. But the destruction would not be immediate; if he had wished to destroy them immediately, he would have smoked a long cigar, not a short one.

A few weeks later, the prophecy came true; the batteries of the UCLA recorder leaked acid and destroyed the wires, while Olsen's own recorder began to mangle tapes and broke beyond repair when he tried to fix it.

This raises the obvious question of whether a shaman may use his powers to harm people. The answer, it seems, is yes—but in doing so, the shaman also harms himself. In an "Interview with a Killing Shaman" a shaman named Ashok from western Nepal tells the Danish anthropologist Peter Skafte how, when business partners swindled him, he became angry and "directed a deadly mantra against my partners."[26] All three died, one falling ill, one catching dysentery, and one being hit by a car. Ashok was horrified, since he had vowed to the gods that he would only use his powers to serve others. "And my fears came true. My little son and daughter became ill with terrible fevers and died within a month."[27]

(According to the European magical tradition, the same is true of western witchcraft; the witch who uses his/her powers to cause harm will become the victim of a boomerang effect.)

Fernando Payaguaje, a Secoya shaman from Ecuador, dictated a book to his grandsons, who translated it into Spanish and published it under the title *The Yage Drinker* (yage being ayahuasca). In this, the shaman explains how yage can teach withcraft. "Some people drink yage only to the point of reaching the power to practice witchcraft. A much greater effort and consumption of yage are required to reach the highest level, where one gains access to the visions and power of healing.

To become a sorcerer is easy and fast. I did not aspire to that, but to become the most wide and knowledgeable."[28] And he tells how, once he had achieved this level "I felt able to practice witchcraft and to kill others, even though I never did, because my father's advice contained me: 'If you use that power now, you could kill someone, but then you would never get over being a sorcerer'."[29]

American anthropologist Michael F. Brown studied the practices of the Jivaro Aguaruna Indians of Peru and noted that they regard sorcery as a deliberate attempt to murder, and believe that sorcerers should be executed. Sorcerers, like shamans, use "spirit darts"; the sorcerer uses them to inflict suffering on his enemies, while the shaman uses them to frustrate the evil activities of the sorcerer.

It should be noted that all shamans—and their patients—believe that all life-threatening illness is the result of sorcery. This, of course, will strike westerners as preposterous. Yet one western anthropologist, Edith Turner, recorded how, in 1985 she witnessed a curative ritual in Zambia in which she felt so close to the participants that she saw the "harmful spirit," a large blob of grey plasma, emerge from the female patient's back. "Then I knew the Africans were right, there is a spirit affliction, it isn't a matter of metaphor and symbol, or even psychology."[30] And she says of the grey blob: "it was a miserable object, purely bad, without any energy at all, and much more akin to the miserable ghosts of suicides."[31] It sounds as if the "blob" was some kind of energy vampire.

Graham Townsley, a British anthropologist, lived among the Yaminahua Indians of the Peruvian Amazon in the early 1990s and heard about a "secret language" among shamans. He set out to decode it, and to learn to overcome the "force field" between his own cognitive framework and that of the shamans.

He explains that the central notion of the Yaminahua is that of yoshi, meaning roughly spirit or animate essence. Everything in the world is given its essence by its yoshi. The yoshi is subject to the influence of other yoshi, which explains illness.

But yoshi are not only the essence of things or beings; they also have an independent existence in a suprasensory realm, and in this realm they are always ambiguous, "like and not like," "the same but different."

Man consists of three parts: his body, then a social self associated with reason and language, then an entity that is neither social nor human, and that mingles easily with other yoshi. The yoshi involves the fundamental sameness of the human and nonhuman, which is why human can be transformed into nonhuman, men into animals.

Singing is the essence of shamanism and the instrument of the shaman's power. Under the influence of ayahuasca, the Yaminahua shaman learns "to sing, to intone the powerful chant rhythms, to carefully thread together verbal images couched in the abstruse metaphorical language of shamanic song, and follow them. A song is a path—you make it straight and clean then you walk along it."[32] The shaman's healing power originates in his song, his koshuiti—kosh is an imitation of the sound we make when we breathe in hoarse, staccato breaths.

The language of the koshuiti is made up of unusual words for common things. The songs are metaphoric, an analogy of the real situation that the song is intended to influence. "Confronted by an illness, a shaman sings a song to the moon, to an animal, or perhaps chants a myth."[33] He is chanting to the nonhuman yoshi who populate his visionary experience. And the language is "densely metaphoric."

Night becomes "swift tapirs," the forest becomes "cultivated peanuts," fish are "peccaries," jaguars are "baskets," anacondas are "hammocks." The result, Townsley says, is that the sense makes absolutely nonsense to nonshamans. Fish are "white collared peccaries" because of the resemblance of the fish's gills to the white dashes on this type of peccary's neck, and jaguars are "baskets" because of the resemblance of the loose-woven fibers of the basket to the jaguar's stripes. The Yaminahua shamans call this "twisted language." The songs are intended, with their imagery, to create the clarity of visionary experience. The shaman says that normal words would make him "crash into things."[34]

All this brings to mind the experiences of an American schoolteacher who went to Hawaii in 1917 and began to study the old religion of the Hawaiian Indians, the Huna, which was guarded by priests named Kahuna, and found its secret in its language.

His name was Max Freedom Long, and he would tell his story in a remarkable book called *The Secret Science Behind Miracles*. Born in 1890, he graduated from UCLA and went to Hawaii as part of a program to teach the children of government officials. Working in a remote valley, he set out to learn all he could about the ancient Huna religion, now forbidden by the white Christian authorities. Long met a museum curator named William Tufts Brigham, who told him that the Kahuna could kill by means of the "death prayer." And Long heard a story of a Christian minister who challenged a Kahuna to a contest of prayer and was disconcerted to find that his congregation was dying one by one of some strange paralysis. Then the minister persuaded someone to teach him the death prayer, and the magician died within three days. Long also heard of a youth who had entered a forbidden temple to show he was not afraid, but whose legs became useless, so he had to be carried home. He had to go to a Kahuna to be cured.

Back in America, it struck him that he might learn some of the basic secrets of the Kahunas through their language. Since Hawaiian words are built from shorter words, it ought to be possible to gather important clues from their sacred terms. He looked up "spirit" and found there were two words, Unihipili and Uhane. And he remembered that Christian missionaries declare that man has two souls.

Later, Long discovered that the Hunas believe that man has, in fact, three souls; besides the Unihipili and Uhane, there is one called the Aumakua. He concluded that the Unihipili is what Freud called the unconscious—man's "lower self." The Uhane is the conscious everyday self—what might be called the "middle self." And the Aumakua is what might be called the "higher self," or the "superconscious mind." So, in addition to his unconscious mind, man has a superconscious mind, which is as far above everyday consciousness as the unconscious is below it.

The psychical researcher F. W. H. Myers had suggested a similar theory in his classic work *Human Personality and Its Survival of Bodily Death*. Myers called the "self" that is able to exercise unknown powers the "subliminal self." In his 1961 introduction to a reissue of Myers's book, Aldous Huxley suggested that it might be simpler to say that man has a Freudian unconscious—a kind of basement—a conscious ego, and a superconscious attic, of which we are all totally ignorant. These three "selves" seem to correspond to the three selves of the Hunas. The low self, say the Hunas, lives in the solar plexus, and its purpose is the manufacture of a vital force called mana.

Mana is a life force that is created from food and is used by the two higher selves when stepped up in vibratory rate.

Although the low self is the servant of the middle self, it is often refractory and disobedient. It likes its own way. It is naturally violent and emotional like a spoilt child. The middle self, say the Hunas (i.e., "us") should try to discipline the low self and raise it, rather than descend to its level, as self-indulgent people do. The human beings who give way to the tantrums of the lower self are simply storing up trouble for themselves. This can be seen in most criminals (particularly sex criminals). According to the Hunas, the high self could be regarded as man's guardian angel, and it knows the future and can control it. So it sounds as if the high self is the part of us that is in charge of synchronicity and such things as dream precognition.

The middle self—the "everyday you"—can, in fact, get in touch with the high self. But the problem is that it has to do so via the low self. It is as if the telephone line passes down through the low self before it goes up to the high self. And since the low self is usually in a state of negative emotion, the crackling on the line makes it difficult to communicate. It is only when the low self has achieved a state of calm, or has been disciplined to behave itself, that it is possible to get through to the high self, and to learn the future.

The death prayer, according to Long, works through "low selves" that have become detached, usually through death. These low selves are, for example, responsible for poltergeist disturbances. They are what are known as earthbound spirits, stupid but not particularly malevolent.

Middle selves that have become detached after death have no memory—since memory is a function of the low self. These are what are called ghosts, and they exist in a kind of permanent present, unable to escape it.

It would, however, be a mistake to assume that the low self is simply a kind of juvenile delinquent. In fact, Long's students came to refer to the low self as "George" and pointed out that George can be extremely useful. He has all the penetration of a child, so that if one asks George what he thinks of a certain person, he is likely to go straight to the point. The middle self may feel that the person is intelligent and convincing; George can see at a single glance that he is a crook.

According to Long, it is possible to get in touch with George and hold conversations with him. A person who has established this kind of close relation with "George" is in a far better position for establishing a fruitful relation with the high self.

The high self, as already stated, can foresee the future and may well be the person who is responsible for those precognitions that J. W. Dunne wrote about in *An Experiment with Time*.

According to Dr. Brigham, the Kahunas can also look into the future and change it for their clients. But this is only possible if the client is not under the domination of the low self, because the low self tends to change its purposes and objectives from moment to moment. Long writes:

"Just how this mechanism works is uncertain, as it belongs to the next higher level of consciousness, but the Kahunas spoke of the forms as 'seeds,' which were taken by the Aumakua (high self) and made to grow into future events or conditions.

"The Kahunas considered it of great importance for the individual to take time out at frequent intervals to think about his life and decide in exact terms what he wished to do or wished to have happen. The average person is too much inclined to let the low self take the helm, which is dangerous because it lives under the domination of the animal world where things happen illogically and as if by accident. It is the business and duty of the middle self, as guide for the low self, to use its power of inductive reason and its will (to control the low self) in making plans for the task of living and seeing that proper efforts are made to work according to those plans."

Long adds: "A large part of the Kahunas' magical practice in days gone by was aimed at seeing what crystallized future lay ahead for the client, then procuring changes in that future to make it more desirable."[35]

Long actually made use of a Kahuna magician—a woman—during the Depression, in 1932, when a camera shop he owned was in danger of going bankrupt. After telling him that he must visualize with great clarity what it was he wanted, she explained how to make a prayer to the high self, so that it would be quite unambiguous. With her help, Long was able to sell his camera shop for a satisfactorily high sum. She ended by foretelling that Long would write eight books, which proved to be accurate.

After such an experience, Long was naturally anxious to establish where the Hunas came from originally, and whether their magical practices were known elsewhere. But that was made doubly difficult by the fear of the "death prayer." When people became the victims of the death prayer, they first lost the use of their feet, then of their legs, and then the paralysis gradually spread upwards until they died.

Dr. Brigham told Long a story about a young Hawaiian boy who accompanied him on an expedition up Mount Mauna Lowa to collect plant specimens, and how, halfway up the mountain, the boy began to experience paralysis in his feet, then in his legs. Other Hawaiians who were in the party assured Brigham that the boy was the victim of the death prayer and, on questioning, the boy admitted that the old Kahuna in his village had warned everyone to have no dealings with the white people, on pain of death.

An old man among the Hawaiians begged Brigham—who was regarded as a magician in his own right—to counter the death prayer. Brigham, who was quite sure that he had no magical powers, finally had to agree. He knew that the agents who carried out the orders of the Kahuna were supposed to be spirits—"low selves" separated from the rest of the being by death. But these spirits are also highly suggestive. Brigham stood above the sick boy and began to argue with the spirits, telling them that he realized that they were fine and intelligent creatures, and that it was a great pity that they had been enslaved by the Kahuna. He told them that their real destiny was to go to heaven and that, in killing the boy, they were simply obeying the will of an evil man. Some of the listening Hawaiians actually began to cry, because they were so moved by Brigham's argument.

Finally, Brigham ordered the spirits to go back and attack the Kahuna. After a very long wait, Brigham felt a strange sensation as if all the tension had gone out of the air. At that moment, the boy discovered that he was able to move his legs. Not long after Brigham went to the boy's village and was told that the Kahuna was dead—it had happened on the night Brigham had wrestled with the spirits. The Kahuna had awakened with a scream and begun to fight off spirits, but because he had failed to put protection on himself, he was vulnerable and died before morning.

It can be seen why Long had so much difficulty in learning anything about the religion of the Kahuna, and the death prayer.

Long also tells the story of a boy who, in a spirit of bravado, walked into a "forbidden" temple in the forest, and became paralyzed from the waist down. A Kahuna priest had to be called in to free him from the "curse."

It was some time after reading this that I came upon a novel called *The Empire of Darkness* by the French Egyptologist Christian Jacq and was struck by a sudden insight. It is the first of a trilogy called *The Queen of Freedom*, about the princess Ahhotep of Thebes, who in the seventeenth century BC had led a revolt against the foreign invaders called the Hyksos, the "Shepherd Kings."

In the seventh chapter, Princess Ahhotep disregards the advice of the priests of Amon and enters the temple of the goddess Mut at Karnak to ask her help in fighting the invaders. Jacq writes: "Yes, this temple was intensely alive. . . . It exuded power in its own right. . . ."[36] But although terrified and convinced she might die, she enters the sanctuary of the goddess, whost statue is in the form of a lioness. She prays aloud, but "The only answer was silence. But it was not the silence of the dumb, for Ahhotep sensed a presence like that of a landscape which spoke to the soul. . . ."[37] But when Ahhotep tries to take from the statue the sceptre of power, it burns her hand, and she falls unconscious.

Suddenly, it struck me that when Jacq says that the temple is alive, he meant it literally, and was saying what Emil Shaker had said to me in the temple of Edfu. These temples had real power, like the power that had struck down the boy in the temple on Hawaii. This was not some primitive superstition, but the same recognition of the power of "invisibles" that Harner and Narby had become aware of in South America. For the first time, I felt I understood the religion of Ancient Egypt.

After the publication of his first book, *Recovering the Ancient Magic*, Max Freedom Long received a letter from a retired English journalist named William Reginald Stewart, who was able to throw an interesting light on the possible history of the Hunas.

Stewart had been in Africa, working as a correspondent for the Christian Science Monitor, when he heard about a woman who possessed magical powers, and who belonged to the Berber tribe, the aboriginal people of North Africa. Stewart was so interested in these stories that he hired guides and set out to find the tribe in the Atlas Mountains. There he discovered the female magician, who was known among her fellow Berbers as a Quahuna—obviously a variant of the Hawaiian word. With a great deal of persuasion, he was adopted by the tribe, and also made the adopted son of the magician. Her name was Lucchi, and her seventeen-year-old daughter was also beginning to train as a Quahuna, so Stewart was allowed to become a second pupil.

According to Lucchi, there were originally twelve tribes of people who had magicians called Quahunas, and they once lived in the Sahara desert when it was green and fertile. Then, said Lucchi, the rivers had dried up and the tribes had moved into the Nile valley. It was there that they used their magic to build the Great Pyramid. They became the rulers of Egypt and were highly regarded because of their magic.

Lucchi went on to tell how the prophetic powers of the Quahunas enabled them to see that a time of intellectual darkness was due to fall on the earth, and that the secret of their magic might be lost. So the twelve tribes began to hunt for isolated lands to which they might go to preserve their secret (for which the Hawaiian word is "huna"). The world was explored—not physically, but by psychic means. Eventually, they discovered that the islands of the pacific were empty and made their way there via a canal to the Red Sea, then along the African coast and across India. But the twelfth tribe decided to stay in Africa and moved to the Atlas Mountains. There, they lived for centuries, preserving the secret and using its magic, until the only Quahuna left was Lucchi.

Much of what Stewart learned from Lucchi corresponded closely with what Max Freedom Long had said in his book. Stewart also described Lucchi's magical powers, how she was able to heal, control the weather, and exercise control over animals.

Then, Lucchi was suddenly killed. Two raiding parties began to shoot at one another, and a stray bullet struck the last of the Quahunas. This was before the First World War, and it was thirty years later that Stewart read Long's first book and contacted him.

It would seem possible, then, that Kahuna magic originated in Africa, before the building of the Great Pyramid, and that it had spread from there to the Pacific.

Long comments that Hawaiian legend states that the Hawaiians once lived in a homeland far away, and that they saw the land of Hawaii by "psychic sight." Their voyage began at the "Red Sea of Kane," and they then moved from land to land in large double canoes.

Long also adds that traces of Kahuna magic can be found in India.

The notion of "curses" really working sounds absurd to the western mind. But skepticism is likely to dissolve in the face of actual contact, and this is what happened to the eminent psychical investigator Guy Lyon Playfair when, as a university graduate, he went to Rio de Janeiro as a schoolteacher in 1961. In *The Flying Cow* Playfair describes how he became interested in a healer named Edivaldo, who could open a patient's stomach with his hands and perform operations, after which he would close up the wound, which would become sealed again.

Edivaldo operated on Playfair's stomach, and Playfair could feel his hands inside him. Playfair felt no pain, only an anesthetized sensation, and after Edivaldo had closed up the wound, there was a thin red line on his midriff. After a second similar operation, Playfair's problem was cured.

Playfair describes how he joined the Brazilian equivalent of the Society for Psychical Research and investigated a number of poltergeist cases. As a result, he quickly reached the conclusion that poltergeist activity is not simply a matter of "RSPK," "recurrent spontaneous psychokinesis," as most western paranormal investigators assume, but that poltergeists are "spirits" (although he does not rule out the RSPK explanation in certain cases). And he discovered in Brazil that umbanda (or spirit magic) specialists can put spells on people and induce poltergeists to invade their homes.

He investigated a series of disturbances that had been going on for six years, which was finally cleared up by a team led by a candomblé magician (candomblé being a Brazilian equivalent of voodoo). In a chapter of his book *The Indefinite Boundary* called "The Psi Underworld," he gives several examples of hauntings induced by "black magic."

Playfair himself, fortunately, had never been the subject of such a curse. But it happened to his friend David St. Clair, who describes it in his book *Drum and Candle*. St. Clair had been living in Rio de Janeiro for eight years and had a comfortable apartment with a fine view. He also had an attractive maid named Edna, a pretty, brown-colored girl. She was, he assures the reader, a maid and nothing more. Her life had been hard; deserted by the father, her family had been brought up in a shack in a slum.

She was obviously delighted with the comfort and security of her job with St. Clair. She joined a folk-dance group and, after a television appearance, became something of a local celebrity. And one day, St. Clair told her that he had decided it was time for him to leave Brazil. Edna was now doing so well that he had no doubt she would easily find another job; he told her he would give her six months' wages.

It was then that things began to go wrong. A book he had written failed to make any headway; his typist made a mess of it, then fell ill so that it sat in her desk drawer for weeks. A New York publisher rejected it. An inheritance he was expecting failed to materialize. His plans for moving to Greece had to be shelved. A love affair went disastrously wrong, and a friend he asked for a loan refused it. He even fell ill with malaria.

One day, he met a psychic friend in the Avenida Copacabana; she took one look at him and said: "Someone has put the evil eye on you. All your paths have been closed."[38] A few days later, another friend wrote to say he had been to an umhanda session, and a spirit had warned him that one of his friends was in grave danger: due to a curse, all his paths had been closed.

An actor friend immediately divined that it was Edna who had put the curse on him. St. Clair thought this absurd. To begin with, Edna was a Catholic and had often expressed her disapproval of Spiritism and umbanda. But his actor friend told him he had attended a spiritist session where he had been assured that David St. Clair's apartment was cursed. But how would Edna go about doing that, St. Clair wanted to know. All she had to do, his friend replied, was to go to a quimbanda— black magic—session and take some item of his clothing, which could be used in a ritual to put a curse on him. And now that his friend mentioned it, St. Clair recalled that his socks had been disappearing recently. Edna had claimed the wind was blowing them off the line.

St. Clair told Edna he believed himself to be cursed; she pooh-poohed the idea. But he told her he wanted her to take him to an umhanda session. After much protest, she allowed herself to be forced into it.

That Saturday evening, Edna took him to a long, white house in a remote area outside Rio. On the walls were paintings of the devil, Exu. Toward midnight, drums started up, and the Negroes sitting on the floor began to chant. A ritual dance began. Then the umbanda priestess came in like a whirlwind—a huge Negress dressed in layers of lace and a white silk turban.

She danced, and the other women began to jerk as if possessed. The priestess went out, and when she came in again, was dressed in red, the color of Exu/Satan. She took a swig of alcohol, then lit a cigar. After more dancing, she noticed St. Clair and offered him a drink from a bottle whose neck was covered with her saliva. Then she spat a mouthful of the alcohol into his face.

After more chanting, a medium was asked who had put the curse on him. She replied: "The person who brought him here tonight! She wants you to marry her. Either that, or to buy her a house and a piece of land. . . ."[39] The priestess ordered Edna to leave. Then she said: "Now we will get rid of the curse."[40] There was more ritual drumming and dancing, then the priestess said: "Now you are free. The curse has been lifted, and it will now come down doubly hard upon the person who placed it on you."[41] When he protested, he was told it was too late—it had already been done.

Three days later, St. Clair received a telegram from a magazine, asking for a story; he had suggested it to them months before but they had turned it down. Now, unexpectedly, they changed their minds and sent him money. A week later, the inheritance came through. The book was accepted. And ten days later he received a letter asking if his broken love affair could be restarted where it had left off. Then Edna became ill. A stomach-growth was diagnosed, and she had to have an operation, for which St. Clair paid. But her health continued to decline. She went to see an umbanda priest, who told her that the curse she had put on St. Clair had rebounded on her, and that she would suffer as long as she stayed near him. She then admitted trying to get him to marry her by black magic, after which she declined his offer to buy her a house or an apartment, and walked out of his life.

So the worldview of the shaman, based on the notion of the reality of spirits, receives support not only from many anthropologists, but from an increasing number of those engaged in psychical research.

As we shall see in a later chapter, such evidence was accepted by Charles Hapgood, and almost certainly played a part in convincing him of the existence of "advanced levels of science that may go back 100,000 years."

NINE

ENOCH'S BURNING MOUNTAINS

In the first two centuries of the Christian era, a strange work called the *Book of Enoch* was widely read and was assumed to be a part of the Old Testament. I think that early readers saw it as a strange kind of adventure story, in which the hero—the prophet Enoch—is taken by angels on a tour of the heavens, including a place very like Hell. It also had a certain scandal appeal, since its rebel angels, called the Watchers, decided to try out the delights of sex with earthly women and begat on them a race of unruly giants.

Then, for no reason that has ever been discovered, the *Book of Enoch* vanished. Was it suppressed by the Church? Whatever the reason, it had soon acquired the reputation of being the kind of book that should not be left out where the children could get hold of it.

It was rediscovered toward the end of the eighteenth century, when a Scotsman named James Bruce found it in a monastery in Abyssinia (now Ethiopia). Bruce was a Freemason of the Canongate Lodge of Kilwinning, and his quest may have been inspired by a romantic desire to track down the Ark of the Covenant, which one tradition claims to have been brought there.

Bruce made his way to Gondar, the capital of Abyssinia, on Lake Tana, and found an extraordinary people who might have been descended from the badly behaved giants of the *Book of Enoch*; they ate raw steaks sliced straight off a living cow, had the testicles of their enemies hanging from their lances, and broke off in the midst of feasts to have sex on the floor. Bruce, who was huge and bearded, found favor with the king and was appointed a military commander. In due course he did some exploring, riding to what his guide assured him was the source of the White Nile, but which actually turned out to be only the source of the lesser Blue Nile.

In a monastery he came upon an epic called the *Kebra Nagest* (Book of the Glory of Kings), which told how King Solomon fathered a child with the Queen of Sheba, who had her capital in Abyssinia. Their son finally returned to Abyssinia, taking the Ark of the Covenant with him.

In the same monastery Bruce discovered the *Book of Enoch*, which was believed to be written by the prophet Enoch, the grandson of Adam and great grandfather of Noah. In fact, it was written about 200 BC; but its description of seven burning mountains that descended out of the sky and fell into the sea, causing a flood, was believed by Professor Alexander Tollmann to be based on a tradition about the comet of 7600 BC.

Since the Flood is an important event in the Freemason's version of ancient history, Bruce must have felt he had stumbled on something that would make him famous among his fellow masons. He brought the book back with him to London, where his tales of his uninhibited hosts were received with the deep skepticism of envious stay-at-homes; Doctor Johnson virtually called him a liar. His great book *Travels to Discover the Source of the Nile* was also badly received, although it is impossible to feel much sympathy, since Bruce had employed a poverty-stricken clergyman as his amenuensis on a promise of later payment, then tried to fob him off with five guineas. Bruce, thoroughly embittered, died at the age of sixty-four, in 1794, after tripping on the stairs and falling on his head.

The *Book of Enoch* was finally translated into English in 1821, just in time to catch the Romantic revolution, with its fascination for rebel angels and forbidden couplings.

At that point in my research, I came upon *Uriel's Machine* by Christopher Knight and Robert Lomas and was fascinated by their account of the section in the *Book of Enoch* called "The Book of the Heavenly Luminaries," which is basically a treatise on astronomy. Enoch is taken on a journey by angels to a land in northerly latitudes. The only clue to its whereabouts is that in this latitude, the day is longer than the night by a ninth part, and the day amounts exactly to ten parts and the night to eight parts; they concluded that this wintry land is between about 51 and 59 degrees longitude, within which we find Stonehenge in Wiltshire, New Grange in Ireland, Callanish in the Hebrides, and various other prehistoric observatories.

These were built by a people known as the Grooved Ware People, after their ceramics. Is it coincidence, Lomas and Knight ask, that in a chapter of the *Book of Enoch* dealing with astronomy, the latitudes of several prehistoric observatories is given? At a certain point in this chapter, Enoch is transported toward a mountain of "hard flint rock" in the west.

"And I saw six portals in which the sun rises, and six portals in which the sun sets and the moon rises and sets . . . also many windows to the right and left of these portals."[1]

Lomas and Knight were reminded of Stonehenge, with its "portals" between the stone uprights of the trilithons.

In the early 1960s, the British astronomer Gerald Hawkins had started to investigate the possibility that Stonehenge might be a kind of Stone Age computer, constructed to calculate the moment of sunrise and moonrise over an 18.6 year cycle. His *Stonehenge Decoded* became an immediate bestseller, although some astronomers were unconvinced. In fact, its ideas are now generally accepted, and in the 1970s, the work of Professor Alexander Thom on ancient stone circles lent support to Hawkins's theory.

The basic notion is that by standing in the center of the circle, you can face the sunrise (or moonrise) and foretell the season according to its position behind the "markers."

Lomas and Knight decided to try and construct a "Uriel machine" on a Yorkshire hilltop—in fact, what amounted to a simple observatory. They returned repeatedly to take their observations of sunrise or sunset

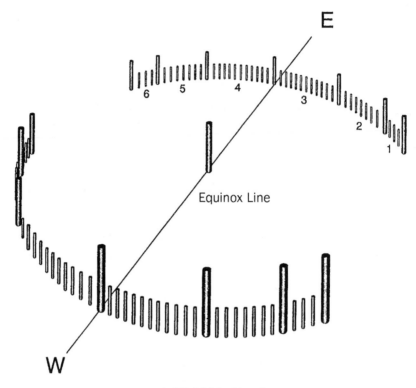

A "Uriel Machine."

from the center of the ring to the horizon and stuck markers in place. They persisted for a year and ended with two curved rows of posts, facing one another. And they learned—as ancient "henge" builders had learned—that the year does not divide neatly into four by solstices and equinoxes. Because the earth's orbit around the sun is an ellipse, there are 182 sunrises from the winter to the summer solstice, but 183 from the summer to the winter solstice. And there is the same disparity between the spring to the autumn equinoxes.

Their observations enabled them to learn why the ancient monument builders—these "stone age Einsteins"—had chosen as their unit of length what Alexander Thom called the "megalithic yard"—32.64 inches. In fact, Thom admittted he had doubled the basic unit he found in all the megalithic sites—16.32 inches—to bring it closer to our modern yard.

Lomas and Knight found that their "machine" registered the length of the year as 366 days (between one winter solstice and another), and this led them to fix a "megalithic degree," a 366th portion of the earth's revolution. They set their posts a megalithic degree apart and found that a star took 3.93 minutes to move from one upright to the next.

The megalith builders almost certainly used a pendulum as their clock. The time a pendulum takes to complete one swing is, of course, determined by its length. Lomas and Knight discovered that for the pendulum to swing 366 times in 3.93 minutes, it had to be exactly 16.32 inches long. This is obviously why the "stone age Einsteins" chose 16.32 inches as their basic unit. Lomas and Knight had solved the problem that baffled Thom.

But Uriel's "machine" (amounting in effect, to a primitive Woodhenge of posts) could not only be used as a calculator of sunrises and moonrises, but as an observatory for measuring comets. It could determine, quite simply, whether a comet was on course to hit the earth.

Lomas and Knight suggest that this was an important part of the purpose of these early observatories. Two postholes in the Stonehenge car park, aligned east-west, indicate that the earliest Stonehenge was set up about 8000 BC, more than three centuries before the impact of Tollmann's comet, which left a layer of sand over Scotland and sea shells on top of Snowdon. There is also archaeological evidence that two more postholes were set up a thousand years later.

The discovery of Lomas and Knight answers critics of the megalithic yard who protest that it is highly unlikely that there could have been a common measure used over thousands of square miles and dozens of centuries. They were thinking in terms of a megalithic yard made out of iron or wood, and carefully copied by everyone else. In fact, all primitive man had to do was to set up two wooden posts on a hill, with a megalithic degree between two of them, and adjust their pendulum so it swung 366 times as a star moved between one post and the next. The pendulum would then be a megalithic yard long.

All of this came into clearer focus when I stumbled upon a book called *Historical Metrology*, by A. E. Berriman, an engineer with an obsession about weights and measures.

Berriman points out that the basic Greek measurement is the stade (from which the word stadium derives), which is about the length of a football pitch, 185 meters. And amazingly enough, there are precisely 216,000 stade in the polar circumference of the earth. That happens to be sixty times sixty times sixty. Or 360 times sixty. It is easy to see at a glance that each degree of the earth's circumference must be sixty stades long. A degree is made up of sixty minutes, so each minute is one stade long. A minute is made up of sixty seconds, so each second is a sixtieth of a Greek stade. And this happens to be a hundred Greek feet.

This is staggering, for the classical Greeks did not know the size of the earth—until Eratosthenes worked it out, around 250 BC, with the aid of a deep well in Syene. Yet their measuring system proves that they took their stade from some civilization that did know the size of the earth. The likeliest candidate would seem to be the Sumerians, who invented the minute with sixty seconds and the hour with sixty minutes. But the Sumerians were not great seafarers, so it seems unlikely that they discovered the size of the earth. Hapgood's ancient sea kings—that is to say, the "Atlanteans"—seem a more likely candidate.

Lomas and Knight had joined the Freemasons out of curiosity; they wanted to know about the origins of its rituals. It is generally assumed that Freemasonry dates back to the Guilds of the Middle Ages, a kind of Trade Union of the builders of cathedrals like Chartres and St. Denis. But close study of its rituals convinced Lomas and Knight that they are far older, dating back to the Jerusalem Church in the time of Jesus and his brother James, and that the traditions of Freemasonry are older still, extending back to the flood of 9600 BC.

Such a notion is not hard to accept. If memories of the flood can be found in the myths of the Indians of western Canada, then there is no reason why they should not have been preserved in the religious traditions of the Middle East, and descended via the Hebrews, and then the Christians.

Lomas and Knight were particularly intrigued by one of Scotland's most remarkable religious monuments: Rosslyn Chapel, near Edinburgh. I visited this when Joy and I were in Edinburgh in May 1996. It had been built by a Templar named William St. Clair in the mid-fifteenth century and was an amazing place, seeming pagan rather than Christian. The walls and pillars were covered with sculptures of vines and a riot of carved flowers and fruits. And the pagan figure known as the Green Man seemed to be everywhere.

What was he doing in a Christian church? In mythology he represents the rebirth of vegetation every spring, and pagan festivals revolved around him.

In my book *Mysteries*, written twenty years earlier, I had discussed the ancient religion of the moon goddess Diana, which had been driven out by Christianity, yet refused to die. As noted earlier, an eccentric scholar named Margaret Murray had even suggested that witchcraft was really a religion based on this ancient worship of Diana, and that witch trials in which the Devil is described as having presided over a Witches' Sabbat were really pagan fertility rituals, presided over by a high priest dressed as the god Pan, with a goat's feet and horns.

I found myself wondering if William St. Clair (or Sinclair, as it was spelled later), the man who had built Rosslyn, was as pious a Christian as he was supposed to be.

There was obviously some mystery attached to the place. To begin with, there could be no possible doubt about the representation of sweet corn, or of the plant called aloes cactus, also a native of America, which looks rather like a lily and has a bitter flavor. But Rosslyn had been built half a century before Columbus discovered America.

On the train back to Cornwall I read a book I had bought in the Rosslyn bookshop, *The Hiram Key* by Robert Lomas and Christopher Knight, which centered around Rosslyn. It reinforced my suspicion that William St. Clair may have been the guardian of some curious—and non-Christian—mystery.

Modern Freemasons are inclined to believe that their odd ceremony of initiation—with a noose round the neck, a slipper on one foot and the other trouserleg rolled up to the knee, and a series of incomprehensible questions and answers—are pure invention. Lomas and Knight came to believe that they are, in effect, a secret code. They concluded that Freemasonry can trace its origins back to the medieval organization known as the Knights Templar, and through them to the Flood.

The Templars are so called because their original headquarters was in the basement of Solomon's Temple in Jerusalem (or rather, the remains of the Temple, which was destroyed by the Romans in AD 70, only four years after Herod had rebuilt it).

Jerusalem fell to Christian knights in 1099, as a result of the First Crusade. Twenty years later, nine French knights from the area of Troyes approached King Baldwin II of Jerusalem and told him they had sworn to protect the roads and make them safe for Christian pilgrims; they asked if they could establish a home on the Temple Mount, and Baldwin gave them a plot of land that included the Temple's "basement," which they turned into a stable.

But oddly enough, the nine knights showed no sign of organizing themselves to protect pilgrims (and in any case, nine men would hardly have formed an effective patrol). Instead, they spent the next seven years excavating their "stable" and scarcely ever ventured outside. They were obviously looking for something. One of their tunnels was found by Israeli archaeologists in the 1970s.

But searching for what? When the Romans destroyed the Temple, they carried off its treasures. Could there have been the remains of that treasure concealed under the Temple?

Whatever they were searching for, they do not seem to have found it, and in 1126, seven years after starting their excavations, Hugh de Payens, the leader of the knights, returned to France. It looked as if the attempt to found an order had been a failure.

Then a rescuer appeared. Bernard of Clairvaux—later Saint Bernard—was a Cistercian and one of France's most powerful churchmen, even though he firmly refused to be promoted above the rank of abbot. He was also the nephew of one of the nine knights, Andre de Montbard. And Montbard had accompanied Payens back to France.

Two years later, a synod was convened in the town of Troyes, whose purpose was to persuade the Church to back the founding of the Order of Knights Templar. And this came about in 1128, when the "Order of the Poor Soldiers of Christ and the Temple of Solomon" was founded, and made answerable only to the Pope. And with the support of St. Bernard, recruits and money poured in, until the Templars became the wealthiest order in Europe.

The Second Crusade was initiated by Bernard of Clairvaux, after the fall of Edessa in 1144, but it ended in failure; the Moslems under Saladin were to recapture Jerusalem in 1187. And during the next century, seven more Crusades failed to restore power to the Christians. The fall of Acre in 1291 completed their defeat. And the Knights Templar lost their raison d'être.

But they did not lose their power—or their wealth (based partly on exemption from taxes). With a new Grand Master, Jacques de Molay, they licked their wounds on the island of Cyprus and wondered what to do next. The problem was that Cyprus was insecure, with the Moslems raiding Limassol and taking captives, who had to be ransomed. The Templars considered returning to France; but there were problems. The king, Philip the Fair (1265–1314) was in conflict with Pope Boniface VIII. And since the Templars regarded the Pope as their master, their return to France would be unwelcome to the king.

In fact, the whole order was unwelcome to the king, who felt they were—like their papal master—arrogant nuisances. (This may have been because he had once applied to join them, and been rejected.) It was Philip who won this round. When the pope threatened to depose Philip, the king denounced Boniface as a heretic and finally had him taken prisoner in his own house; Boniface died soon after being rescued.

When his successor, Boniface IX, showed signs of taking up the struggle where Boniface VIII left off, Philip arranged to have him poisoned. Then he had his own candidate, Archbishop Bertrand de Gotte of Bordeaux, placed on the papal throne.

Philip laid down a number of preconditions for supporting Bertrand's candidacy. One of these was that the new pope should move the seat of the papacy to France. But another precondition was held in reserve and has never been revealed. It was almost certainly that the pope should not oppose his plan to arrest the Templars and seize their money.

Bertrand became Pope Clement V in 1305. And the king immediately began to plan one of the most amazing coups in history. It was to arrest all the Templars—fifteen thousand of them—now living in France, and accuse them of heresy. It could be compared to a modern king plotting to arrest all the officers in the army, the navy, and the air force.

What is so incredible is that it succeeded. Sealed orders went out about four weeks before the swoop, and the Templars were arrested on Friday, October 13, 1307.

The Templars were accused of homosexuality, worshipping a demon named Baphomet, and spitting on the cross. Under appalling tortures—such as being held over red hot braziers—many confessed. The Grand Master Jacques de Molay himself confessed. But at their sentencing on March 18, 1314, Molay withdrew his confession, declaring that it had been forced from him by torture. The king was so enraged at having his plans thwarted that he immediately ordered Molay, and his friend Geoffrey de Charney, who also withdrew his confession, to be roasted alive over a slow fire.

This happened on the following day, on an island in the Seine called the Ile de Palais. It is said that Molay called upon the king and the pope to meet him before the throne of God within a year. Within three months both were dead—Philip gored by a boar during hunting, Clement of a fever.

But not all the Templars were captured. Their fleet was moored at La Rochelle, and on the day before the swoop, the ships sailed away—and vanished. The commander of one of these ships was the Seigneur de Gotte, who was related to the Pope, Bertrand de Gotte. It looks as if Bertrand had tipped him off about the forthcoming coup.

We know what happened to at least one of the ships. It was commanded by a knight named Henri de St. Clair, who settled in Scotland, and in due course, one of his descendants built Rosslyn Chapel.

Perhaps the most interesting speculation to emerge from all this is that other ships of the Templar fleet sailed across the Atlantic, nearly two centuries before Columbus, and one later returned to Scotland. It is hard, otherwise, to explain the sweet corn and aloes carved on the walls of Rosslyn Chapel.

But there is another question, equally baffling. If the Templar fleet knew about the existence of America, where did they learn about it? They must have read manuscripts or seen maps that told them of its existence—"maps of the ancient sea kings." Where would they have found them? The obvious possibility is: buried in the basement of the Temple in Jerusalem, when the Templars were living there and excavating the "stables."

And who would have hidden them there? Clearly not the Jewish priests, who were mainly concerned with hiding the Temple treasures from the Romans.

However, in the year of the Jewish revolt—AD 66—there were others who were equally anxious to preserve their treasures. The Essenes were a religious sect who had withdrawn into the wilderness to signalize their disapproval of Israel's priestly dynasty, the Hasmoneans or Maccabees. These were descendants of the guerrilla warrior, Judas Maccabeus who, two centuries earlier, had led the revolt against the Syrian overlords. When Judas was killed in battle, his brother Jonathan took over; in due course he became High Priest and founded a dynasty. Orthodox Jews were outraged, for the Law stated that High Priests should be descended from Aaron, and they formed an opposition party, the Pharisees.

But the Essenes, led by a prophet who called himself The Teacher of Righteousness, went further and set up their own community at Qumran, in the desert near the Dead Sea caves. They seem to have lived in tents and used the caves for storerooms. Nearly two thousand years later, many Essene scriptures were found in the caves and became famous as the Dead Sea Scrolls.

Lomas and Knight accept the widely held theory that Jesus was an Essene, and that his younger brother James succeeded to the title of Teacher of Righteousness. Jesus was crucified after an attempt to raise a revolt against the Romans, and priests threw James from the wall of the Temple, then stoned him to death. But when the Emperor Vespasian came with his son Titus to suppress the Jewish revolt of AD 66, the Essenes prepared to fight to the death and—Lomas and Knight argue—hid their most valuable scrolls in the Temple. Most died in their fight against the invaders, and Titus razed the Temple to the ground and carried off its treasures to Rome. But the tradition of the hidden scrolls was somehow preserved—we shall consider the most startling theory of how this came about in the next chapter—and when the Church called for a crusade to conquer the holy land, heirs to that tradition seem to have seen their opportunity to regain the lost scriptures.

Their first priority would be to get them translated. One of the knights, Geoffrey de St. Omer, knew an old scholar named Lambert, now known as Lambert of St. Omer, and probably took some of the scrolls to him around AD 1119. The evidence is that Lambert is now best known for a copy of a drawing called *The Heavenly Jerusalem,* which shows all the basic symbols of Freemasonry—the twin pillars, the three Masonic squares, and compasses—five centuries before it is supposed to have been founded in Europe.

Lomas and Knight point out that the notion of a Heavenly Jerusalem (or New Jerusalem) was found in the Dead Sea Scrolls, based on Ezekiel's vision. Their argument is too complex to summarize here, but they conclude: "With the discovery of the Heavenly Jerusalem scroll . . . we were now certain that the Templars did find the secrets of their Order inscribed upon the scrolls buried by the Nasoreans (or Essenes of Qumran . . .)."[2]

If this scroll was one of the parchments found under the Temple, it would confirm that Freemasonry was known to the Essenes.

Now Lomas and Knight turned their attention to Palestine in the time of Jesus. And discoveries began to come thick and fast.

To begin with, it soon became clear that the Christian Jesus of Nazareth and the Jesus known by his contemporaries were two completely different figures. In fact, the town of Nazareth did not even exist in Jesus's day. Jesus was known as "Jesus the Nazorean," not the Nazarene. And the Nazoreans were what we today might describe as Jewish Puritans. They were strict vegetarians, rejected animal sacrifice, and refused to recognize the divine inspiration of Moses. Charles Guignebert says that "in certain respects they resembled the Essenes," but Lomas and Knight argue convincingly that they were the Essenes.[3]

Lomas and Knight also discovered that Nazoreans still survive in southern Iraq in a sect called the Mandaeans. Are they Christians? No, not quite. Their devotion is not to Jesus, but to his cousin John the Baptist. Their opinion of Jesus is extremely low—they regard him as a rebel and heretic who betrayed secrets that had been entrusted to him.

In a book called *A History of Secret Societies*, Arkon Daraul comments that the Mandaeans "follow an ancient form of Gnosticism, which practices initiation, ecstasy and some rituals which have been said to resemble those of the Freemasons."[4]

Moreover, the Mandaeans practice a special handshake and have a ritual in which—as in Freemasonry—the candidate rises from the dead.

Lomas and Knight felt that this amounts to evidence that Freemasonry is a great deal older than the seventeenth century, and it is difficult not to agree with them.

Now we come to their startling and highly unconventional views on Christianity.

They argue that Jesus was not simply a preacher of universal love; he wanted to get rid of the Romans and was prepared to lead a revolt to do it. His views outraged many people.

"Everything points the same way; Jesus, or Yahoshua ben Joseph as he was known to his contemporaries, was a deeply unpopular man in Jerusalem and at Qumran. His agenda was much more radical than his family and most other Qumranians could understand. As we will go on to show, all the evidence suggests that most people backed James, including Mary and Joseph."[5]

The Essenes, Lomas and Knight state, accepted Jesus and John the Baptist as the two messiahs, the "two pillars" that are so basic to Freemasonry. Qumran means an arched doorway, and the arch that joins the pillars is God.

With the death of John the Baptist, Lomas and Knight argue, Jesus became more radical, and he also took on his cousin John's role of the "second pillar." This upset the Qumranians. (I must stress that Lomas and Knight cite historical texts for even their most outrageous assertions.) Jesus spent the period of his ministry (which was only a year) gathering followers, as he preached in remote places where the Romans would pay no attention.

Then he decided it was time for action. He rode into Jerusalem on an ass, to fulfill a prediction of the prophet Zachariah that the king would arrive on a donkey. Then he went to the Temple and caused a riot, attacking the money changers. After that he retreated to the nearby village of Bethany and waited for the revolution.

The Romans issued a wanted poster for Jesus, which still survives, describing him as short (about four foot six), bald-headed, and hump-backed.[6] His brother James was arrested first, then Jesus was arrested in Gethsemane, just across the valley from the Temple. From there he would have been able to see the two pillars of the eastern gate, with the arch that joined them—the two pillars of the New Jerusualem that were, in effect, himself.

The implication seems to be that he was not expecting to be arrested. He had struck the first blow, an act that he believed would soon echo across all Judaea, and bring people flocking to his banner. Then, with the help of Jahweh, he would do for his people what Judas Maccabeus had done nearly two centuries earlier. But he had underestimated the Romans and their Jewish underlings. They decided to nip this rebellion in the bud.

An old friend of mine, Hugh Schonfield, an eminent Jewish scholar, was firmly convinced that Jesus did not die on the cross, but was given a drug that made him appear to be dead; he argues this case convincingly in *The Passover Plot*. Henry Lincoln, Richard Leigh, and Michael Baigent take a similar line in *The Holy Blood and the Holy Grail*.

So Jesus was crucified at the age of thirty-three, and his body placed in a specially prepared tomb. But two days later, the body had disappeared, and some of the disciples saw him alive. But the date is a matter of dispute. Jesus was almost certainly born in 7 BC. This means that the Millennium was actually in 1993.[7]

The next step in the story is the coming of Saul, a Romanized Jew. He changed his name to Paul when he became a Roman citizen (and not, as usually stated, when he became a Christian convert). Then he was given the job of stamping out the remains of the Jewish freedom movement. He began to do this about ten years after Jesus's crucifixion, in AD 43, and among his first victims were the sect of Mandaeans, who ended in Iraq. Seventeen years later, he was struck blind on "the road to Damascus" and became the chief exponent of Christianity.

This would not have been Damascus in Syria, where he would have had no authority, but probably Qumran, also referred to as Damascus. Lomas and Knight suggest he was going there to persecute Jesus's brother James, now known as James the Just. And it was Paul who, on recovering his sight, became romantically enthralled by the doctrine that would later be labeled Christianity.

James was probably startled when the persecutor came to Qumran and begged to know all about his brother Jesus. What James—and other members of the community—told Paul seems to have inspired him to create his own religion based upon Jesus. When, in due course, the Qumranians realized what the new convert was preaching, they nicknamed him "the spouter of lies."

According to Paul, there are two versions of the life of Jesus: Paul's own, and that of James the Just. Paul's own version was that Jesus was the son of God, and had died on the cross to save man from the consequences of the sin of Adam. This version was designed to appeal to Gentiles, particularly those (like the Romans) who valued Greek culture. Paul's Jesus was a kind of Greek god who had died to guarantee his followers entry into heaven.

James and his Nasoreans were also known as Messianists, for they were still awaiting the Messiah, and some seemed to believe that the martyred revolutionary Jesus would return from death and lead a military revolt against the Romans. (These extremists also became known as Zealots.) The Messiah they awaited would be an orthodox Jew, like

Judas Maccabeus. They also believed—as Jesus had done—that the end of the world was about to arrive, and that they alone would be saved.

But Paul's Christianity—which he carried abroad to the Gentiles—had more appeal. I note in *A Criminal History of Mankind*:

"This new version of Christianity appealed to gentiles as much as Jews. Anyone of any sensitivity only had to look at the Rome of Tiberius, Caligula, and Nero to understand just what Paul meant about the fall of man. These sex-mad drunkards were a living proof that something had gone wrong. And the Roman matron who took up prostitution for pleasure revealed that Eve had fallen just as far as Adam. The world was nauseated by Roman brutality, Roman materialism, Roman licentiousness. Christianity sounded a deeper note; it offered a vision of meaning and purpose, a vision of seriousness. For the strong, it was a promise of new heights of awareness. For the weak, it was a message of peace and reconciliation, of rest for the weary, of reward for the humble. And for everyone, it promised an end to the kingdom of Caesar, with its crucifixions, floggings and arbitray executions. The Christians hoped it was a promise of the end of the world."[8]

Ironically, it was the Jewish revolt of AD 66 that led to the triumph of Paul's Christianity over James's Messianism. And it was sparked—at least in part, according to the Jewish historian Josephus—by the murder of James by priests in AD 62. Nero was forced to send his general Vespasian to put down the revolt. When Nero committed suicide, Vespasian was proclaimed emperor by his troops.

Vespasian returned to Rome and left his son Titus to continue the siege of Jerusalem, which fell in September AD 70. The Temple was burned, the rebels—including the Messianists—massacred, and the treasures of the temple carried back to Rome. And now there were no Messianists, Paul's religion of the crucified savior—which he had carried abroad—had no rivals and went on to conquer the world.

Christianity was such a highly successful religion because it preached the end of the world—Jesus had said that Armageddon, the final battle between good and evil, would take place within the lifetime of people then listening to him. Assuming some of his listeners were children, that meant that event could be expected by about AD 90.

Jesus was, by modern standards, suffering from delusions when he believed that God had told him that the end of the world was about to take place—just as the Jews were suffering from delusions when they started the revolt with the total certainty that Jahweh would not allow his Temple to be invaded by foreigners. But when AD 90 came and went without Armageddon, no one noticed. To begin with, the Christians were being persecuted by one of the most vicious Roman emperors so far, Vaspasian's other son Domitian, who insisted on being addressed as Lord God, and killed thousands of Christians for refusing to accept his divinity. He was assassinated in AD 96.

For the next two centuries the fortunes of the Christians varied, but as often as not, they were persecuted—emperors found it convenient to have someone to throw to the lions, for the amusement of the populace. Since the Christians were mostly slaves and the downtrodden, they were regarded with little sympathy by those who were better off. When Pliny the Younger decided to find out about Christianity by questioning his two young slave girls, who happened to be deaconesses, he found it perfectly natural to torture them. He was later apologetic about this, reporting that he had found nothing against them except that they were in the grip of a "distorted and boundless superstition."[9] On the whole, Lomas and Knight would concur.

Pope Leo X also agreed; he is quoted by Lomas and Knight as saying: "It has served us well, this myth of Christ."[10]

In the year AD 312, the persecuted minority called Christians could hardly believe their luck when the emperor Constantine made Christianity the official religion of the empire. Constantine's own explanation is that he saw a cross in the sky before he fought the crucial Battle of the Milvian Bridge, and the words "In this sign shall ye conquer."

That story is thrown into doubt by the fact that Constantine himself did not become a Christian; he remained a follower of the sun god Sol Invictus, instituted by the emperor Aurelian. But he did conquer—he was fighting his brother Maxentius—and threw Maxentius's body into the Tiber. And the Christians were in the position of some poor relation who suddenly becomes sole heir to immense wealth.

Constantine's "conversion" seems to have been entirely political. In the previous century there had been more than seventy emperors in seventy years, mostly assassinated. All over the empire, the barbarians were in revolt. The emperor Diocletian seized power in AD 284 and held the empire together by sheer strength of will and brute force. He flung bands of steel around the empire and ordered towns and villages that garrisoned his troops to feed them for nothing. His people were taxed as never before. Even so, he had to appoint three other "emperors" to help him rule the empire. But when he decided to retire and remove the bands of steel, the empire immediately began to fall apart.

Something had to be done, and it was Constantine—son of one of Diocletian's fellow "emperors"—who saw how to do it. Perhaps the inspiration came to him before the battle of the Milvian Bridge and explains why he said he had seen a vision. He realized that what the empire needed was not a vast army but a new religion. His choice of Christianity was probably due to the fact that his mother Helena—a British princess—was a Christian. Although Christianity had spread throughout his empire, it was very much a minority religion—only one in ten of his subjects was a Christian. On the other hand, there were a few Christians in virtually every town and village. And if he handed them power, then he had a supporter in every town and village, and a fellow emperor in every city big enough to have a bishop.

It worked—but then, Constantine found himself with another headache. These gentle, peace-loving Christians began to assail one another as violently as the Jews of three centuries earlier. The cause of contention was much the same as in Jerusalem: half the Christians regarded the other half as "collaborators." The emperor Diocletian had persecuted Christians and ordered them to hand over their holy books, and many had preferred that to martyrdom. Now the noncompromisers wanted to see them punished.

When a council of bishops held at Arles failed to heal the breach, the harassed emperor fled to Byzantium, no doubt regretting his folly in handing power to these squabbbling fanatics. But Byzantium was just as bad; there the main cause of contention was the view of an Alexandrian priest named Arius, who had made the apparently unexceptionable observation that Jesus, while the son of God, was not God himself. But by that time, Paul's romantic view of Jesus had taken such a hold that this sensible and moderate notion was regarded as blasphemous.

Constantine decided to put a stop to this irritating dissension once and for all. In 325 he called a council at Nicaea, in Turkey, and summoned church leaders from all over the empire. Then he sat down with them, and more-or-less ordered them to decide exactly what constituted Christianity. Arius lost the argument, and his views were condemned as "the Arian heresy."

He was sent into exile, and Christianity was defined by the Nicene Creed, which stated that Jesus was "one in being" with God the Father, while the Holy Ghost came a poor third, since it simply "proceeded" from the Father and Son. And so Jesus, whether he liked it or not, was transformed into a god—a notion that, as an orthodox Jew, would have shocked him profoundly.

Constantine, who was not a Christian and could not have cared less what they decided, was delighted that they had made up their minds, and would stop killing one another and undermining the security of the state. (His daughter Constantia was less sure and intervened to have Arius recalled from exile and reinstated.) His mother Helena proved invaluable, for she discovered the "true cross" complete with the plaque about the "King of the Jews." The spot where Jesus was crucified was identified, and so was his tomb. Helena also identified the spot where God spoke to Moses from a burning bush, and dozens of other places mentioned in Holy Scripture, in all of which she had a church built. Naturally, all became tourist attractions.

This was just a beginning. As Lomas and Knight put it: "The early Roman Church set about the task of destroying everything that did not meet its required dogma. Truth was unimportant; what the Church wanted to be was so, and everything contradictory to that was removed."[11]

In 415 AD, a screaming Christian mob, led by the Patriarch Cyril, burned down the library of Alexandria. The scholar Hypatia, one of the chief mathematicians of her day, was stripped naked and her skin flayed from her bones with abalone shells. Cyril was in due course canonized.

And so the Roman Catholic Church continued where the caesars left off and even forged a document called the Donation of Constantine, which claimed that the Church should have absolute authority, not just in spiritual matters, but in the affairs of this world, too. The Church had tasted power and it liked it—and was determined to hang on to it.

Understandably, the Church totally rejected this view of the founding of Christianity and continued to do so, virtually unopposed, until 1947. Then a discovery made in caves close to Qumran, on the Dead Sea, provided a challenge that threatened to shake it to its foundations.

At some date in early 1947, a Bedouin shepherd boy, searching on the cliffs at Qumran for a lost goat, found an opening that was invisible from below. He threw a stone, and there was a sound of breaking pottery; so he clambered in and dropped on to the floor of a cave. It contained a number of earthenware jars, each about two feet tall.

One of the jars proved to contain leather rolls wrapped in crumbling linen. For poor Arabs, the jars were more valuable than their contents, so several jars were removed and used for water, and some of the scrolls burned as fuel, when one of them reached a Christian shopkeeper. He in turn showed it to his archbishop. Finally, some scrolls reached an archaeological institute run by Dominicans in Jerusalem, which concluded they were forgeries. It was not until March of the following year that William F. Albright, of Johns Hopkins University, pronounced that some scrolls dated from 100 BC.

In fact, other ancient scrolls had been discovered two years earlier, in Nag Hammadi, in Egypt; but I shall delay discussion of these until the next chapter.

As more Dead Sea Scrolls came to light in Qumran, they were transferred to the Palestine Achaeological Institute, known as the Rockefeller Museum, in Jerusalem, under the guardianship of the rigidly conservative Dominican Father Roland de Vaux. They had still aroused no great interest in the scholarly world, for it was assumed that they were simply ancient copies of known books of the Old Testament, like Isaiah. And as de Vaux recognized their real significance, he also realized that it was in the interest of the Church to keep it that way. For in effect, the Dead Sea Scrolls revealed that the Roman Catholic Church had been built on a foundation of lies.

By 1954, all this was about to be threatened by a maverick scholar named John M. Allegro, the British nominee of an international team of scholars. To begin with, Allegro naively assumed that he was working with completely objective scholars who would not mind in the least releasing the news that the scrolls proved that Jesus was not the son of God but a Jewish rebel. But when it became clear that the incredibly slow pace at which the discoveries were being published was part of a cover-up, and that the chosen material was chosen for its unimportance, he decided to do something about it.

Allegro was not the first to realize that the scholars were engaged in skulduggery. The American literary critic Edmund Wilson wrote an article about the scrolls for the *New Yorker* in 1955, which was such a success that he decided to write a book. Wilson was a leftist and an anti-Catholic and soon realized what was happening. He pointed out that there seemed to be a certain dragging of feet, and a tension between the academic team at the Rockefeller Musem, and some independent scholars like Professor Andre Dupont-Sommer of the Sorbonne, who had pointed out five years earlier that the Teacher of Righteousness who is described as being crucified in the Dead Sea Scrolls sounded very like Jesus. He was amazed at the bitterness of the replies of his Catholic opponents.

In 1956 John Allegro gave three radio talks in the north of England on the Scrolls and advised a friend on de Vaux's team not to become a theologian because "by the time I've finished there won't be any Church left for you to join."[12]

His broadcasts caused little stir in England but were picked up by the *New York Times,* which stated that some of the early Qumran documents seemed to show the origins of Christianity a hundred years before Jesus. *Time* magazine followed with an article called "Crucifixion Before

Christ." By now Catholic scholars were in full defensive posture. They had dismissed Edmund Wilson as an ignorant amateur, but a scholar who was a member of the team was more dangerous.

Their next move amazed Allegro. They wrote a joint letter to the *Times* denouncing him and denying his assertions about "the teacher" and his crucifixion; they claimed that there was nothing of the sort in their texts. Allegro was baffled that they wanted to go public with the row, since it seemed contrary to their whole policy of playing down the scrolls. What he failed to grasp was that this was the first step in a move to totally discredit him; in his naivety, he still thought of himself as a member of the team and continued a friendly—if argumentative— correspondence with de Vaux and others.

Then there was the sensitive question of the Copper Scroll. In 1952, this was found in a Qumran cave, with writing indented on it. It was in two fragments, both rolled up, and was so brittle that it could not be opened. A friend of Allegro, Professor H. Wright-Baker of Manchester College, devised a machine for slicing it into strips. And it proved to be a list of treasures from the Temple.

Again, de Vaux's team was embarrassed. The Essenes were supposed to be enemies of the Sadducees who ran the Temple, but this find indicated otherwise. The international team had been insisted that the Essenes were an isolated cult who were irrelevant; that was clearly not so.

This was not the only reason de Vaux wanted to keep the scroll secret. If talk of hidden treasure was publicly announced, thousands of Bedouins with spades might descend on Qumran. So Allegro saw the point when told to keep his own counsel. And, assuming that it would be published sooner or later, he did as he was asked. He even kept quiet about it in a book he was writing on the Dead Sea Scrolls. But when the official communiqué was finally released in May 1956 and stated that the treasure was probably fictional and, in any case, was not associated with Qumran, Allegro felt he had been stabbed in the back.

At least the controversy turned Allegro's book *The Dead Sea Scrolls* into a bestseller. So he naturally agreed when the BBC suggested making a program based on it. But when the BBC team arrived at the Rockefeller Museum they were met with a blank refusal to cooperate. And when told that, in that case, the program would be made without their help, they admitted that it was not the program they objected to but Allegro.

In spite of all this, the program was completed at the end of 1957. Then transmission was delayed until the end of 1959, when it went out in a late night slot. Allegro assumed, probably rightly, that the BBC had been "got at" by the international team.

It looked as if Allegro had won when he persuaded the Jordanians to nationalize the Rockefeller Musem; they did this at the end of 1966. Then came the Six Day War of 1967, and Jerusalem became Israeli property. And Israel had no wish to upset the pope. So the Rockefeller team could dawdle to its heart's content.

And now, amazingly, Allegro played straight into the hands of his opponents. In 1970, he produced a book called *The Sacred Mushroom and the Cross*, which argued, on philological grounds, that Jesus had never existed; he was a symbol of godhead evoked by psychedelic mushrooms ingested by some contemporary fertility cult. This sounds preposterous—particularly in view of Allegro's familiarity with Essene scrolls that left no doubt that Jesus—or at least a crucified Teacher—was a real person. Neither can this extraordinary aberration be blamed on Allegro's own drug taking, for he was not even a drinker or smoker.

Whatever the reason, Allegro destroyed himself and handed victory to the Rockefeller team. He never regained academic respectability nor popular favor. He died unexpectedly in 1988 at the age of 53. (His chief enemy de Vaux had been dead since 1972.)

It is a pity that he was unable to live another two years, and see the self-destruction of one of the most prominent members of the de Vaux team, the editor in charge of publication John Strugnell. Like most of the team, Strugnell was violently anti-Semitic. And when, in November 1990, the Israelis appointed one of their own scholars, Emmanuel Tov, to act as joint editor of the project to publish the Scrolls, Strugnell told an interviewer that he regarded Judaism as "a horrible religion . . . a Christian heresy."[13] He added that the only solution was a mass conversion of the Jews to Christianity. His remarks were reported world wide, and within weeks he had been dismissed.

The battle for access to the Scrolls was not won until September 1963. Then the Huntingdon Library in California dismayed the Rockefeller team by announcing that it possessed a complete set of photographs of the Scrolls, which had been commissioned in 1953, before de Vaux had succeeded in establishing his stranglehold. De Vaux's team asked for their return and were ignored. And the Huntingdon declared that it intended to make microfilm copies available to scholars for as little as $10. So, in effect, the Scrolls were finally published.

According to Lomas and Knight, the original Jerusalem Church, which began with the Essenes, vanished when Titus burned down the Temple and slaughtered the Essenes who were left. But the tradition survived in various documents. Lomas and Knight came upon a letter by Clement of Alexandria, a second century theologian, which spoke of a secret gospel, and of secret ceremonies conducted by Jesus himself.

We may recall the Mandaeans, the Nasoreans (i.e., Essenes) who escaped to Persia before Titus's massacre of rebels, who worshipped John the Baptist, regarding Jesus as a traitor, and whose rituals resemble those of the Freemasons. Their ceremonies seem to support Lomas and Knight's arguments that Freemasonry can be traced to the Esssenes and their Jerusalem Church.

In other words, the Essenes practiced initiation ceremonies, into which only special selected candidates were admitted, and which involved a ritual death and resurrection as in Freemasonry.

Soon after the beginning of the Jewish revolt of AD 66, a strange thing had happened, which is still not fully understood by historians. Before Vespasian was sent to Palestine, a Roman named Cestus Gallus arrived with a powerful military force and made his way to Jerusalem, encountering little resistance. The Romans besieged the Temple and breached the walls. Then they changed their minds and withdrew. The astounded Jews could only assume that Jahweh had decided to help them, as he had helped the Israelites escape from Egypt. They harassed the retreating Romans and killed around six thousand of them.

Rome soon took its revenge and sent Vespasian, who proceeded to destroy the Jewish cities and towns one at a time, to leave no refuge for the rebels. It took more than four years but ended in Roman victory and Jewish defeat.

It is almost certain that it was while Cestus was marching on Jerusalem that the Essenes decided to conceal their holy scriptures. The less important ones they cut into slices and hid in jars in the caves overlooking the Dead Sea. But the most valuable documents they hid beneath the Temple. These scrolls, Lomas and Knight speculate, are the ones discovered by the Templars.

But William St. Clair built Rosslyn two centuries before the first Freemasons are recorded in England. How do we even know that St. Clair was a Freemason?

Lomas and Knight uncovered much evidence at Rosslyn, which they describe in their books *The Hiram Key* and *The Second Messiah*. But one of the most convincing pieces of evidence is this carving they found on the wall outside Rosslyn.

This shows a Freemason ceremony, with the candidate blindfolded, and with a noose round his neck. The man who holds the rope is a Templar, with the cross on his tunic. It leaves no doubt that St. Clair was a Templar, and that the Templars were also Freemasons. In fact, Lomas and Knight believe that the building of Rosslyn marks the first appearance of Freemasonry in England.

Lomas and Knight began to look into the history of the St. Clairs of Rosslyn. It seemed that William St. Clair was a Norman who came over at around the same time as William the Conqueror in 1066. He was known as William the Seemly. His son was Henri St. Clair, and he went off on the First Crusade in 1095 and fought alongside Hugh de Payens, marching into Jerusalem with him. And Hugh married Henri's niece Catherine St. Clair. So the connection of the St. Clairs with the Templars was very close indeed.

When the Templar fleet sailed from La Rochelle in 1307, some Templars went to Scotland, where an abbey named Kilwinning had been built in the first great days of Templar power, around 1140. It was just

An outline of the carving at Rosslyn showing a Templar Knight
initiating a candidate into Freemasonry.

south of Glasgow and was the Templar's major center. This would be a natural refuge, particularly since the St. Clair family lived not far away, in Roslin. Robert the Bruce, king of Scotland, had been excommunicated by the pope, so Templars had nothing to fear in Scotland.

One of the main arguments of *The Hiram Key* is that Rosslyn Chapel was built in deliberate imitation of Herod's Temple (which, remarkably enough, was only about the size of a parish church), and as the home of the precious scrolls, which were the most important "treasure" of the Templars. They argue that even the unfinished outer wall at Rosslyn, which looks as if the building was simply abandoned at that point, was a replica of an unfinished wall in Herod's rebuilding of Solomon's Temple.

In 1447, while Rosslyn Chapel was being built, there was a fire in the keep of Roslin Castle. William St. Clair was frantic—until he learned that his chaplain had managed to salvage four great trunks full of charters, whereupon, says the record, "he became cheerful."

Lomas and Knight point out that it sounds odd to value four trunks of "charters" more than his castle keep—not to mention his wife and daughter, who were also inside. But if these trunks contained the secret scrolls from Jerusalem, which would be buried in Rosslyn Chapel, his curious priorities become understandable.

All this seems to indicate clearly that William St. Clair was a Freemason, and that there is a direct link between the Essenes and Freemasonry. This would also explain why the Catholic Church has always been so hostile to Freemasonry. The Essenes were rebels against the Jewish religious establishment; Jesus himself was a rebel who wanted to lead a revolt against the priests and the Roman occupiers. He was crucified for wholly political reasons. St. Paul invented his own religion, which Shaw characterized as "Crosstianity," and which is still the religion of the Catholic Church. The Templars knew the truth; they rejected the notion that Jesus was the Son of God. That is why they were accused of spitting on the cross and tortured to death. That is why Rosslyn is not a Christian church but is full of images of the Green Man.

But a major question remains. Why is Rosslyn a replica of Solomon's Temple? Why is Solomon's Temple so central to Freemasons? And why is its architect, Hiram Abif, so important to Freemasonry? In the ceremony of initiation, Hiram's murder by three workmen is reenacted, after which the candidate is resurrected.

As he is resurrected, certain words are spoken aloud. They sound like gibberish: "Ma'at-neb-men-aa, Ma'at-ba-aa."

But Christopher Knight happened to know that ma'at is an ancient Egyptian word. It meant originally "ordered and symmetrical," like the base of a temple. Then it came to mean righteousness, truth, and justice, concepts that play such a central role in Freemasonry. Knight realized that the "gibberish" is ancient Egyptian, meaning "Great is the master of Ma'at, great is the spirit of Ma'at."[14]

It seems that Hiram, who came from Tyre, was not just the architect of the Temple, but the Master Builder who directed operations. And he was attacked and killed by three of his own workers, who struck him three blows, apparently because he refused to divulge the secret signal that would have enabled them to claim a higher rank than they actually possessed (and thus higher wages). It all sounds highly unlikely—surely workers on the Temple could not get away with such a crudely conceived swindle? Lomas and Knight had a strong suspicion that the story of Hiram Abif concealed some important historical truth.

Moreover, why is the ritual of Freemasonry so full of hints that its origin lies in ancient Egypt? Why is the Great Pyramid one of its central symbols? The forefathers of modern America, all Freemasons, were responsible for placing the pyramid symbol on dollars bills.

Since there are so many connections between Jews and Egyptians in the Old Testament, Lomas and Knight felt that their answer probably lay in historical events in which both figured. And such events would probably have taken place long before Solomon built the Temple.

Now according to the *Book of Genesis*, the Jews came into existence after Jacob had wrestled with the angel, and his name was changed to Israel. His twelve sons gave their names to the twelve tribes of Israel. The date, as we shall see in a moment, seems to have been some time in the middle of the sixteenth century BC.

The Jewish historian Josephus had identified the so-called Hyksos, or Shepherd Kings, with the Hebrews of the Old Testament. The Hyksos were, in fact, a mixed group of Semitics and Asiatics who moved into Egypt around 1750 BC—not as warriors, but as refugees from drought. They seized power around 1630 BC and ruled until they were thrown out a hundred and eight years later, as a result of a revolt that began at Thebes (now Luxor). And although modern scholars do not feel that Josephus was completely accurate, there seems little doubt that the ancestry of the Jews includes the Hyksos.

The Hyksos kings ruled northern Egypt ("Lower Egypt"), but Thebes was ruled by a traditional pharaoh, Sequenenre, whose eldest son inaugurated the revolt.

Lomas and Knight were inclined to wonder: was there an Egyptian pharaoh to whom the story of Hiram Abif might apply?

Indeed, there was—and only one. It was Sequenenre himself.

It seemed that the Hyksos pharaoh of this time was called Apophis or Apopi. Christopher Knight remembered a book of Egyptian liturgies called *The Book of Overthrowing Apopi*, full of magic spells to get rid of him. Moreover, the Hyksos kings increased their unpopularity by worshipping the storm god Set, whom most Egyptians regarded as the god of evil.

When a pharaoh ascended the throne, he went through a ceremony whose purpose was to make him into a god—specifically, into Horus, son of Osiris. And when he died, he became Osiris, and there was an important ceremony called "the Opening of the Mouth," when his mouth was levered open with an adze, so his soul could rejoin his fellow gods in heaven and take on the task of interceding for his people.

Why should Apopi want to know the secret ceremony? Because after two centuries the Hyksos had been thoroughly "Egyptianized," they believed that the ritual would turn the pharaoh into a god. They saw themselves as upstarts, but they wanted to become truly Egyptian. And the pharaoh Apopi naturally wanted to become a god. (At that stage, of course, the Hyksos had every reason to assume that they would still be ruling Egypt a thousand years hence.)

Sequenenre was murdered with blows on the head; we know that from his mummy. Lomas and Knight include a gruesome photograph of it with gashes on the skull and one eye missing. The person with the most obvious motive for murdering him would be the Hyksos pharaoh Apopi.

If Sequenenre was the original of Hiram Abif, then the secret the three murderers tried to force from him would be the ritual to make a newly crowned pharaoh into Horus.

In the scenario of Lomas and Knight—based on masonic ritual—

Sequenenre was approached by three men, named Jubela, Jubelo, and Jubelum, whose task was to make him divulge the secret ritual. He refused, probably with some angry and contemptuous words—kings do not like being threatened—whereupon the three ruffians went beyond their instructions and killed him with three blows. (This is also a basic part of the Masonic tradition—they were not instructed to kill Hiram Abif, but only to force the secret from him.)

Lomas and Knight even add the fascinating speculation—based on Sequenenre's dates—that Apopi's "grand vizier," who was behind the plot to force Sequenenre to divulge the secret ritual, was Joseph, son of Jacob, whose brothers sold him into slavery. They go further and speculate that two of the murderers were Joseph's brothers Simeon and Levi. The third murderer, they believe, was a young priest of Sequenenre's temple, who was dragged into the plot with the threat that Apopi meant to destroy Thebes, and that the only way of averting this would be to divulge the "god-making" ritual.

Lomas and Knight discovered some extraordinary physical evidence to support their theory. The mummified head of Sequenenre, as already noted, showed marks of violent blows, one of which had destroyed his eye. But entombed beside the pharaoh was another mummy, whose state had baffled Egyptologists. Although the flesh had been mummified by the dry air of the tomb, the inner organs had not—as is usual—been embalmed. He had been castrated, and his face bore an expression of agony. He had clearly been wrapped in bandages while still alive and had died of suffocation.

There could be little doubt that this was one of the murderers of the pharaoh. The fact that he was killed so horribly and buried beside Sequenenre suggested that he was not a "hyksos," but some member of the pharaoh's entourage who was being punished for treachery. The other two murderers—foreigners—would simply be executed.

But why the castration? Because when the god Horus avenged the murder of his father Osiris in a battle with Set, Horus lost an eye, and Set lost his testicles. So to punish a treacherous priest in this way would be oddly appropriate—particularly since Sequenenre had lost his eye.

Sequenenre's son Kamose avenged his father's murder by fomenting the rebellion that drove the Hyksos out of Egypt. Kamose became the founder of a new Egyptian dynasty. And the ritual of the murder and resurrection of Osiris, which would be used at his coronation, would be enriched by a new level of meaning—the death and resurrection of Sequenenre. (Whether the actual god-making ritual survived is, of course, questionable.)

If Lomas and Knight are correct in believing that the pharaoh who made Joseph the governor of Egypt was Apopi—and the dates seem to support it—then the murder of Sequenenre was of even deeper significance. For, as we have seen, Joseph's father Jacob became Israel, the founder of the Jewish people. If Joseph and his family were among the Hyksos who were driven out of Egypt, then the murder of Sequenenre also created the Jewish nation.

That would certainly help to explain why the murder of Sequenenre was regarded as so important by the Jews that it was transformed into the murder of Hiram Abif, the architect of Solomon's Temple.

Now we can begin to glimpse something of the bold and imaginative sweep of the theory put forward by Lomas and Knight. In researching the history of Freemasonry, they seem to have made a string of extraordinary discoveries.

The identification of Hiram Abif with Sequenenre was only the first. With the murder of Hiram Abif, Egyptian mythology was metamorphosed into Jewish mythology. And this implies that some form of Freemasonry had survived from the time of Sequenenre, which involved a ritual death and resurrection.

For me, this was further confirmed by Lomas and Knight's references to the prophet Enoch. In *The Hiram Key* there are merely three brief references to him. Toward the end of its sequel *The Second Messiah* there is a passage about the thirteenth degree of Scottish Freemasonry, which "tells how, in times long before Moses and Abraham, the ancient figure of Enoch foresaw that the world would be overwhelmed by an apocalyptic disaster through flood or fire, and determined to preserve at least some of the knowledge then available to man, that it might be passed on to future civilizations of survivors. He therefore engraved in hieroglyphics the great secrets of science and building on to two pillars: one made of brick and the other of stone.

"The Masonic legend then goes on to tell how these pillars were almost destroyed, but sections survived the Flood and were subsequently discovered—one by the Jews, the other by the Egyptians. . . ."[15]

So according to the Masons, the origins of Freemasonry—the two pillars that play a central part in its rituals—can be traced back to Enoch.

When I first read *The Hiram Key* I assumed that this was simply another more-or-less fictional attempt to establish the ancient lineage of Freemasonry. But by the time I finished *The Second Messiah* I was less inclined to be dismissive. It seemed to me that Lomas and Knight had made an extremely plausible case for the Egyptian origin of Freemasonry, and for some secret knowledge that could be traced through Solomon's Temple, the Essenes, and the Templars.

Lomas and Knight also emphasize that the tradition of Enoch and the Flood is of central importance to masonry. And in their third volume, *Uriel's Machine*, Enoch is virtually the central character. As already noted, Lomas and Knight argue that the Flood was caused by the impact of a comet in 7640 BC, and that the ancients were able to anticipate this impact by using "Uriel's machine." There are also no less than thirty-two references to the planet Venus, which, they explain, "symbolises rebirth in Judaism, Freemasonry, and many other ancient traditions."[16]

We can see, then, a convergence of masonic tradition and the arguments of this book about ancient civilization.

To recap what we have discussed in this chapter: Lomas and Knight produced compelling evidence to suggest that the Egyptian ritual for which Sequenenre was murdered was one of the secrets of the Essenes, which was hidden beneath the Temple after the crucifixion of Jesus—in whose story resurrection also plays a central part.

The Essenes, who guarded the secret, were wiped out by Titus, and the Temple was destroyed. Lomas writes of a ritual of Freemasonry that "has a retrospect that tells of the fall of the Nasoreans in AD 70, and how the progenitors of Freemasonry left Jerusalem at that time to spread across Europe."[17] Lomas also says that these survivors "believed they were preserving the bloodlines of the two Messiahs of David and Aaron, who would one day arrive and establish the kingdom of God on earth."[18]

Jesus, whom the Baptist Mandaeans (descendants of the Essenes) regard as an imposter, was raised to the status of a god by St. Paul. And when Constantine used Christianity to bind his collapsing empire together, the Resurrection became the Church's most powerful claim to supernatural authority.

It was this authority that would destroy most of the Templars in 1307. But the Templar fleet escaped, and some ships sailed to America. Other Templars went to Scotland, where an abbey named Kilwinning had been built in the first great days of Templar power, around 1140. It was just south of Glasgow and was the Templar's major center. This would be a natural refuge, particularly since the St. Clair family lived not far away, in Roslin. Robert the Bruce, king of Scotland, as we have noted earlier, had been excommunicated by the pope, so Templars had nothing to fear in Scotland.

One of the main arguments of *The Hiram Key* is that Rosslyn Chapel was built in deliberate imitation of Herod's Temple (which, we may recall, was only about the size of a parish church), and as the home of the precious scrolls, which were the most important "treasure" of the Templars. They argue that even the unfinished outer wall at Rosslyn, which looks as if the building was simply abandoned at that point, was a replica of an unfinished wall in Herod's rebuilding of Solomon's Temple.

And what of the man who built the Temple, Hiram Abif? As I read Lomas and Knight on Hiram Abif, I found myself thinking about another interesting connection. Hiram was, as noted, from Tyre. And having visited Tyre on a trip to Lebanon, I knew that it was a Phoenician city, and that the Phoenicians were not worshippers of Jahweh. Why would Solomon want a Phoenician architect?

Presumably because Hiram of Tyre was the best man for the job.

All the same, it seemed odd. The chief Phoenician god was Baal or Bel, whom the authors of the Old Testament regard with suspicion and dislike. And their leading female deity was Astarte, also called Ashtoreth and Ishtar.

In *The Temple and the Lodge*, Michael Baigent and Richard Leigh make an astonishing assertion: that "modern archaeological research confirms that Solomon's Temple . . . bears an unmistakeable resemblance to the actual temples built by the Phoenicians." They go on: "It is even possible to go a step further. Tyrian temples were erected to the Phoenician mother goddess Astarte . . . hilltops and mountains—Mount Hermon for example—abounded with her shrines."[19] And they point out that King Solomon is also described (I Kings III) as offering "sacrifice and incense on the high places."[20]

Lomas and Knight draw attention to the fact that Solomon's religion was not strictly orthodox. When he grew old "his wives swayed his heart to other gods . . . Solomon became a follower of Astarte."[21] (I Kings XI.) They even state that the famous Song of Songs is a hymn to Astarte. They then ask the astonishing question: "Was [the Temple] dedicated to the God of Israel, or was it dedicated to Astarte?"[22] The question may seem academic until we recall that Astarte was known to the Greeks as Aphrodite, the goddess of love (from which we get the term aphrodisiac) and to the Romans as Venus. So the man who built Solomon's Temple was a worshipper of Venus, and his employer also had leanings in that direction. The pagan goddess must be regarded as the key to the next chapter of this strange story of ancient rituals.

Venus is not only the goddess of love but of magic. And the reason for this is a striking peculiarity connected with its orbit that distinguishes it from all the other planets.

If we imagine the earth as the center of the solar system (as the ancients believed it was) it becomes obvious that there will be moments when every planet will be "eclipsed" by the sun, when the sun comes between the planet and the earth. Mercury, for example, is "eclipsed" three times a year, and if we draw lines between these three points in the heavens, they form an irregular triangle. Mars is "eclipsed" four times, and the figure is an irregular rectangle. In fact, all the planets make irregular figures—except Venus. And this makes a perfect five-sided figure, or pentagram.

And if we draw a five-pointed star inside the pentagram, the result is a figure known to every magician in history, the pentacle, a figure that is often used to symbolize man, since it seems to have two arm, two legs, and a head. A famous drawing of Leonardo, the *Vitruvian Man,* shows a spreadeagled man in the shape of a five-pointed star.

Venus is also the goddess who presides over the world's most ancient religion, nature worship. This was the religion practiced in Tyre, and of which King Solomon was an unlikely votary. According to the Freemasons, Solomon's Temple was designed by a worshipper of Venus, Hiram of Tyre.

The nine knights who founded the Templars were undoubtedly Christians, not worshippers of Venus. But their subsequent history, and the final destruction of the Templars, makes it clear that they were certainly not believers in the Savior theory of St. Paul, or in the Christianity of the Nicene Creed. They held the same religious beliefs as the unknown draughtsman who drew The Heavenly Jerusalem. To use a word that was not invented until William St. Clair built Roslin in 1554, they were Freemasons.

But who were they? From whom did they inherit these ancient beliefs?

A startling answer to that question was proposed in 1982 in a book called *The Holy Blood and the Holy Grail,* by Richard Leigh, Michael Baigent, and Henry Lincoln. But although Leigh and Baigent occupy the leading position on the title page, the man who stumbled upon this story was the third, Henry Lincoln.

The story told of a village priest named Béranger Saunière, whose parish was in the Languedoc, north of the Pyrenees. He was very poor— his income was about six pounds sterling a year, on which he supported himself and his housekeeper. The village was called Rennes-le-Château.

TEN

THE MAGIC LANDSCAPE

When the Rennes-le-Château village church was being repaired around 1891, six years after Saunière's appointment, a workman found four wooden cylinders containing rolls of paper inside a square Visigothic pillar that held up the altar stone.

Two of the papers proved to be genealogies of local families, allegedly linking them with the Merovingians, a dynasty of kings that had ruled France—less than successfully—from the fifth to the eighth centuries AD. The other two were Latin texts from the New Testament, but written without spaces between the words.

They were fairly obviously in code—in fact, the code of the shorter text was so straightforward that Henry Lincoln saw it at a glance as he looked at the reproduction in a book called *La Tresor Maudit* (*The Accursed Treasure*) by a journalist called Gèrard de Séde. Some letters were raised above the others, and when these were written down consecutively, they read: "A Dagobert II roi a Sion est ce tresor et il est la mort" or "this treasure belongs to King Dagobert II and to Sion, and he is there dead."[1] Sion was Jerusalem, and the last phrase could also mean "and it is death."

Dagobert was a seventh-century French king of the Merovingian dynasty. The author of these parchments was probably a predecessor of Saunière named Antoine Bigou, who had been cure of Rennes-le-Château at the time of the French Revolution.

Saunière took the parchments to his bishop, who was intrigued enough to send him to Paris to consult with various scholars. There he went along to the church of St. Sulpice and talked with its director the Abbé Bieil. He also met Bieil's nephew, a young trainee priest named Emile Hoffet. Hoffet was involved in a circle of "occultists" who flourished in Paris in the 1890s (and some of whom J. K. Huysmans portrays in his "Satanist" novel *Lá Bàs*).

Hoffet introduced Saunière to a circle of writers and artists that included the poet Mallarme, the dramatist Maeterlinck, and the composer Debussy. Sauniere also—probably through Debussy—met the famous soprano Emma Calvé and probably became her lover. (Saunière was far from an ascetic.)

Before leaving Paris, Saunière visited the Louvre and bought reproductions of three paintings, including Poussin's *Les Bergers D'Arcadie*— The Shepherds of Arcadia—which showed three shepherds and a shepherdess standing in front of a tomb on which are carved the words "Et in Arcadia Ego," usually translated "I (death) am also in Arcadia." (The original title of the painting was Happiness Subdued by Death.)

Back in Rennes-le-Château three weeks later, Sauniére hired workmen to raise a stone slab set in the floor in front of the altar—it dated from around the time of Dagobert II, who had lived at Rennes-le-Château in the far-off days when it was a flourishing town. They discovered two skeletons and "a pot of worthless medallions."[2] Sauniére sent his helpers away and spent the evening in the church alone.

Now Sauniére committed an odd piece of vandalism on a grave in the churchyard—that of a distinguished lady named Marie de Blanchefort— and obliterated its two inscriptions.

But he was unaware that the inscriptions had already been published in a little book by a local antiquary. One contains the words "Et in Arcadia Ego" (in a mixture of Greek and Latin letters) on either side of the slab. The other is curious in that it contains four unexplained lower case letters, three e's and two p's, and four capitals, TMRO.[3] From the small letters only one word can be formed—epée, sword—while from the capitals, the only word that emerges is Mort, death. Epée proved

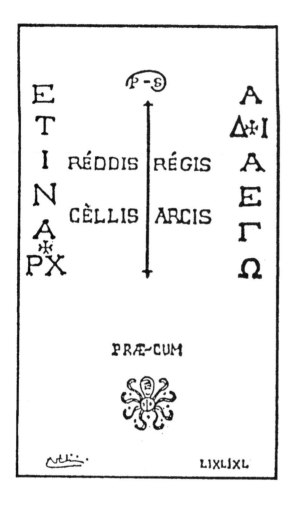

CT GIT NOBLe M

ARIE DE NEGRe

DARLES DAME

DHAUPOUL De

BLANCHEFORT

AGEE DE SOIX

ANTE SEpT ANS

DECEDEE LE

XVII JANVIER

MDCOLXXXI

REQUIESCAT IN

PACE

(P.S.) PRAE-CUM

The inscriptions on the tombstone of Marie de Blanchefort.

to be the "key word" to decipher the second parchment Sauniére had found in the column.

And suddenly, Sauniére was rich. He built a public road to replace the dirt road to the village, and a water tower. And he built himself a villa with a garden, and a Gothic tower to house his library. Distinguished visitors came regularly, including Emma Calvé and the Austrian Archduke Johann von Habsburg, cousin of the emperor Franz-Josef. His many guests were superbly fed and wined by his young peasant house-keeper, Marie Denarnaud. He also restored and redecorated the village church, but in appalling taste—its glaring colors recall Disneyland.

Inside the door the visitor encounters a crouching, club-footed devil. This, apparently, is Asmodeus, the legendary guardian of Solomon's treasure. And at the foot of a hill on which Christ is succoring the afflicted lies an incongruous money bag. The layout of the quotation "Come unto me all ye that labor and are heavy laden . . ." also has an anomaly: the first two letters of "accablé" (burdened) are smaller than the rest of the word, and a faint line links them to the last letter of the previous word, the "s" of "etes," so we read SACCABLES, which sounds like "sac a blés"—bag of corn. Corn is French slang for gold. Moreover, the original quotation does not say "accablés" but "affligé"—afflicted. Sauniére has changed it so he can get in the pun about the bag of gold.

The Stations of the Cross are also full of incomprehensible oddities—like a mysterious figure who is turning his back on Pontius Pilate, and holding up a golden egg. In Station 2 a young man picking up a stick is totally irrelevant. So is a soldier holding up his shield against the sky in Station 6.

The Devil is half-sitting on a throne carved out of a rock that the villagers would all recognize as a nearby rock known as "The Devil's Armchair." They would also know that beside this rock there is a spring known as "The Spring of the Circle." The Devil seems to be underlining the name by joining his right thumb and index fingers to form a circle. Sauniére is obviously playing games—or trying to tell us something.

The bishop who came to bless the church was obviously disturbed and puzzled by it and never came again. But at least he was friendly. A new bishop was openly hostile, and when Sauniére refused to divulge the source of his wealth—saying merely that it was from a wealthy penitent who inisisted on anonymity—the bishop ordered his transfer to another parish. Sauniére refused to be transferred, and another priest was appointed in his place. (Oddly enough, when the bishop took his complaint to Rome, the Pope found in Sauniére's favor. . . .) In 1905 the French goverrnment—which was anticlerical—began to make his life uncomfortable by accusing him of being an Austrian spy—it seems that part of his regular income came from Austria.

In 1917, Sauniére died of cirrhosis of the liver; he was 65. The priest who attended his deathbed is said to have been so shocked at his final confession that he refused to administer extreme unction.

His housekeeper lived on in the villa and died in 1953. She had sold the villa in 1946 and told its purchaser that one day she would tell him a secret that would make him rich and powerful; but a stroke left her speechless.

This was the remarkable story Henry Lincoln read in Gérard de Sède's book. There were obviously many questions. Had Sauniére found a treasure? Or had he learned some secret that led certain wealthy patrons to wish to silence him with large sums of money? Was he a blackmailer, or simply a member of a small group who shared some closely guarded secret?

There was yet another possibility—that the treasure might have been that of the Templars, concealed to keep it out of the hands of Philip the Fair. Not far from Rennes-le-Château is the Chateau of Bézu, whose owner was the Signeur de Gotte, who escaped with the Templar Fleet from La Rochelle.

On his return to London, Lincoln succeeded in interesting a friend at the BBC in the story, and the two of them went to Rennes-le-Château. Gérard de Sède had agreed to act as a consultant on the program, and was able to provide the key to decoding the second mystery parchment. It was an incredibly complex code, which involved a technique known to cipher experts as the Vigenère process. The alphabet is written twenty six times, the first beginning with A, the second B, the third C, and so on. The key word MORT EPÉE is placed over the parchment, and the letters are transformed using the Vigenère table.

The "noble Marie de Blanchefort" text (which Sauniére had tried to destroy) is then used as another key word, and finally, the letters are placed on a chess board and a series of knight's moves produces a message which may be translated: SHEPHERDESS NO TEMPTATION TO WHICH POUSSIN AND TENIERS HOLD THE KEY PEACE 681

WITH THE CROSS AND THIS HORSE OF GOD I REACH THIS
DEMON GUARDIAN AT MIDDAY BLUE APPLES.

This, presumably, is what had led Sauniére to his fortune, although
it is hard to see how.

In his subsequent television program *The Priest, the Painter and
the Devil*, Lincoln has a suggestion. In the original parchment, he had
noticed certain letters that were smaller than the others. These spelt out
the words "rex mundi," king of the earth. This led him to suppose that
the Cathars, a sect of medieval heretics who were bloodily suppressed by
the Church, played some part in the story.

Like other heretical sects such as the Bogomils and Albigensians and
the Waldenses, the Cathars believed that everything to do with the spirit
is good and everything to do with matter is evil—a belief also known
as Manicheeism—and that therefore this world was not created by God
but by the Devil. In 1244, the Cathars of the Languedoc were virtually
wiped out after a siege of their stronghold on top of a mountain called
Montségur and were burned alive at the foot of the mountain.

But three months before their surrender, two men escaped carrying the "treasure" of the Cathars and slipped through the lines of the
besiegers. No one knows the nature of this treasure, but it is clear that
two men could not have carried much in the way of gold and jewels. So
Sauniére's wealth cannot have been Cathar treasure, unless he found it
elsewhere.

Which means we can probably dismiss the Cathars as a solution to
this mystery. It is true that they may be described as Gnostics—from the
Greek gnosis, meaning knowledge—and that the writers of the so-called
Hermetic books (of which the most famous is the *Emerald Tablets of
Hermes Trismegistus*) are also known as Gnostics. But these early Gnostics do not regard matter as evil. The Essenes seem to have belonged to
this latter group. But there is no connection between Essene gnosticism
and that of the Cathars. So we shall drop the Cathars from the story.

The Marie inscription ends with the letters P.S. This, Lincoln learned
from de Sede, stood for Priory of Sion, Sion meaning Jerusalem. And
in the Bibliothéque Nationale in Paris, Lincoln found that a number of

pamphlets and documents had been deposited since 1956, many written under pseudonyms like "Anthony the Hermit."

One of these documents spoke about a secret order called the Priory of Sion and gave a list of its Grand Masters, which included the alchemist Nicolas Flamel (reputed to have made gold), Leonardo da Vinci, Isaac Newton, Claude Debussy, and, more recently, Jean Cocteau. Sauniére, we recall, had met Debussy on the trip to Paris.

And according to these documents—collectively known as The Secret Dossier—the Priory of Sion was the inner hierarchy of the Knights Templar. The Dossier claimed that the Priory had continued to exist even after the Templars were destroyed.

This suggested to Henry Lincoln that Sauniére had not found a treasure—but that his wealth came from holding an important position in the Priory of Sion. In fact, many known facts point to this conclusion. According to Henry Buthion, who owned the hotel that was once Sauniere's Villa Bethanie, Sauniére was often short of cash and failed to pay 5,000 francs that he owed the makers of some expensive furniture he ordered for the Villa. He certainly died penniless, but that may have been because he simply allowed large sums of money to be paid direct to his housekeeper Marie Denardaud. Still, a man with a hidden treasure does not run short of cash, even if he banks it. Much of Sauniére's cash seems to have come from Austria, which is why the French government suspected him of spying.

Eventually, Lincoln's television program got made and was broadcast in 1972 under the title *The Lost Treasure of Jerusalem*, but by now so much material had come to light that it was clear that a second program was going to be required.

Perhaps the most intriguing hint of all came soon after the program was transmitted. A retired Church of England vicar wrote to tell Lincoln that the "treasure" was not gold or jewels, but a document proving that Jesus was not crucified in 33 AD, but had still been alive in AD 45.

Lincoln went to see him. The clergyman obviously wished he had kept his mouth shut. But he finally admitted that his information had come from an Anglican scholar named Canon Alfred Lilley. And—

Lincoln's heart must have leapt as he heard this—Lilley had maintained close contact with scholars based at St. Sulpice and had known Emile Hoffet, who had introduced Sauniére to Debussy.

This obviously raised a fascinating possibility. If Debussy was, indeed, a Grand Master of the Priory of Sion, could he have shared the belief that Jesus did not die on the cross? And was that Sauniére's secret, which so shocked the priest who listened to his final confession?

It certainly began to look more and more as if this was the answer. We may recall that when Sauniére left Paris, he purchased some copies of paintings from the Louvre, among them *Les Bergers d'Arcadie, The Shepherds of Arcadia,* which shows three shepherds and a shepherdess standing by a tomb bearing the words "Et in Arcadia Ego."

While they were filming the first program, de Sède told Lincoln that the actual tomb used in the painting had been discovered at Arques, not far from Rennes-le-Château. And in fact, the tomb, although it had no Latin inscription, was otherwise identical, even to the stone on which the shepherd is resting his foot in the painting.

Nicholas Poussin's The Shepherds of Arcadia.

Nicolas Poussin (1594–1665) was one of the most distinguished painters of his time; although born in Normandy it was in Rome that he won fame and spent most of his life. For a short time he had served Louis XIII and Richelieu.

Poussin's *The Shepherds of Arcadia* came into the possession of Louis XIV, after his agents had been trying, with great tenacity, to lay their hands on it for some time; yet when the king finally became its owner, he kept it locked away in his private chambers; rumor has it that he was afraid that it might reveal some secret if it was displayed more publicly. Yet the painting itself seems to offer no clues as to why the king wanted it so badly, or why he then kept it from the eyes of the world.

What we do know, however, is that in 1656, the king's Minister of Finance, Nicolas Fouquet, sent his younger brother Louis to Rome to see Poussin, and that Louis then wrote to Nicolas: "He and I have planned certain things of which in a little while I shall be able to inform you fully; things which will give you, through M. Poussin, advantages which kings would have great difficulty in obtaining from him, and which, according to what he says, no one in the world will ever retrieve in centuries to come; and furthermore, it would be achieved without much expense and could even turn to profit, and they are matters so difficult to enquire into that nothing on earth at the present time could bring a greater fortune nor perhaps ever its equal. . . ."[4]

What can he be talking about? "Nothing on earth could ever bring a greater fortune" sounds like a treasure—except that he also says it could "even turn to profit," which suggests that he means something else after all.

What is certain is that the king, who was only five years old when he came to the throne, nursed an increasing dislike of his brilliant and ambitious finance minister. Fouquet became immensely wealthy, and according to his assistant Colbert, he managed this by cooking the books every afternoon. In 1661, Louis had Fouquet arrested, and he was eventually imprisoned. (Some historians have suggested that he was the famous Man in the Iron Mask, but he died 23 years before the mysterious prisoner.)

Is it possible that when Fouquet sent his brother Louis to see Poussin, it was with treasonous intent?

Indeed, it is. And that possible treason leads us to another encounter with the Priory of Sion.

The Merovingian king Dagobert II, born in AD 651, was kidnapped as a child and taken to Ireland, while a usurping major domo took his place. But he returned to France—in fact, to Rennes-le-Château—now married to a Visigothic princess named Giselle. He reclaimed the throne but was murdered in 679 as he lay asleep under a tree. The Church certainly played some part in the assassination, but his major domo, Pepin the Fat, was also involved.

Pepin was the grandfather of the famous warrior Charles Martel, who turned back the Moslem invasion of France at the Battle of Poitiers, and saved Europe from becoming Moslem. His son, Pepin the Short, seized the throne and inaugurated the Carolingian dynasty, whose most famous member was his son, the great Charlemagne. The descendants of Dagobert were understandably resentful about being deprived of the throne, and there was always a movement in favor of their restoration—rather like the Jacobites in England.

Like the Jacobites, they were a lost cause. But one Merovingian descendant achieved a fame that rivaled that of Charles Martel or Charlemagne. He was Godfrey de Bouillon (1058–1100), duke of Lorraine, the man who led the First Crusade and recaptured Jerusalem—the knight who became the first king of Jerusalem.

There can also be little doubt that he was the founder—or one of the founders—of another dynasty, the Priory of Sion—or, as it was first known, the Order of Our Lady of Sion. And soon after the capture of Jerusalem, an Abbey of Sion was built on the Temple Mount, and its occupants were known as the Order of Our Lady of Sion. According to the Secret Dossier, the Order was founded in 1090, nine years before the fall of Jerusalem. Five of the nine original Templars were members. So it seems probable that the Templar order sprang out of the Order of Sion.

Lincoln cites evidence to show that the two orders soon grew apart. It seems that the fabulous power and wealth of the Templars made them headstrong, "like unruly children."[5] And matters came to a head in 1187, when a Templar named Gerard de Ridefort led the knights into a rash encounter with the Saracens, and lost Jerusalem—this time forever.

At this point, it seems, the Order of Sion lost patience with the Templars and broke with them. The Order now changed its name to the Priory of Sion. One of the major aims of the Priory was to restore the Merovingians to the throne of France. When the Templars were destroyed in 1307, the Priory continued to exist—no doubt because it was such a well-kept secret.

So this could well explain why Louis XIV was anxious to get rid of his minister Fouquet, and to get his hands on Poussin's painting. If the "secret that king's could not draw from him" was the secret of the Priory of Sion, Louis may well have been worried. His uncle, Gaston d'Orleans, had been married to the duke of Lorraine's sister, and there had been an attempt to depose Gaston's elder brother, Louis XIII, in favor of Gaston. In which case, the Merovingian blood would once again have flowed in the veins of the kings of France.

The attempt failed. But since Louis XIII was childless, it looked very much as if Gaston would nevertheless inherit the throne. Then, to everyone's amazement, Louis XIII produced a son—at least, his wife Anne of Austria did. There were many people who believed that Cardinal Richelieu was the true father, or perhaps that he had employed a "stud." Some suggest that this stud was Richelieu's captain of musketeers, Francois Dauger, and that it was Dauger who thus frustrated the designs of the Merovingians and the Priory of Sion to wrest back the throne.

Francois Dauger had two sons, named Louis and Eustache. Many people commented on the resemblance between these brothers and Louis XIV. This is understandable if, in fact, the Dauger sons were the king's half brothers.

But Eustache was a ne'er-do-well, always in trouble. Both Louis Dauger and Eustache were eventually arrested, Louis for an affair of the heart, Eustache for general hellraising. But Louis was released and continued to rise in the world. Eustache disappeared and may well have been the Man in the Iron Mask. (It was actually a velvet mask, and if indeed Eustache was the mystery prisoner, he may have been forced to wear it because of his resemblance to the king.)

His offense may have been to try and blackmail the king "Release my brother or else. . . ." Or he may have got involved with the Priory of Sion and the Merovingians, who would have been delighted to learn that Louis XIV had no right to be on the throne because he was illegitimate.

We may mention, in passing, that the Habsburgs were also members of the house of Lorraine, and therefore prime candidates for membership of the Priory of Sion. And we may recall that one of Sauniére's guests was Johann von Habsburg, and that Sauniére received money from Austria.

It sounds as if Sauniere's visit to St. Sulpice introduced him to people who were willing to share their secret, and give him generous financial support as the present incumbent of Dagobert's ancient stronghold.

But this complex and fascinating story has another amazing twist. We have seen that Lincoln learned from a retired clergyman that the "real treasure" was the knowledge that Jesus did not die on the cross, and this knowledge came from St. Sulpice. If St. Sulpice was the Paris headquarters of the Priory of Sion, then it may well be that Sauniére's secret—the secret that shocked the priest who attended his deathbed—was that Jesus had not died on the cross, and that therefore the Christian Church had been built on foundations of sand, since it was based on the notion that Jesus died on the cross to save man from the burden of Original Sin.

When Lincoln was working on the BBC program *The Shadow of the Templars*, he was suddenly struck by a startling thought. He and two researchers, Richard Leigh and Michael Baigent, were joking about a legend that the mother of King Merovec, the founder of the Merovingian line, had been impregnated by a sea creature, and one of them quipped that the story sounded "fishy." Suddenly, Lincoln and Leigh looked at one another as they were seized with the same suspicion. Fish—the symbol of Christianity. Could the legend mean that the lady had been impregnated by . . . a symbol of Christianity, a direct descendant of Jesus?

The Merovingians kings claimed that they reigned "by right of blood"—royal blood—not by being anointed by the Church. Was the bloodline they were so proud of that of Jesus himself?

Then who was Jesus's wife? In the village of Les Saintes Maries de la Mer, there is a yearly ceremony held to celebrate the arrival of Mary Magdalen in France, bearing the True Cross and the Holy Grail. The church in Rennes-le-Château is dedicated to her and has two statues of her carrying the cross and the Grail. Sauniére built a library called the Tour Magdala—the Magdalen Tower. Mystics of the Middle Ages identified her with the planet Venus—the goddess of love.

In December 1945, near the Egyptian town of Nag Hammadi, an interesting discovery threw new light on Mary Magdalen. Two peasants who were digging for fertilizer in a graveyard at the foot of a cliff came upon a jar buried at the base of a boulder, which contained a number of parchments written in Coptic—ancient Egyptian written with Greek letters. These proved to be unknown Christian gospels, many contemporary with those of the New Testament. They had titles like *The Gospel of Philip*, *The Gospel of Thomas*, and—most significantly—*The Gospel of Mary*. This is not the Virgin Mary, but Mary Magdalen. Mary is seen encouraging the disciples after the resurrection of Jesus and is quite obviously the most important among them. *The Gospel of Philip* refers to Mary as Jesus's "companion," and the original Greek word means consort.

The notion that Mary Magdalen was married to Jesus is not so surprising; all Jewish rabbis and preachers were not only permitted but expected to marry.

In the New Testament Mary is referred to only once; she is a reformed prostitute who dries Jesus's feet with her hair. The Nag Hammadi gospels indicated that she was, like Jesus, a descendant of a royal line, the House of Benjamin. (Jesus, of course, was of the House of David.)

When the New Testament was first assembled by bishops who had been appointed by Constantine, all reference to Mary as Jesus's wife was censored, and she was reduced to a reformed prostitute. The Gospels of Mary, Philip, Thomas, and the others were collected and destroyed. But someone took care that the Nag Hammadi gospels survived in a clay urn.

And they indicate that Mary was married to Jesus. In Leonardo's painting of *The Last Supper*, she is sitting at the right hand of Jesus. The painting had also been censored, and Mary Magdalen changed to a man, but when it was cleaned in 1954, the disciple on Jesus's right hand was seen to be a woman. (Leonardo, of course, is listed in the Secret Dossier as one of the Grand Masters of the Priory.) And St. Peter, who hated her—as the Nag Hammadi Gospels make clear—holds out his hand in a threatening gesture. And a disembodied hand holding a dagger also threatens her.

It was all this that led Lincoln and Leigh to speculate that Jesus and Mary Magdalen had come to France, and founded the blood line of the Merovingians. There are dozens of legends of Mary, from Marseilles to Rennes-le-Château, where the church is dedicated to her. Perhaps the tomb that Poussin painted was, in fact, the tomb of Jesus? It was this extraordinary speculation—and Lincoln insists that it is merely a speculation—that made *The Holy Blood and the Holy Grail* an instant bestseller.

By now, Lincoln had learned, through the detective work of a BBC researcher, that the most important living member of the Priory of Sion was a man named Pierre Plantard. Plantard was indeed the name of a noble family that was of the Merovingian line. A meeting was arranged, and Lincoln invited Plantard to view the second Rennes-le-Château film, *The Priest, the Painter and the Devil.*

He proved to be a kindly and courteous elderly gentleman—born in 1920—and a group of his followers were present. The closest seemed to be a marquis named Philip de Cherisey. Lincoln was to learn that de Cherisey was responsible for much of the Secret Dossier deposited in the Louvre.

Sitting behind them, Lincoln was pleased to observe that they became suddenly attentive when the film showed an image of one of the parchments, in which Lincoln had detected the form of a pentagram.

Lincoln also noticed something odd about the geometry of Poussin's

Shepherds of Arcadia. Looking for the "secret" that seems to have alarmed Louis XIV, he noticed that the staff of the shepherd on the right is neatly cut in two by the shepherd's arm. And the distance from the top of the staff to the shepherd's pointed finger was precisely this same "half measure." He soon noticed other "half measures" throughout the painting. The picture had obviously been designed geometrically.

Lincoln showed the painting to Professor Christopher Cornford, of the Royal College of Art. And Cornford found something even more fascinating. The structure of the painting was based on the geometrical proportion known as the "Golden Section" (and called by the Greek letter phi).

At first sight, this sounds like a rather boring definition from a school geometry book. In fact, it is a notion of such overwhelming and profound importance that it would be easy to devote a whole book to it. Basically, it is a way of dividing a line so that the proportion of the short part to the long part is the same as the proportion of the long part to the whole line, as in the following figure:

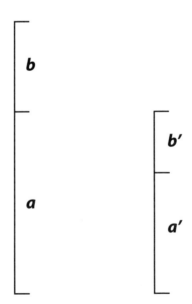

Golden Section ratios.

That sounds like a conundrum from one of those puzzle books you buy to keep the children quiet on the train. Then why is it so important?

Because, for some odd reason, nature uses it all the time. Your body is an example, with your navel acting as the division between the two parts. It can be found in the spirals of leaf arrangements, petals around the edge of a flower, leaves around a stem, pine cones, seeds in a sunflower head, seashells—even in the arms of spiral nebulae.

Artists also discovered it at a fairly early stage, because this way of dividing a picture is oddly pleasing to the eye—in exactly the same way that musical harmonies are pleasant to the ear.

Why is nature so fond of it? Because it is the best way of packing, of minimizing wasted space.

Obviously, there is something very important about this simple-looking fraction. It is, in fact, .618034 . . ., going on forever as some decimals do.

Another form of phi is 1.618. If you wish to extend a line a phi distance, you simply multiply it by 1.618.

We must mention one more piece of mathematics before we can get back to the mystery of Rennes-le-Château. This is a sequence of numbers invented by the mathematician Fibonacci, in which each number is the sum of the preceding two numbers. So if you begin with 0, then the next number is obviously 1, and 0 + 1 equals 1. And that 1 plus the previous 1 equals 2. And that 2 plus the preceding 1 equals 3. And so on (0, 1, 1, 2, 3, 5, 8, 13, 21, 34, 55 . . .).

And now another curious fact. If you take any two Fibonacci numbers, and divide each one by the one after it, the answer gets closer and closer to the "Golden Number," .618034, the bigger the numbers concerned. For example, 2 divided by 3 is .6666. . . . But 34 divided by 55 is .6182. Yet no matter how big the numbers become—even billions or trillions—the number never quite reaches the Golden Number.

It is these Fibonacci numbers that can be found in pine cones, nautilus shells, and spiral nebulae. Why God decided to choose such an odd ratio is anybody's guess. But it is also worth mentioning that the

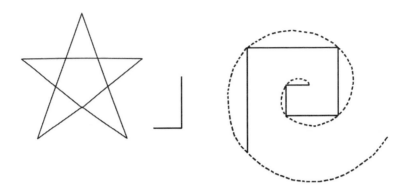

A Fibonacci spiral.

Fibonacci spiral can be derived from a pentacle. If one side of its inner pentagram is placed at right angles to the side of one of the "legs," the Fibonacci spiral can be started from the end of the shorter line.

It seems that God also has some preference for pentagrams.

It is worth adding that, according to Herodotus (in a passage we need to amend slightly to make any sense of what is obviously a copyist's error), the Golden Section can also be found in the area of each side of the Great Pyramid.

When Cornford reported to Henry Lincoln on *The Shepherds of Arcadia,* he explained that he began by looking for one of two "systems" in constant use by classical painters. One is a number system, based on Plato's *Timaeus* (a dialogue about the creation of the universe), which became highly influential in the Renaissance. But the other is a far older system, a geometry based on the Golden Section.

Cornford expected to find the Timaeus system in Poussin's painting, because the Golden Section system was then regarded as extremely old fashioned. In fact, he did find traces of this system. But the basic system used in *The Shepherds of Arcadia* is the Golden Section. The painting is also full of pentagonal geometry.

Consider the following:

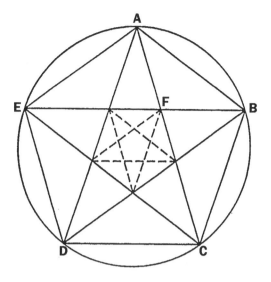

Pentagram in a circle.

The ratio of all its five sides (for example, AB) to its chords (like AC) is the ratio 1:1.618, or phi.

And when Cornford looked more closely, he could draw a pentagram that went outside the painting:

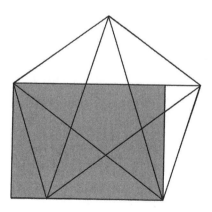

Pentagram extended beyond the parameters
of The Shepherds of Arcadia.

In short, the pentacle was encoded into Poussin's painting. And that led Cornford to make an interesting suggestion. Could the phrase "Poussin holds the key . . ." be anything to do with the landscape around Rennes-le-Château, which is where Sauniére searched for the treasure?

This comment led Lincoln to one of his most important discoveries.

When he looked at an ordnance survey map of the Rennes-le-Château region, one thing was immediately obvious: that three of its key sites—Rennes-le-Château, the Templar chateau of Bezu, and the Blanchefort chateau, were three points of a triangle. And all were on hilltops.

When Lincoln drew the triangle on his map and proceeded to measure its lines, he received a surprise. It was a precise isosceles triangle, that is, with two sides exactly equal. With Bezu at the apex of the triangle, the lines from Bezu to Blanchefort, and from Bezu to Rennes-le-Château, were equal.

This could not be an accident. At some remote point in time, someone had observed that the three hilltops made a precise triangle, and in due course, they had been chosen as part of a secret pattern.

Now Lincoln found himself wondering if, by any remote chance, there were two more hilltops, which would form the rest of a pentagram. Of course, he felt, that would be asking too much. . . .

Yet when he studied the map, he was staggered to find that there were indeed two such hilltops, in precisely the right places. The eastern one was called La Soulane, and the western one Serre de Lauzet. And when the five hilltops were joined up, they formed an exact pentacle.

It was obviously an amazing natural freak. But there was one more surprise to come. When Lincoln looked for the center of the map, he found that it was marked by another hill, called La Pique.

Admittedly, although the summit of La Pique looked on the map like the dead center, it was actually 250 yards to the southeast of center. But that was to be expected. After all, this was not a man-made landscape. It was incredible enough that La Pique fell at the center of the pentacle.

So this was the basic secret of Rennes-le-Château: that it was part of a sacred landscape. Perhaps this is why Rennes-le-Château was chosen by Dagobert as his home (and why his son Sigisbert fled there after his father's murder). The royal blood of the Merovingians was associated with a magic landscape.

I was dubious until I read Lincoln's Key to the Sacred Pattern and realized that this is a natural "magic landscape"—as Henry Lincoln recognized.

Oddly enough, M. Plantard refused to confirm Lincoln's insight. Although it was obvious that he and Cherisey were startled that Lincoln had discovered the pentagonal geometry in the Sauniére parchments, Plantard would simply not enlarge. On the contrary, when Lincoln asked him about the hidden codes in the parchments, Plantard made the incredible remark that the parchments were "confections" concocted by his friend Cherisey. For what purpose? For a ten-minute television film made some years previously.

Quite rightly, Lincoln refused to swallow this. The incredible complexity of the code left no doubt that it had taken a very long time and a great deal of skill to prepare.

So why did Plantard try to throw dust in his eyes? For there seems little doubt that it was Plantard's original aim—and that of the "Priory"—to bring this mystery to public attention; the aim, presumably, to place the Merovingian descendants in a good position if France should get tired of being a republic. De Sède originally told Lincoln: "We hoped it might interest someone like you."[6] Yet now Lincoln had got his teeth into the subject, and had discovered the pentagonal geometry, Plantard seemed to feel he had been a little too successful and wanted to backtrack.

In 1991, Lincoln made another important discovery. He had been contacted by a Danish television producer who had been born on the island of Bornholm. Erling Haagensen had become fascinated by Bornholm's fifteen churches, which dated from the thirteenth century (the time of the Knights Templar), and the fact that they often seemed to be associated with ancient megaliths—in fact, some megaliths were actually built into the church walls. Now Lincoln had been toying with the idea that perhaps some of the Rennes-le-Château pattern had been laid out in megalithic times. And when Haagensen told him that the geometry he had identified on Bornholm was pentacular, Lincoln became convinced that they were each "uncovering a different portion of the same mystery."

Moreover, Haagensen found the English mile present in the Bornholm geometry. For example, if Haagensen's geometry was correct, the distance between two of the churches, Ibsker and Povlsker, should be exactly seven miles. And it was.

Why miles? In a chapter called "The Measure," Lincoln lays out some curious but highly convincing facts.

The French meter, which came into use in 1791, was one ten millionth of the distance from the North Pole to the equator. Lincoln shows that an old English measure called the rod, pole, or perch (which is three hundred and twentieth of a mile) is also a precise measure of the earth's surface: one pole (198 inches) multiplied by itself (i.e., squared) is a kilometer (39,204 inches).

When this ancient pole (198 inches) is multiplied by 1.618, the Golden Section, the result is 320, the number of poles in one mile.

So there is a mathematical connection between the British pole and the kilometer, and between the pole, multiplied by the Golden Section, and the mile.

Lincoln also cites Berriman's *Historical Metrology*—the book that mentions that the Greek stade proves the Greeks knew the exact size of the earth. Berriman asks: "Was the earth measured in remote antiquity?" and sets out to demonstrate that it was, bringing in ancient Egypt, Babylon, Sumer, China, Persia, and many other cultures. He argues that ancient weights and measures are derived from measuring the earth— which of course, means in turn that ancient people had already measured the earth.

The book must have struck Berriman's contemporaries as hopelessly eccentric. He says that one measure was a certain fraction of the earth's circumference, that a measure of land area (the acre) was based on a decimal fraction of the square of the earth's radius, and that certain weights were based on the density of water and of gold. It sounds as if Berriman is positing the existence of some ancient civilization, which vanished without a trace, except for these ancient measures.

This, of course, is consistent with Hapgood's comment that history does not necessarily proceed steadily in a forward direction. It might pause, or even backtrack. This in turn was the basis of his assertion that a civilization with high levels of science existed a hundred thousand years ago.

Lincoln came upon a Norwegian named Harald Boehlke, who had made some remarkable discoveries about Norwegian distances. Norway was pagan until a thousand years ago, and with the coming of Christianity, scattered trading posts disappeared and gave way to larger centers, which became cities. And Boehlke's researches seemed to establish that these new cities—Oslo, Trondheim, Bergen, Stavangar, Hamar, Tonsberg—were placed in what looked like quite arbitrarily-chosen spots—for example, Oslo in what was simply a backwater.

No one has the slightest idea why Stavangar was chosen as a cathedral town. But distances seem chosen for some mathematical reason: Oslo to Stavangar, 190 miles, Oslo to Bergen, 190 miles, Tonsberg to Stavangar, 170 miles, Tonsberg to Halsnoy, 170 miles, and so on. Moreover, the position of the old monasteries again shows a pentagonal geometry. It looks as if the Church was using some secret geometrical knowledge in creating the new Christian Norway.

Lincoln also identified a "church measure" of 188 meters and appealed in a French magazine for examples of it, as well as of pentagonal geodesics. A mathematics teacher named Patricia Hawkins, who lived in France, was able to find no less than 162 "church measures" linking churches, hilltops, and those roadside crucifixes called Calvaries, in the Quimper area of Brittany.

Lincoln begins the last chapter of *Key to the Sacred Pattern*:

"We are confronting a mystery. The structured landscape of Rennes-le-Château and its association with the English mile (as well as the mile's apparent link with the dimensions of the Earth) are easily demonstrated, with a multitude of confirming instances. The measure and the geometry are evident. The patterns are repeatable. The designs are meaningful. All this was created in a remote past, upon which the phenomenon is shedding a new light."[7] And he goes on to plead for historians and archaeologists to turn their attention to the evidence.

Now by "patterns," Lincoln is not simply talking about the pentacle of mountains or the circle of churches. His own study of the Rennes-le-Château area revealed many patterns that could only have been created by deliberate intent. The "holy place" of his title is "the natural pentagon of mountains, and the artificial, structured Temple that was built to enclose it."[8]

I must admit that I took some convincing. I only have to see a map covered with lines drawn all over it to groan and close the book. But Lincoln soon had me convinced. For example, he has a diagram centered on Rennes-le-Château church, with lines drawn from it to surrounding villages, churches, and castles. Straight lines ran from some distant church or chateau, straight through Rennes-le-Château church, and out the other side to another chateau or church.

One of his most convincing discoveries is of a grid pattern. When

All roads lead to Rennes-le-Château.

lines were drawn connecting various sites, they were found to run parallel to one another—not only from left to right, but up and down. Moreover, the lines were the same distance apart:

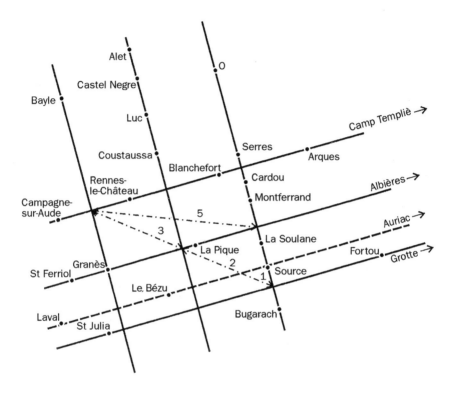

Grid of Rennes-le-Château and environs.

What is more, the unit measure on this grid is the English mile.
(Lincoln prints lists of distances that are in miles; for example, Rennes-
le-Château to Bezu, precisely four miles, Rennes-le-Château to Soulane,
precisely 4 miles.)

He also made a discovery that may throw a new light on Saunière's
unexplained fortune. Many of his alignments went through the tower
Saunière had built as his library, the Magdala Tower. This tower is
placed as far to the west as Saunière could go—he built it on the edge of
a sheer drop and added one more important alignment to what Lincoln
calls "the Rennes-le-Château temple."

There is an even more interesting piece of information. Not long before his death in 1917, Sauniére had commissioned another tower—sixty meters high. We do not know where it was to be located. But Lincoln points out that one of the most important alignments of the area is the "sunrise line," which runs from Arques church, through Blanchefort, to Rennes-le-Château. This line was the one that first got Lincoln looking for English miles. It was almost six miles long.

If it was to be exactly six miles long, it would end on the slope below the Magdala Tower. But since it is on a slope below the Tower, it would have to be higher than the Tower if the landmarks—Blanchefort and Arques church—were to be seen from its summit. Is this where Sauniére meant to build his new tower?

If so, it only underlines what we already know—that the whole area has been deliberately laid out with a geometrical logic that reminds one of the streets of New York.

Soon after Sauniére had discovered the parchments, he spent a great deal of time rambling around surrounding hillsides, claiming he was collecting stones to build a grotto. Most commentators suspect that he was looking for treasure. But there is now a more likely possibility: that on his trip to Paris he had learned the secret of the geometry of the "Temple" and was now familiarizing himself with it. Then he built the Magdala Tower, completing the "sunrise" alignment.

He went as far west as he could—but the slope of the landscape frustrated him. So it seems highly probable that, twenty-five years later, he prepared to build a second tower, sixty meters high, which would complete the "sunrise line."

So it sounds as if Sauniére's discovery of the parchments led to his being appointed custodian of the "Temple," probably by Debussy, with the money to build more landmarks.

What Lincoln has done, with his thirty-year investigation of Rennes-le-Château, is to demonstrate the existence of some ancient science of earth measurement. Since medieval times, this science seems to have been in the custody of the Church (and we must naturally suspect the involvement of the Templars). But Lincoln is inclined to believe that it may be far older—dating back to the age of the mega-liths. This immediately reminds us of Alexander Thom and his "stone age Einsteins."

Berriman seems to be making the same point in *Historical Metrology*. His argument, as noted above, is that prehistoric measurement was geodetic in origin—that is, was derived from the size of the earth.

Berriman is full of puzzling facts, like the precise number of stade in the earth's circumference, and that the area of the great bath of Mohenjo Daro, in the Indus Valley, is a hundred square yards.

He also mentions that a piece of shell was found in the Indus Valley with fine saw cuts marking a linear scale, and that the distance between two specially marked lines is precisely two Sumerian shusi. (The shusi is two thirds of an inch.)

Here is another curiosity: the Romans had a land measure called a jugerum, which is five eighths of an English acre (as the French meter is five eighths of an English mile). And it is exactly 100 square English "poles." Again, we are faced with the idea that ancient measures are not dependent on the whim of some ancient king's land surveyor, but on a tradition stretching back into the dim past, and based on an exact knowledge of the size of the earth.

As to this "English connection," Lincoln has an amusing but fasci-nating speculation. Early in his investigation into Rennes-le-Château, he went to the Bibliothéque Nationale with Gerard de Sède. And de Sède suggested he should request a book called *Le Vraie Langue Celtique* (*The True Celtic Tongue*) by the Abbé Henri Boudet, priest of nearby Rennes-les-Bains, a close friend of Sauniére.

There is strong evidence that Boudet was Sauniére's paymaster. Plantard's grandfather went to visit Boudet in 1892, and Boudet, not only passed on more than three and a half million gold francs to Sauniére (or rather, to Sauniére's housekeeper Marie Denardaud), but more than seven and a half million gold francs to Bishop Billard, the man who appointed Sauniére, and who was obviously in on the secret. Since a gold franc was worth thirty-five modern francs (and there are about nine francs to the pound sterling), Sauniére received more than the equivalent of thirteen million pounds (over twenty million dollars) and his bishop more than twice that amount.

Lincoln was able to obtain Boudet's book and found it baffling as well as funny. Boudet seemed to think that the original language of mankind before the Tower of Babel was English—or rather, Celtic. This part of Boudet's book Lincoln describes as "linguistic tomfoolery." And since Boudet was known to be an intelligent man, Lincoln suspects he has his tongue in his cheek. But the volume then turns into something far more interesting. Boudet goes on to discuss the complex megalithic structures of the area. The subtitle of the book is *The Cromlech of Reines-les-Bains*—a Cromlech is a megalith made up of a large flat stone resting on two upright stones, rather like a huge dining table.

It looks as if Boudet's job was simply to hint at the mystery of the whole area, and imply that it dates back to megalithic times. But Lincoln is inclined to suspect that his intention is also to tell his reader that one major key to the secret of the area lies in English—perhaps in English measures, such as the English mile. And is Boudet hinting that the original measures of mankind are English—such as the mile?

Rennes-le-Château differs from other sacred sites in being centerd on a natural pentacle. This would have been enough to guarantee that it would be regarded as sacred.

How long has this been so? Lincoln is certain that it has been sacred for at least a thousand years, for the "temple"—consisting of churches, castles, and villages—must have been designed at least a thousand years ago.

That raises an obvious question. The pentacular structure of the mountains of the area can only be seen from the air or on a good map. But we know that there were no good maps a thousand years ago, except portolans, which covered the sea. Land maps were crude in the extreme.

But we have also seen Hapgood's evidence that there were maps—even of Antarctica before the ice—that dated from thousands of years before Christianity.

Now Berriman's evidence, demonstrating that the Greek stade indicates a civilization that knew the exact size of the earth, seems to point to the Sumerians. They invented the sixty-minute hour and the sixty-second minute. But that raises another problem. How would the Sumerians have known the exact size of the earth?

The answer is: using the method employed by Eratosthenes in 250 BC, using the shadow of the tower in Alexandria. But it is not necessary to take two places 5,000 stade apart; it can be done with two upright poles stuck in the ground a few miles apart.

It seems clear that the ancient Egyptians knew of some such method, since they encoded the size of the earth into the measurements of the Great Pyramid. The fact that the Sumerians counted in sixties indicates that they also knew it.

But if we had asked Plato where this knowledge of the size of the earth came from, he would probably have replied: Atlantis. And so, in all probability, would Hapgood—until the last year of his life, when he became convinced that "advanced levels of science" dated back one hundred thousand years.

It is true that the idea sounds totally absurd. Until, that is, we recall Maurice Chatelain's argument that the Nineveh number was a factor of the two even larger Quiriga numbers, and that Chatelain concluded that "the Mayas and the Sumerians must have had direct connection with each other *or that they shared a common origin*" (my italics).[9] And that common origin, Chatelain suggests, was more than sixty thousand years ago. . . .

Lincoln's researches on the alignments of the Rennes-le-Château area were further explored by the art historian Peter Blake, whose interest in the subject was piqued when he was looking at Luigi Signorelli's painting *The Education of Pan*, which was commissioned by Lorenzo de Medici. Blake noticed that the painting, commissioned in 1492, contained a pentagram. Familiarity with Lincoln's analysis of *The Shepherds of Arcadia* made its structure immediately apparent.

This obviously raises the question of whether Lorenzo de Medici was also privy to the secret of the Templars and the Priory of Sion. Since he was part of the great humanist tradition, this seems highly likely.

And if we bear in mind that he was also a patron of Leonardo, and that Leonardo is listed as a Grand Master of the Priory of Sion from 1510 to 1519, it becomes almost certain.

Blake also noted that the pentagram in *The Education of Pan* is identical with the one Henry Lincoln found in one of the Sauniére parchments found in the church of Rennes-le-Château.

Poussin's *The Shepherds of Arcadia* was commissioned by Cardinal Guilio Rospigliosi, who would later become Pope Clement IX. So it seems likely that Rospigliosi was also a member of the Priory. And if that seems unbelievable for a man who became pope, we only have to bear in mind that Pope Leo X, who made the remark: "It has served us well, this myth of Christ," was Giovanni de Medici, the son of Lorenzo.[10]

Cardinal Rospigliosi also commissioned Poussin's *A Dance to the Music of Time*, painted in 1638. This is the last of the paintings he commissioned from Poussin, and Blake sees it in many ways as the most significant. It shows Hermes playing his lyre, and four female figures dancing in a circle holding hands, their backs toward one another. Two sculpted heads, probably Jesus and John the Baptist, are back to back on a marble column. Across the picture, on the same level, is a plinth, and the line that connected them is obviously the upper line of a pentagram. Above them, Orion sweeps across the sky in his chariot. Unlike the pentagram in *The Shepherds of Arcadia*, this one is neatly contained within the picture.

Blake has noted a color code in *Shepherds* in which a Jesus figure is associated with red. He goes on to argue that this also applies to *A Dance to the Music of Time*. The woman to the right of the central figure is dressed in red and blue, implying both Jesus and the Virgin Mary. The central figure, a woman in a gold skirt, he associates with harvest. Blake suggests that the harvest borne by the woman is a child—which seems to be supported by a child in the right hand corner of the picture—and that this painting hints at the notion that the woman, associated with Jesus and motherhood, has borne Jesus a child.

There is one more painting in which he finds hints that Jesus was a father, *The Deluge*. This, the last of four paintings on the four seasons, and therefore representing Winter, seems so odd that it almost signals hidden meaning. It shows a family struggling ashore from a stormy sea. One figure dressed in red is being pulled to shore by an ass, making the identification with Jesus fairly plain. There is a female figure dressed in gold, like the one from *A Dance to the Music of Time*, and she is holding a child, also dressed in red, and hinting clearly at the notion that Jesus is the father.

A snake on a rock is seen by Blake as a symbol of wisdom, like the pyramid in the background of the painting. Could all this hint at Jesus and his family arriving on a strange shore, intended to represent France? It is very hard to see what this painting might otherwise represent.

It was commissioned by the Duc de Richelieu, the nephew of Cardinal Richelieu, the minister of Louis XIII, and the Grey Eminence behind the throne. Richelieu became the King's First Minister in 1624, and although he had been ordained a priest in Rome seventeen years earlier, he took the side of the Protestants in a dispute between the Spanish Hapsburgs and Swiss Protestants and expelled the papal troops from France. The King's mother, Marie de Medici, was horrified and tried to persuade her son to dismiss Richelieu. But Louis was a weakling who was tired of being bullied by his mother and realized that Richelieu was his salvation. When he chose Richelieu, his mother and brother fled to the Netherlands, then occupied by Spain.

Now Richelieu held Poussin in the highest esteem, so much so that he exerted pressure to make Poussin return from his beloved Italy to become a member of the Royal Academy of Painting. Poussin went, much against his will, in 1640, and was relieved to be allowed to return to Italy two years later. It is probable that he became a member of the Priory of Sion while he was in Paris and, on his return to Italy, embarked on the commissions for Cardinal Rospigliosi. Richelieu continued to visit Poussin in Italy.

This, of course, raises the suggestion that Richelieu was himself a member of the Priory of Sion, and this explains why he was on the side of the Protestants rather than the Catholic Church. In which case, was it Richelieu who inducted Poussin into the Priory?

If Richelieu was indeed a member of the Priory, then he obviously did not share its desire to restore the Merovingians to the throne, for he is generally believed to have been behind making sure that Anne of Austria became pregnant, and so kept the descendants of Pepin the Short on the throne.

Why should that be so? Presumably because it made no real difference to Richelieu whether a Merovingian or a Carolingian was on the throne; the House of Lorraine was no more likely to tell the world the truth about Christianity than the House of Bourbon (to which Louis belonged) was. And with the House of Lorraine on the throne, Richelieu would lose his power. So he helped to preserve the House of Bourbon by ensuring that it had an heir.

But if Richelieu was indeed a member of the Priory, it merely underlines the astonishing fact that so many of the most remarkable men of their time regarded the popes and princes of the Church as a dynasty of impostors, and would have been glad to see the end of Roman Catholicism.

When Peter Blake had worked out the pentagrams in Poussin's *The Shepherds of Arcadia* and *A Dance to the Music of Time*, and in Signorelli's *Education of Pan*, he tried applying them to the landscape around Rennes-le-Château and was delighted to find that they fit. The pentagram from Signorelli fit neatly on to a number of hilltops, and so did the pentagram from *The Shepherds of Arcadia*. As to the pentagram from *A Dance to the Music of Time*, Blake turned it at an angle of 90 degrees to the other two, since it was a female-dominated painting and again found that its vertices rested on hilltops. And the intersection of the pentagrams fell on a hill at the end of a valley. Nearby was a rocky spur on a hilltop called Estagnol, which in Old French translates as "The Lamb of the East."

Blake drove to the spot and found it to be a finger of stone at the top of an escarpment, with a ten-meter drop on its far side. He could see a massive stone slab lying at the bottom, leaning against the cliff face. There was a hole full of moss on one side of the slab. Blake tore this out and opened up a meter-square gap. Inside he found a cavity with a flat earth floor. He crawled through a triangular cave, noticing that underneath the earth on its floor there was a bed of flat stones. He pulled one of these out and saw that it was rough and irregular underneath. This floor had obviously been carefully laid.

At the far end of the cave there was an opening, which led out into the daylight. A few yards further along, he found another stone slab leaning against a triangular opening, and inside it, yet another cave.

These two caves, Blake believes, are the tombs of Jesus and Mary Magdalen.

Let me try to summarize this extremely complex story.

According to Lomas and Knight, Freemasonry is a tradition of knowledge that extends back to the flood of 7600 BC. This was caused by the impact of a large body from space, which broke into "seven burning mountains," as reported by the prophet Enoch.

Around 1530 BC, the pharaoh Sequenenre was killed by three employees of the Hyksos rival pharaoh Apopi, who wanted to force him to divulge the ritual for transforming the pharaoh into a god. They failed, and the new pharaoh, Sequenenre's son, led a revolt that drove the Hyksos out of Egypt in 1522 BC. His father's killer was probably a Hebrew. But by six centuries later the story had been altered, and Hiram Abif, the Tyrian architect of Solomon's Temple, had become the victim.

Solomen had been tempted from the religion of Yahweh by some of his Phoenician wives and made sacrifices to the goddess Astarte, one of the names of Venus. His Temple was built on the lines of a temple to Astarte.

In 587 BC, the Jews were dragged off into their Babylonian captivity by King Nebuchadnezzar and were not allowed to return until fifty years later. In exile, they had dreamed of a Messiah, or Anointed One, who would lead them to victory and establish the kingdom of God on earth. They hoped that Zerubbabel, who rebuilt the Temple, would declare himself the Messiah, but he had no ambitions in this direction.

When Alexander the Great became their ruler, many hoped that he was the Messiah. But when one of the Seleucids—Alexander's successors—set up a statue of Zeus in the Temple, it led to the revolt of Judas Maccabeus, whose family became the hereditary priesthood.

This led a disgusted group of religious conservatives called Essenes to move into the wilderness at Qumran, where they lived ascetic lives. Their leader was called the Teacher of Righteousness, and he worked miracles, claimed to be the Messiah, and was executed, about a century before the coming of Jesus. The similarities between this teacher and Jesus are so great that the scholar G. R. S. Mead wrote a book called *Did Jesus Live 100 BC?*

Jesus himself was the eldest of a family of four brothers and two or more sisters. His father Joseph was a Pharisee, one of those Jews who insist on strict observance of the law. Jesus would turn his back on this sect, feeling it to be barren. His second cousin, John the Baptist, was the son of a priest named Zechariah, who was of the Abijah sect (Abijah was a descendant of Aaron). At a fairly early age John went into the wilderness—since his parents were old when he was born, it seems likely he was orphaned early. And since the Essenes took in orphans—they lived in chastity, so had no other way of sustaining their numbers—it is likely that the "wilderness" means Qumran. The presence of his cousin among the Essenes may also explain why Jesus and his younger brother James became attached to the sect.

Jesus was crucified because he was intent on leading a rebellion that would drive the Romans out of Judaea. King Herod was not only a friend of Rome; he also had a group of rich Jewish admirers, known as Herodians, who were perfectly happy with the Roman occupation. So Jesus was playing a dangerous game, with enemies on both sides. When the uprising he hoped to lead failed to materialize, Jesus was condemned and crucified.

However, crucifixion was not quite the agonising ordeal most of us suppose. Except for those condemned for the worst kind of treason, it did not involve being nailed to a cross but tied with ropes around the wrists and ankles. Moreover, a man sentenced to crucifixion was usually left on the cross for days until he was dead; Jesus was left for only six hours, because it was Passover the next day—a Sabbath—and the law did not allow men to remain on the cross over Passover.

Then a wealthy member of the Sanhedrin—the Jewish council—went to Pilate and obtained permission to take down the body of Jesus, whose death had deeply impressed him, and put it in his own tomb, which was nearby. Jesus was conveyed to a tomb, but Joseph of Arimathea was to suffer several years imprisonment for his open support. According to another New Testament scholar, Barbara Thiering (in *Jesus the Man*) Jesus was then revived with an antidote to the poison he had been given on a sponge.

What then happened, if Lincoln, Baigent, and Leigh are correct, is that Jesus was taken across the Mediterranean, probably to Marseilles, and there continued his ministry. According to Barbara Thiering, he made a final journey to Rome, where he died some time after AD 64, when he would be seventy-one.

This, then, was why the tradition that Jesus had died on the cross was never accepted in the region of Aireda (which became Rennes-le-Château), where he spent much of his later life.

Why, in that case, is there not a strong tradition regarding Jesus, as well as of Mary Magdalen, in the south of France? Perhaps because King Herod was also exiled to Gaul by Caligula, where he died in AD 69. It would not be good sense for a fugitive from the law to attract too much attention.

Peter Blake, as we have seen, believes he has found the tombs of Jesus and Mary Magdalen side by side, and that their location is coded into Poussin's paintings.

This, then, is probably the knowledge "that kings would have great difficulty in obtaining from him," particularly Louis XIV, who belonged to the wrong dynasty.[11]

The next question concerns the Merovingian dynasty. When Henry Lincoln set out to research them he found that details were lacking, due to the assiduity of the Church in censoring the records. But we know that it was founded by a Frankish king named Merovech (or Merovée), who was crowned in AD 448. So he would be a contemporary of King Arthur. His kingdom would have extended over most of France, from Marseilles in the south to the Ardennes in the north. This seems to be the person whose legendary origin gave Henry Lincoln and Richard Leigh the insight that led to *The Holy Blood and the Holy Grail*: that the fish that impregnated Merovech's mother might symbolize the founder of Christianity, as it did in the early days. Lincoln cites a tradition that Merovingian monarchs were occult adepts, and that they were often called "the sorcerer kings." This would certainly explain why they found such significance in the Rennes-le-Château area, with its natural pentagram of hills.

Lincoln mentions that the tomb of Merovech's son, Childerich I, was found in the Ardennes in 1653 and contained great treasures, including various objects obviously associated with sorcery—a crystal ball, a severed horse's head, and a golden bull's head. There were also three hundred bees made of gold. Oddly enough, Napoleon insisted on these bees being attached to his coronation robes. And his interest in the Merovingians is also indicated by the fact that he commissioned a genealogy of the dynasty; the genealogy was later used in the documents deposited in the Bibliothéque Nationale.

The myths surrounding the Merovingians included the notion that they originated in Arcadia, in Greece—presumably explaining the inscription on the tomb in *The Shepherds of Arcadia*.

And so, in due course, a descendant of the Merovingians, Godfrey of Bouillon, led the first Crusade, and after his death, his brother, Baldwin I, gave the members of the Priory permission to move into the stables. We presume they found there what they were looking for—the scrolls the Essenes had been allowed to conceal in the Temple, including the Heavenly Jerusalem scroll with its Masonic symbols. These were transported back to France and may have been stored in the Château of Bezu, in the midst of Cathar country. (Lincoln mentions that St. Bernard, who had traveled to the area intending to preach against the Cathars, was less appalled by the heretics than by the corruption of his own church, and praised the purity of their morals.)

When the Templars were arrested by Philip the Fair, their fleet escaped with the scrolls, which ended at Roslin. But the Priory, under Edouard, Comte de Bar, continued its secret existence.

Freemasonry finally came into the open in 1640. This was preceded by the strange affair of the Rosicrucians. In 1614, the publication of a pamphlet called *Fama Fraternitas* (or *Fraternal Declaration*) of the Meritorious Order of the Rosy Cross caused a sensation all over Europe. It purports to describe the life of a mystic-magician of the fifteenth century named Christian Rosenkreuz, who lived to be 106, and whose body was preserved—undecayed—in a mysterious tomb for the next 120 years. The pamphlet goes on to invite all interested parties to join the Brotherhood and tells them that they only have to make their interest known (by word of mouth or in writing) and they will be "contacted." Hundreds of people published their willingness to join; but, as far as is known, no one ever received a reply.

The *Fama* was followed by two more "Rosicrucian" works, the *Confessio* (1615), and a larger work called *The Chemical Wedding* (1616). These intensified the Rosicrucian fever. The author is believed to be a Protestant theologian named Johann Valentin Andrae, who is most certainly the author of *The Chemical Wedding*, although he denied writing the other two. He seems to have started as an idealistic young man who hoped to launch a new spiritual movement, since—like so many other people at that period—he felt that it was time for a new beginning. And, significantly, he is listed in the Secret Dossier as one of the Grand Masters of the Priory of Sion.

Finally, in Scotland and in England, an organization that called itself the Freemasons came into being around 1640. The Catholic Church hated it, but in the early days—particularly in Scotland—there seem to have been as many Catholics as Protestants in the organization.

The full implications were not understood until after the Second World War, when the Priory of Sion, under Pierre Plantard, decided that it was time to go public, and secured its greatest publicity coup when Henry Lincoln found Gerard de Sède's book and persuaded the BBC to make a documentary.

The book that eventually resulted, *The Holy Blood and the Holy Grail*, became an international bestseller.

Yet it still only reached a cultured minority, prepared to immerse themselves in the history of the Merovingians. Then, in 2003, Dan Brown's novel *The Da Vinci Code*, which included an account of the story of the Priory of Sion, reached the largest audience so far and brought the history of Jesus and the Templars to millions of readers. It is probably the most widely read attack on Catholicism since Martin Luther. But Brown evidently decided that including Sauniére and Rennes-le-Château would complicate the story too much, and Sauniére's name is kept only for the curator of the Louvre who is murdered in the first few pages.

And that, at the time of writing, is the latest episode in this strange story that is the history of Christianity.

ELEVEN

PRIMAL VISION

As I researched this book, my mind kept returning to Hapgood's phrase "advanced levels of science that may go back 100,000 years." What did he mean by "advanced levels of science"? We are fairly certain that our Cro-Magnon ancestors had no steam engines or electric lights.

Or could Hapgood have meant something quite different? After all, Stonehenge and Tiahuanaco reveal high levels of science without anything that looks like technology.

In *Time Stands Still* by Keith Critchlow, there are some extraordinary facts about Babylonian mathematics. These were calculations about the sides of Pythagorean triangles—the amazing thing being that, in spite of the Babylonian's crude number system, they seemed to have no difficulty in multiplying a huge number like 18,541 by itself, the product of which exceeds 343 million. Yet apparently they did not even possess the simple algebra for working out the hypoteneuse of a right-angle triangle.

Critchlow concluded that people in the remote past possessed some sort of "immediate perception of the general relationships existing between these numbers."[1] In other words, they saw the answer, as you and I can see that two times two equals four.

That sounds absurd—until we remember the story of six-year-old Benjamin Blyth who took only half a minute to work out how many seconds he had been alive, including leap years.

A British autistic savant named Daniel Tammet has provided some of the answers. Explaining how he can instantly calculate, say, 377 multiplied by 795, he describes how he can "see" numbers as shapes, colors, and textures. "When I multiply numbers together I see two shapes. The image starts to change and evolve, and a third shape emerges. That's the answer. It's mental imagery. It's like math without having to think."[2] In short, the work is done by the right side of his brain, the side that deals with shapes and forms. Tammet's powers developed when he had an epileptic attack at the age of three—an attack that must have damaged the left hemisphere of his brain, and transferred dominance to the right.

This also helps to provide an answer to the question raised in chapter 2—what Robert Graves "saw" when he sat on the school roller and suddenly "knew everything."

He speaks of "sudden infantile awareness of the power of intuition, the supra-logic that cuts out all routine processes of thought and leaps straight from problem to answer."[3]

So he is describing a flash of intuition, right-brain awareness, the "bird's eye view." And what the "bird" sees is all the complexities and contradictions of human existence suddenly resolved in a simple vision of wholeness. Gurdjieff's disciple Ouspensky had such an experience—almost certainly induced by nitrous oxide—which he describes in a chapter called "Experimental Mysticism" in *A New Model of the Universe*.

He wrote: "Everything is unified, everything is linked together, everything is explained by something else and in turn explains another thing. . . . The new world with which one comes into contact has no sides, so that it is impossible to describe first one side and then the other. . . ."[4]

This is why Graves became so confused when he tried writing it down; he was trying to find a "starting point" that did not exist. And when he persisted, he came down to earth with a bump and the vision simply disappeared.

What is being suggested is that Benjamin Blyth and the creator of the Nineveh number were able to access this bird's eye view at will, whereas modern man is in the same position as Graves after he has come down to earth. Everything is now separate, disconnected.

In *From Atlantis to the Sphinx*, I spoke about the anthropologist Edward Hall, who spent years studying North American Indians, and who tells how one of his students decided to film a group of children in a school playground. After watching this film several times, Hall's students began to sense an underlying beat. And when a rock music enthusiast saw the film, he took a tape from his collection and played it alongside the film. The children seemed to be dancing to the rock music, as if they had been choreographed. They were apparently dancing to some underlying rhythm of which they were unconscious. This is why Hall calls his book *The Dance of Life*.

And Schwaller de Lubicz declared in his book *Sacred Science*: "Every living being is in contact with all the rhythms and harmonies of all the energies in his universe."[5]

In *From Atantis to the Sphinx* I also spoke of a book called *The Infinite Harmony* by Mike Hayes, in which he explains his own discovery of a connection between music and the DNA code. At the time, neither I nor Mike Hayes were aware that this insight had already been recorded by Dr. Martin Schonburger, a Jungian, in 1976, in a book called *The I Ching and the Genetic Code*, inspired by Dr. Marie-Louise von Franz, or discussed by the Tai Chi specialist, Graham Horwood, in his book *Tai Chi Chuan and the Code of Life*.

Hayes was attending classes on the genetic code at Leicester University, and when he heard that the four bases form into triplet codes, called RNA codons, in sixty four ways, he recalled that the *I Ching* or *Book of Changes* has sixty-four "hexagrams," or groups of six lines, each formed of two "trigrams" consisting of broken or unbroken lines.

Now he learned that each of the triplet units of RNA links up with another triplet in the DNA molecule. So the double helix of the DNA molecule is made of sixty-four hexagrams, just like the *I Ching*. He found himself wondering if Fu Hsi, the legendary creator of the *I Ching*, might have gained access to some fundamental insight into the code of life. In which case, there ought to be eight trigrams hidden in DNA. When he learned that indeed this was so, Hayes began to suspect he had stumbled on something important.

He had also been intrigued to learn that there are twenty amino acids necessary for the manufacture of protein, with two more coded instructions for "start" and "stop"—twenty-two in all. And he recalled that Pythagoras had regarded the number twenty-two as sacred because it represented three musical octaves. (The octave has seven notes—doh, re, mi, fa, soh, la, ti, and another doh to complete the octave and begin the next.) And obviously, these octaves also involve the mystical number three.

Pythagoras, of course, is recognized as the first of the great "number mystics."

The ancient Egyptians went to enormous lengths to encode their knowledge—we have seen that the height and base of the Great Pyramid encode the size of the earth. And Mike Hayes points out that in the antechamber to the King's Chamber, there is a granite relief whose area is exactly equal to the area of a circle whose diameter is the length of the antechamber floor. Moreover, when this length is multiplied by pi, the result is precisely the length of a year—365.2412 pyramid inches. Such architecture obviously sprang from the ancient Egyptian belief that numbers encode the structure of the universe.

As Mike Hayes studied the major world religions—he had become interested in Islam when living in Iran—he was struck by the important part played in them by the numbers three, seven, and twenty-two. The number pi, the relation of the diameter of a circle to its circumference, is twenty-two divided by seven. In *The Infinite Harmony* there are dozens of illustrations of the recurrence of three, seven, and twenty-two, and Hayes calls these, and other numbers, "the Hermetic code." He argues that this Hermetic code is an evolutionary code—that is, it is something to do with the way life manifests itself and tries to move to higher evolutionary levels.

It becomes possible to see why Narby's comment that all the shamans of the world agree that contact with spirits is achieved via music may have a far deeper significance than it first appeared to.

The *I Ching* works, according to Jung, by means of what he called synchronicity, or meaningful coincidence. Like Jeremy Narby, Jung accepts that we are living in an "intelligent universe," not in the dead universe of nineteenth-century science. When the *I Ching*—or whatever meaningful principle lies behind it—is consulted with the necessary seriousness of intent by throwing three coins, it provides the appropriate response by referring to one of sixty-four hexagrams. (When Jung wrote his Introduction to Richard Wilhelm's translation in 1951, he had been secretly consulting it for more than thirty years.)

All this begins to offer us some insight into the question of Hapgood's "advanced levels of science" in remote times. We can see that if Hapgood had read Narby's book, he would have agreed that the Quirishari's insight into the properties of eighty thousand plants qualifies as advanced knowledge. And so does the Egyptian ability to encode the length of the year—to four decimal points—in a square granite relief.

What is being implied here by Narby, by Edward Hall, by Mike Hayes, by Jung and by Schwaller de Lubicz, is that nature is full of significances to which we have become blind.

It is almost impossible for modern man to understand how he can be "blind." We see what is in front of our noses, and we could not see more even if we opened our eyes as far as they will go.

But there is another kind of blindness, which William James describes in his essay "On a Certain Blindness in Human Beings." James recounts how he was being driven, in a buggy, through the mountains of North Carolina, and looking with revulsion at the newly cultivated patches of land (called coves) and reflecting how ugly they were. He asked the driver what kind of people lived here, and the driver replied cheerfully: "We ain't happy unless we're getting one of these coves under cultivation."[6] And James suddenly woke up to the fact that these homesteaders regarded each cove as a personal victory, and saw it as beautiful.

We become blind to things by imposing our concepts on them and looking at them with a kind of indifference, which arises from our conviction that we know what they are already. James was quite sure that the coves were ugly, without seeing that the ugliness lay in his own eyes.

But even when we know this, it is still very difficult for us to grasp just how the ancient Egyptians—or our Cro-Magnon ancestors—somehow saw the world quite differently, and might consequently have developed their own "high levels of science." The following example should make it clearer.

One of the few men to whom this "ancient seeing" came quite naturally was the poet Goethe. And Goethe's vision of science can enable us to grasp what it is all about.

It would simplify what follows if I explain how I happened to stumble on Goethe's vision of science.

I had been an admirer of his work ever since my teens, when I first read Faust in the old Everyman edition. His vision of a scholar rendered miserable by his sense of the meaninglessness of life struck a deep chord with me at the age of sixteen. Good English translations of his work are rare, but over the years, I went on to collect every volume I could lay my hands on.

A few years ago, I came across a translation of *Goethe's Theory of Color* but was of two minds whether to buy it. I knew Goethe was an enthusiastic amateur scientist but felt that basically he was no more than that—an amateur. All the same, I bought the book—and it stayed unread on my shelf.

I should have been aware of the risk of dismissing any aspect of Goethe. For example, I knew that he had finally proved correct about the intermaxillary bone. This is a bone in the upper jaw that holds the incisors, and all animals possess it. But in the 1780s, a famous Dutch anatomist named Peter Camper announced that what makes man quite unique is that he has no intermaxillary bone in his jaw. And Goethe, who was an evolutionist long before Darwin or Lamarck, was sure this had to be nonsense. So he proceeded to search through piles of animal and human skulls and found signs of the intermaxillary bone in man, although it was now little more than a seam uniting the halves. But when he announced this to Camper and other scientists, they dismissed him as an amateur. By the time of Darwin, Goethe was recognized to be right, and Camper wrong.

However, where color was concerned, I simply could not see how Goethe could question the accepted theory. We were all taught at school that white light actually consists of the seven colors of the rainbow—red, orange, yellow, green, blue, indigo, violet. And Newton proved this by a simple experiment. He made a small hole in his blind, to admit a narrow beam of light, and then passed this through a prism. And the light split into the seven colors. Surely that is quite conclusive?

Goethe borrowed a prism and set about repeating Newton's experiment. And he immediately came upon an anomaly. If he looked at a white tabletop through the prism, it did not turn into a rainbow-colored table. It stayed white, and the only rainbow colors were around its edges. And this proved to be generally true. Colors only appeared when there was one kind of boundary or edge.

Goethe took a sheet of paper in which the top half was white and the bottom half black. When he looked through a prism at the halfway line, he saw the colors red, orange, and yellow run up into the white half. But when he stared intently at the black boundary, he saw that the darker colors of the spectrum are there—light blue closest to the boundary, then dark blue (indigo), and violet. So the order of the colors does not run in the proper rainbow sequence: red, orange, yellow, green, blue, indigo, violet, but yellow, orange, red, blue, indigo, violet, apparently defying Newton's law.

All this led Goethe to what will seem to us a strange conclusion. If you look at the sky on a hot day, it is deep blue overhead and becomes lighter as your gaze travels toward the horizon, where the atmosphere—loaded with light—is thicker. But if you could travel upward in a rocket, the sky would become steadily bluer and darker until it turned into the blackness of space.

On the other hand, when the sun is directly overhead, it is yellow. As it moves down to the horizon, its light turns to red. So where the sun's light is concerned, the atmosphere produces the three light colors: yellow, orange, and red. Where darkness is concerned (outer space), the atmosphere creates the three dark colors: blue, indigo, and violet.

To express this crudely, Goethe is suggesting that the dark colors—blue, indigo, violet—are made by diluting blackness, while the light colors—yellow, orange, red—are made by thickening the light.

My own reaction, when I read all this, was a desire to tear my hair and throw the book out of the window. Where, I wanted to know, was Goethe's theory superior to Newton's? And anyway, what did it matter?

At that point, my friend Eddie Campbell lent me a copy of *The Wholeness of Nature: Goethe's Way of Science*, by Henri Bortoft, a scientist who had been a pupil of the physicist David Bohm. It looked so difficult that I decided it would take years to read, and I had better buy my own copy—which I then allowed to sit on my shelf for over a year. But when I finally came to read it, I realized that it is among the most important books I had ever bought.

Bortoft's book offered some interesting new facts. To begin with, when Goethe had been observing the colors, he would close his eyes and envisage what he had just seen. He would try to see the colors, in their right order, inside his head, and would do this until he could conjure it up with as much reality as the actual colors.

He was practicing what I described as "eidetic vision." For what purpose? Let Bortoft explain:

"When observing the phenomenon of color in Goethe's way it is necessary to be more active in seeing than we are usually. The term 'observation' is in some ways too passive. We tend to think of an observation as just a matter of opening our eyes in front of the phenomenon. . . . Observing the phenomenon in Goethe's way requires us to look as if the direction of seeing were reversed, going from ourselves toward the phenomenon instead of vice versa. This is done by putting attention into seeing, so that we really do see what we are seeing instead of just having a visual impression. It is as if we plunged into seeing. In this way we can begin to experience the quality of the colors."

And after describing Goethe's way of re-creating the colors in his imagination, Bortoft explains: "The purpose is to develop an organ of perception which can deepen our contact with the phenomenon. . . ."[7]

Goethe called this "active seeing."[8] And this, I would suggest, is the difference between modern man and ancient man. Ancient man, because of his closer contact with nature, was far more accustomed to active seeing.

I happened to be sitting in bed at about 6:30 on a bright summer morning as I read Bortoft on Goethe. Suddenly I understood what he meant. I looked out of my window at the garden, with its trees and shrubs, and deliberately did what Goethe recommends: that is, I tried to see it actively.

This made me aware that when I normally look out at the garden, I am seeing it passively, taking it for granted, feeling I know every inch of it. Instead I tried to suspend all ideas, all preconceptions, and simply to look as if it was somebody else's garden and I was seeing it for the first time.

The immediate effect was a feeling of being drawn into nature. The grass, the trees, the shrubs suddenly seemed more real and alive. Moreover, they seemed to be communicating with me. There was an odd sense of being among old friends, as if I belonged to a club in which I felt perfectly at home.

I also realized that Goethe, like many poets, possessed this kind of perception naturally. In Faust he talks about nature as "God's living garment." In his lyric poetry there is a tremendous, surging vitality that reminds us of certain of Van Gogh's later paintings—*The Road With Cypresses* and *The Starry Night*—in which the trees seemed to have turned into green flames roaring upward toward the sky.

There is a well-known story about how Goethe and the poet Schiller left a rather dull scientific lecture in Jena, and Goethe remarked that there ought to be some other way of presenting nature—not in bits and pieces, but as a living actuality, striving from the whole to the parts. And Schiller shrugged and remarked: "Oh, that's just an idea."[9]

But he was wrong. For Goethe it was not just an idea; it was something he saw when he looked at trees and flowers and grass. They looked alive, as if nature was, in some way, a single organism.

As an exercise, let the reader try looking at a garden with "active seeing." Instead of seeing it as a kind of still life, like a painting, make an effort to recognize that it is in continual motion—very slow motion, but motion nevertheless—and that plants are as alive as insects or birds or bees.

No doubt this was not true for Goethe all the time; like the rest of us, he must have had his periods of fatigue in which he saw things mechanically. But in his wide-awake moments, he seems to have seen nature as Van Gogh painted it.

And, as Bortoft recognized, this is not just a matter of making more effort. It is a matter of developing an organ of perception.

William Blake said: "If the doors of perception were cleansed, every thing would appear to man as it is, infinite."[10] Aldous Huxley quoted it in his book *The Doors of Perception*, in which he recorded his experiences with the psychedelic drug mescalin, during which everything suddenly appeared far more real. This is clearly the kind of thing Bortoft is talking about. But if, as Narby implies, the natives of Quirishari still possess this "organ," modern man certainly lost it centuries ago.

This "organ" is what the German writer Gottfried Benn called "primal vision."[11]

How did we lose it? By developing a kind of mechanical perception to cope with the complications of our crowded lives. Wordsworth understood all about it, as he demonstrates in the "Intimations of Immortality" ode. For a child everything seems new and exciting, "the glory and the freshness of a dream." This is because he lives in the present, and everything appears sharp and clear. Then "shades of the prison house begin to close" upon the growing youth, as life becomes more difficult and demanding. And by the time he reaches adulthood, he is always in a hurry, and the "glory" has faded into the light of common day.[12]

All that this means, of course, is that he no longer puts the effort into seeing things. When a child sits in front of his favorite television program, he turns his full attention on it—so much so that he often fails to hear when you speak to him. And everyone can remember that delightful feeling of listening to the rain pattering on the windows—the novelist Laura del Rivo told me she used to roll herself into a ball and say: "Isn't it nice to be me?" And indeed, it is nice to be you—provided you turn your full attention on it and don't permit any "leakage." But this is precisely what we do as we grow up—we spread our attention too thin and then accept that diluted version of reality as the real thing. And so the "certain blindness" sets in.

Animals don't do that. They live comfortably in the present and turn their total attention to anything that interests them. We "civilized" humans have forgotten how to do this. And we are not even aware we are short-changing ourselves, because we think this is the way things are.

One of the worst effects of this diluted and degraded consciousness is that it fills us with stress, and causes us to direct attention at worries that don't deserve it. And when we occasionally experience a breath of real consciousness, for example, setting out on holiday, we assume that it is simply due to the holiday and fail to draw the lesson that we habitually misuse our powers of attention. The problem is rather like breathing too shallowly until you begin to suffer from oxygen starvation.

According to Princeton psychologist Julian Jaynes, all this began to happen fairly recently. In *The Origin of Consciousness in the Breakdown of the Bicameral Mind*, Jaynes offers the evidence of "split-brain research" to argue that the consciousness of modern man has contracted so much that he now lives in only one half of his brain—the left cerebral hemisphere (which is devoted to language, logic, and "coping" with everyday life). The right half, he claims (which deals with intuitions, insights, and feelings) has become a stranger. And Jaynes suggests that man became a "left brainer" as recently as 1250 BC.

During the great wars that convulsed the Mediterranean during the second millennium BC, the old childlike mentality could no longer cope; man had to become more narrow, more obsessive—and at the same time, more brutal and ruthless. (Tension tends to make us cruel.) And in this new state of mind, man lost touch with the gods, and with his own deeper self. About 1230 BC, the Assyrian tyrant Tukulti-Ninurti had a stone altar built, which shows the king kneeling before the empty throne of the god. But all earlier kings had portrayed themselves sitting beside the god on his throne. Now the god has vanished, and man is "on his own."

It is an interesting theory, and Jaynes argues it very convincingly; but of course, we have no way of knowing whether it is correct. All we can say is that something of the sort must have happened to us at some point during our evolution.

Narby's *Cosmic Serpent* seems to show that this is not true of his Peruvian Indians. Like shamans the world over, they are still in touch with their gods—or at least, know how to get in touch with them. Which raises an interesting question. The Quirishari believe that it is the cosmic serpent that teaches them, and Narby suggests that this cosmic serpent is actually the DNA molecule. Is it their own DNA that teaches them about the properties of plants? Are they able to learn direct from nature, from "God's living garment"?

All this raises another interesting point. Since it is the left hemisphere of the brain that deals with calculation, we tend to assume that this is the mathematical hemisphere. But any good mathematician will tell you that mathematics requires the same kind of intuition as poetry or art. This would explain how Oliver Sacks's subnormal twins could exchange enormous prime numbers. They must have been able to see them, in the same way that Michelangelo could "see" the statue inside a block of marble while it was still in the quarry, or Nicola Tesla could "see" a machine he had not yet even committed to paper. The strange implication would seem to be that, in becoming a "left brainer," modern man actually lost an important part of his rational faculty.

All of which seems to offer interesting glimpses into how our remote ancestors might have possessed "high levels of science" without inventing the concrete mixer.

Everything seems to indicate that high levels of science require intuition rather than reason. Any good scientist would agree. But it also seems to suggest that intuition might be able to create higher levels of science than most scientists would be willing to concede.

In that case, Hapgood's hundred thousand year old culture with "high levels of science" might be less paradoxical than we supposed.

In May 1996 I received in the post a book with the intimidating title: *Extrasensory Perception of Quarks*. The author, Stephen Phillips, was an Englishman who held a doctorate in particle physics and had taught the subject at Cape Town University.

It was while taking his doctorate at the University of California that he wandered into a Los Angeles bookstore and came upon a copy of a book called *The Physics of the Secret Doctrine* by a Theosophist named William Kingsland. Flicking through the pages, he was brought up short by a picture of a hydrogen atom in which the nucleus had three small points. Few scientists would have given it a second glance, for it doesn't look in the least like a hydrogen atom, which (of course) has one electron orbiting its nucleus, like a single planet going round the sun. This diagram showed six circles, joined in two triangles, and each circle containing three "dots." But Phillips knew that the model of the hydrogen nucleus posited by Murray Gell-Mann in 1961 contained three particles, which Gell-Mann called quarks. And Phillips suspected that quarks themselves may be divided into three "subquarks."

Kingsland was reproducing a picture from a book called *Occult Chemistry* by Annie Besant and C. W. Leadbeater, two of the Theosophical Society's most important founder members. It seemed that, through yogic training, they believed themselves able to clairvoyantly discern the basic structure of matter. *Occult Chemistry* came out in 1908; by 1911, Rutherford—and soon after that, Bohr—had described the structure of the atom we still accept, with its nucleus and orbiting electrons. So understandably, no scientist took *Occult Chemistry* seriously—the very title was enough to make a physicist shudder.

But Stephen Phillips was not a typical physicist. He was the son of a Marxist father and a Spiritualist mother, and while his father had given him a four-inch refracting telescope when he was a child, his mother had given him a copy of Madame Blavatsky's *The Secret Doctrine*. So he had maintained an affectionate interest in Theosophy even when he became an expert on superstrings and quarks.

Besant and Leadbeater had pursued their researches by concentrating on various elements, such as gold, platinum, and diamond, and such compound substances as air and salt. They often saw at first a gray mist, which they were able to "magnify" until it was seen as points of light, or "globes of scintillating points, tossing and waving about as if blown by an invisible wind." The points were then seen to be organized in geometrical figures, which were always the same for each element. These Besant and Leadbeater called "MPAs," meaning micro-psi atoms. These are seen to contain "UPAs," ultimate physical atoms, or the ultimate constituents of matter.

Interestingly enough, Besant and Leadbeater noted variant forms of some atoms, such as neon, argon, and krypton; in due course, these would be recognized as isotopes.

What is argued with great conviction in *Extrasensory Perception of Quarks* is that Besant and Leadbeater had not only recognized the existence of quarks, but of even smaller particles. In 1980, when the book was finally published, subquarks were unheard of; yet in 1996, scientists in Fermilab, near Chicago, performed experiments, which strongly suggested their existence.

After *Extrasensory Perception of Quarks* came the even more definitive *ESP of Quarks and Superstrings*, and after that, a magnum opus called *The Image of God in Man and Matter*.

His thesis here is that the kabbalistic Tree of Life should not be regarded as some vaguely symbolic account of reality put together by woolly-minded mystics, but as a scientifically accurate description of the underlying mathematical reality of the universe.

In Kabbalism, the "Tree of Life" is not a real tree, but a symbolic axis that connects earth and heaven, like the shaman's pole. There are ten levels or "emanations," which may seem at odds with the seven or nine levels of shamanism—until we recognize that the basic level is earth (Malkuth), from which it springs, leaving nine levels.

In a letter to me Stephen Phillips wrote:

"When I returned to England in 1976, I immersed myself in the Pythagorean tetractys [an arrangement of dots in the form of a triangle]. As my research deepened, everything began to fall into place. I discovered how the Godnames defined those sections of inner and outer forms of the Tree of Life that encode numbers of cosmic significance, such as the group-theoretical parameters 248 and 496, intrinsic to superstring theory. Remarkably, the number 168, namely, the kernel of the number 1680 of circular turns counted by Leadbeater in a whorl of the UPA (which my first book identified as a subquark), was the very number value of the Hebrew word signifying the physical manifestation

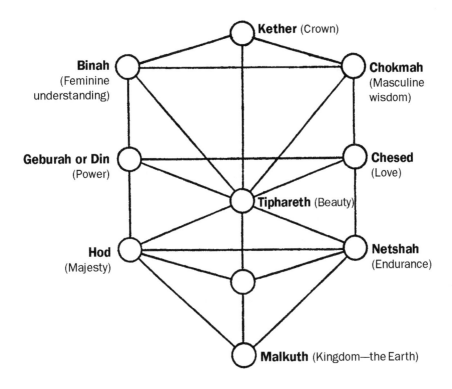

The Tree of Life.

of the Sephirah Malkuth. This was clearly independent confirmation of the objectivity of Leadbeater's clairvoyance. The constant simultaneous appearance of several Godname numbers quantifying aspects of the same geometrical object went beyond coincidence."[13]

It was while looking through *ESP of Quarks and Superstrings* for this chapter that I came upon a letter Stephen had written me some years ago. It contained an account of a "mystical experience" he had had as a child.

"I often went to the local park when I was young, not to play, but to watch the insects and birds. At the age of 9, sitting down in a wood and watching the butterflies darting about and ants crawling up blades of grass, seemingly going nowhere, it struck me that here was a world teeming with purposeful activity that went on whatever humans thought about the meaning of life. As I held the thought, the sense of 'I,' of being separate from the world, began to vanish. Colors and sounds intensified, then lost their significance. I was really all that hive of life, not apart from it. I then felt surrounded by love. Or rather, it seemed that it was everywhere this all-pervading love—I was not experiencng it, for 'I' no longer existed. Images of objects did not register their meaning in my consciousness, for there was only this sea of love. Then I suddenly became aware of being aware. I was back with the insects in the wood. A feeling of exhilaration remained with me for several hours."[14]

Reading this immediately after Narby's book, I was struck by the similarity of what they are saying. Watching butterflies and ants, Phillips might have been in the Peruvian rain forest. And it is interesting that, after reflecting that this world of purposeful activity was independent of our human sense of meaning, Phillips at first experienced an intensification of colors and sounds—what we might call "the Goethe effect," a sudden "active seeing." Then this quickly passed into a sense of the oneness of nature, in which his own identity disappeared. It is interesting to note that Phillips was only nine at the time—an age before the "shades of the prison house begin to close." This vanished as self-consciousness returned—he became "aware of being aware." The left brain was back, and the sense of the wholeness of nature had disappeared.

T. E. Lawrence had once described a similiar experience; it had happened when he was traveling with a party of Arabs: "We started on one of those clear dawns that wake up the senses with the sun, while the intellect, tired of the thinking of the night, was yet abed. For an hour or two, on such a morning, the sounds, scents and colors of the world struck man individually and directly, not filtered through or made typical by thought; they seemed to exist sufficiently by themselves. . . ."[15]

Lawrence complained that his problem sprang out of what he called his "thought-riddled nature"—left brain consciousness. And we can see again that this acts as a kind of filter, like a pair of dark glasses. Without the thought-riddled nature, we would "see things as they are—infinite." That is to say, the normal boundaries of personality would dissolve away.

Neither should we minimize the importance of Phillips's comment that he felt surrounded by a sea of love. Such experiences bring a sense of nature as a living and benevolent force.

Narby's remarks on the Quirishari's familiarity with the properties of eighty thousand plants also brought to mind the work of the great Bengali scientist Jagadis Chandra Bose, which I had first encountered in *The Secret Life of Plants* by Peter Tompkins and Christopher Bird. Bose's most remarkable achievement was to show that there is no hard-and-fast line between living and nonliving things.

Bose, the son of an Indian civil servant, was born in 1858 and proved to be such a brilliant student that his father sent him to England to study physics, chemistry, and botany at Cambridge. But when appointed professor of physics at Calcutta, he ran into the kind of prejudice he was to encounter all his life, the jealousy of colleagues—Indian as well as white—who wanted to see him "kept in his place." He taught without salary for several years until his obvious brilliance caused the authorities to relent. He went on to demonstrate his genius as a physicist by transmitting radio waves before Marconi.

He was invited to England to lecture to the Royal Institution, and the acclaim was so great that the Royal Society recommended a government grant of £40,000 to enable him to set up a research laboratory. Yet once again the envy and backbiting of Indian colleagues blocked him. It was in 1899 that Bose noted an odd fact: that if he overworked his metal coherer for receiving radio waves, it became less efficient. Yet if he allowed it to "rest," it recovered. Bose began to study the boundary between living and "nonliving" things, especially metals.

When Sir Michael Foster, secretary of the Royal Society, came to visit him, Bose showed him a graph. The eminent scientist looked disappointed. "What's new about this? It's been known for half a century."

"What do you think it is?" asked Bose.

"Why, a curve of muscle response!"

"Pardon me," said Bose, "but it is the curve of metallic tin."

"What!" shouted Foster incredulously, leaping to his feet.[16] Bose went on to show him similar results with other metals like iron and copper. He also demonstrated that metals seemed to have memory. A metal surface could be etched with acid, then polished until all trace had vanished. Yet tests could show just where it had been etched.

His next experiment was with leaves; he demonstrated that they could be anesthetized, just like human beings. He even anesthetized a pine tree with chloroform and was able to transplant it to another place without the fatal shock that usually makes such transplanting impossible.

Opposition was still bitter. When he performed his experiments on plants and metals before the Royal Society, he was attacked by the grand old man of physiology, Sir John Burdon-Sanderson, who simply denied that such things were possible. But one of his ex-professors arranged another exhibition before the Linnaean Society, and there Bose triumphed. Yet underhand plotting once more prevented the publication of his results by the Royal Society.

Eventually, Bose won through, even inventing instruments that could show a plant growing from second to second; one device using a beam of light could magnify the "muscular" movements of a plant ten thousand times. Finally, at the age of fifty-nine, he was knighted and was able to open his own Research Institute.

For the remaining twenty years of his life he continued to devise experiments to show that there are no "gaps" in nature: that animal life, plant life, and so-called "inanimate nature," all shade gently into one another. In one lecture he talked about the "pervading unity" of all things and added that it had made him understand "that message proclaimed by my ancestors on the banks of the Ganges thirty centuries ago"—of the oneness that lies behind the multiplicity of nature.[17]

Unlike Goethe, Bose succeeded in convincing his colleagues that he was more than a dreamer. Yet he shared Goethe's fate in the sense that his contemporaries were simply not ready for what he had to say. The result is that one of the greatest scientists of the twentieth century has been virtually forgotten.

It might be reasonable to ask: how could his work be continued? The answer is inherent in Jeremy Narby's *Cosmic Serpent*. The scientist himself must attempt to develop the "shamanic vision," or at least open his mind to its possibility. One metallurgist, Sir Robert Austen, admitted to Bose that he himself had concluded that metals were alive but had been promptly rebuffed when he even hinted at this before the Royal Society. He lacked Bose's advantage: of belonging to a culture that was rooted in the shamanic tradition.

Interestingly enough, this was a view that Charles Hapgood himself came to share in the last years of his life, and expressed in the long Introduction to his last book *Voices of Spirit*.

His starting point was the work of Chandra Bose. In his wide and eclectic reading, Hapgood had come across Bose's book, *Response in the Living and the Non-Living*. He was particularly struck by Bose's demonstration that the metal of his radio receiver could become "fatigued" by too much activity. But he was even more struck by another of Bose's observations: that if he left the receiver for several days without use, it became inert.

Bose comments: "In fact, it had become lazy through lack of stimulation" and had to be stirred back into activity with "a strong shock."[18] Hapgood saw, correctly, that the implications are extraordinary. After all, "metal fatigue" is a familiar concept and can be explained in purely mechanical terms; but "metal laziness" is altogether harder to account for.

Hapgood goes on to speak about the now famous experiments of Cleve Backster, a lie detector expert who, in the mid-1960s, attached his polygraph to the palmlike leaves of a dracaena plant that stood on the floor in his laboratory. He wanted to see if the plant would show less electrical resistance as it sucked up water. To his surprise, it showed more, just like a human being receiving stimulation.

He decided to try burning the leaf with a match—and was startled to see the pen sweep upward on the graph before he struck the match. The plant had apparently read his mind. This was verified when he struck a match with no intention of burning the leaf, and the plant showed no reaction.

He discovered that the plant registered alarm if a dog passed by, and that it registered shock if he dropped live shrimps into boiling water, and appeared to "faint" for a few seconds. It even reacted to the dried blood of a cut finger. Backster had proved that plants have consciousness.

Hapgood goes on to mention the experiments of the Rev. Franklin Loehr, who worked with the parapsychologist J. B. Rhine at Duke University, and demonstrated that plants at which a group directed prayers grew better than plants that were ignored. Ominously, the plants that were prayed against grew poorly and often died—apparently proving the efficacy of "black magic."

Hapgood, always a practical scientist rather than a theoretician, decided to repeat these experiments at Keene State, except that instead of praying, the students were instructed to direct emotion—positive or negative—at the plants. Again, the plants that were exposed to love did better than those that were ignored, while plants exposed to hate did very poorly.

Hapgood's students worked alone, and this led him to an interesting discovery. One very beautiful girl complained that she was unable to influence the growth of plants by love, but that she was very successful in killing those she directed her emotions against.

As he got to know her better, Hapgood understood why. She was an emotionally negative girl, far better at hate than love. "She could let loose the whole of her psychic force against but not for the wretched little seeds. And they didn't have a chance. . . . I got the feeling that in olden times she would have made a very good witch."[19]

Hapgood goes on to discuss the findings of a Yale biologist, Harold Saxton Burr, who discovered that there is a weak electrical field associated with life, and that a fine voltmeter attached to a tree could not only register this field, but noted that it fluctuated during thunderstorms, sunspots, and changes of season. Women show an increase in electrical activity when they ovulate, and one woman who had difficulty becoming pregnant used this knowledge to conceive.

When Burr noted that a frog's egg contains lines of force that develop into a tadpole's nervous system, he concluded that these "fields" actually shape living cells, as a jelly-mould shapes the jelly. He called them L-fields (for life fields).

Burr also discovered that his refined voltmeter could detect cancer in patients—often early enough for the malignancy to be removed before it could develop.

Hapgood points out that Burr's life fields "display all the attributes of what we call purpose, intelligence, spirit."[20] He might, for example, have cited the example of the Microstomum flatworm, described by the zoologist Sir Alister Hardy.

It eats a polyp called Hydra for the sake of its stinging capsules. These "bombs" are designed to discourage predators, but they fail to explode when swallowed by the Microstomum. And when the Hydra has been digested, the "bombs" are picked up in the lining of the flatworm's stomach, passed on to another set of cells, which carry them, like builder's laborers, to the flatworm's skin, where they are mounted pointing outward, like cannons.

Moreover, the flatworm eats the Hydra solely to steal its armory; when it has enough capsules mounted on its skin, it will not touch a Hydra, even if starving. Clearly, an unconscious yet purposeful force is involved here.

A follower of Burr named Edward Russell made an equally remarkable contribution. He noted that the hypnotist Leonard Ravitz had been able to measure the depth of a subject's hypnotic trance with the aid of Burr's voltmeter. This showed that the L-fields of the body can be affected by the mind. Ravitz had also observed that L-fields of mentally unstable people may register the disturbance before symptoms show themselves.

Edward Russell pointed out that since "thought fields" (or T-fields) can affect the life fields, thought must, in some sense, control the life fields. And this, as Hapgood pointed out, amounts to saying that "thought is the primary force in the universe."[21]

Hapgood arrived at the conclusion that materialistic science is, in some sense, holding things upside down. Thought is not some kind of emanation of matter, but a prime cause behind matter. In effect, Burr and Russell had demonstrated the primacy of "spirit," or mind, or whatever one chooses to call it.

Hapgood goes on to discuss psychometry—which, we may recall,

Colonel Fawcett accepted as real—and tells how the "psychic" Peter Hurkos looked at photographs of both his sons, and not only gave an accurate diagnosis of their characters but was able to tell Hapgood that one them had almost died recently when a doctor had failed to recognize a sore spot on his skull as a cancerous growth.

Hapgood's viewpoint was moving steadily closer to the "shamanic," as epitomized in Manuel Cordova and Jeremy Narby. And this led him to some extremely interesting reasoning. He asked himself whether the rain dances and corn dances of the Indians are superstition, or are they genuinely effective. Hapgood reflected: "Our human ancestors have had roughly our own level of intelligence for at least 200,000 years, and probably for ten times as long."[22] He had watched Taos Pueblo Indians in New Mexico dancing for hours in the blazing heat and reasoned that, if it was really superstition and wasted effort, they would have discovered this a long time ago. And now, his own experiments concerning the power of prayer on plants had demonstrated that plants could be affected by the human mind.

It is interesting that Hapgood says that man has been as intelligent as ourselves for at least 200,000 years, and possibly for two million. A discovery made in 1997 adds powerful support to this argument.

Exploring an ancient lake bed at Mata Menge, on the island of Flores (which is east of Java and Bali), a group of paleoanthropologists from Australia found stone tools. The bed of volcanic ash in which the tools were found by Mike Morwood, and colleagues from the University of New England (New South Wales) dated from more than 800,000 years ago, the time of homo erectus. Animal bones from nearby gave the same date. What was unusual is that Flores is a relatively small island, and was not known to be a site of ancient man. The nearest such site is the far larger island of Java, the home of Java Man, who also belongs to our earliest ancestor, homo erectus.

To reach Flores, these primitive men would have had to sail from island to island, making crossings of around a dozen miles. This sounds a modest distance, but homo erectus is regarded as little more than a "glorified chimp," as Morwood put it. If he was able to sail the seas, then he must have been far more than that. Moreover, Morwood argues, the organizing ability required by a fairly large group to cross the sea suggests that homo erectus possessed some kind of linguistic ability.[23]

In other words, ancestors of nearly a million years ago were intelligent enough to collaborate on the building of rafts. And if they had not yet developed the ability to communicate linguistically, then we have to suppose some intuitive, direct communication, some form of telepathy—all of which seems to reinforce Hapgood's speculations about the unexplored possibilities of the human mind.

Now Hapgood had had a curious experience when he was sitting with his friend Ivan Sanderson, the zoologist, in the garden of Sanderson's home. The conversation turned to dissolving clouds, and Sanderson pointed at a large cloud overhead and asked Hapgood to demonstrate. "This put me on the spot," said Hapgood. "It would be humiliating to fail."[24] So he decided to try with a much smaller cloud. He concentrated on it, willing it to dissolve. For a few minutes, nothing happened. Then the cloud thinned and vanished. Claiming it was just coincidence, Sanderson asked him to try again. And Hapgood, to his own surprise, dissolved two more clouds.

That encouraged his train of thought about primitive people. For years now, Hapgood had been battling against some large black ants that invaded his kitchen every spring. One day, as he was thinking of buying ant poison, he found himself wondering why not try communication? So he sat there talking to them in a friendly tone, stressing that it was in their own interest to go away.

The next morning, the ants had gone. Later, when more ants appeared, he got rid of them the same way.

A woman to whom he told this story complained that his method did not work. She had tried it, and the number of ants had only increased. Hapgood asked her what she had done, and she explained that she had ordered them out of her kitchen, calling them "dirty little communists." Hapgood had to explain gently that this method was sure to fail.

In April 1964, Hapgood came upon another phenomenon that aroused all his scientific curiosity. He attended a demonstration of hypnotic regression by a psychologist, Dr. Kenneth Lyons. Lyons regressed a subject named George back to his first day at school, whereupon George's voice changed to that of a child, and he described his day in detail. But after exploring George's life so far, Lyons told him that he wanted him to go back to the last time he was alive, and George told him that his name was James, the date 1618, and that he lived in Cornwall. He went on to describe how he had died in a London prison at the age of seventeen.

Hapgood found it so interesting that he invited Lyons to do a demonstration at Keene State. Both he and his students found the subject fascinating, and these experiments in "past life regression" continued for two years. Hapgood noted: "In every case our subjects, when regressed to the past, described the social conditions of their presumed lives correctly."[25] One student described in detail an ancient method of curing hides; another girl, who knew no French, spoke perfect French when regressed to a past life in France. One 16-year-old boy was asked to go to the Topkapi Palace in Istanbul—where the Piri Reis map had come from—and described it in accurate detail.

Hapgood now found himself wondering whether, if people could be regressed to the past, they could be sent forward to the future. The results were remarkable.

A student named Jay was told to go forward to the following Wednesday. He described the events of the day—luncheon menu, class assignments, tests—in some detail. Asked where he was now, he said he was at the Keene airport, and that he had met a pilot from Montpelier, Vermont, who had been able to clear up the details of a rather puzzling plane crash that had occurred a year earlier.

The following Wednesday evening, Hapgood asked Jay about his day. Jay said that he had been to the Keene airport and described how he had met the flier from Montpelier, who had given him an account of the crash. The remaining details of Jay's day—assignments, etc.—corresponded closely to what he had said the previous Sunday.

Another student named Henry was "progressed" to the following Thursday. He explained that he was going to nearby Brattleboro to get drunk and was going to borrow a friend's car. Progressed a few hours further, he described how he was drinking in a diner with two women, who were making improper advances to him, and criticizing their husbands. But he declined to repeat their remarks, obviously finding them too embarrassing. He described how he had finally arrived home at 2 AM and wakened up the household when the dog barked.

The following Friday, Hapgood saw Henry in the Student Union and said: "I know where you were last night." "I bet you don't," said Henry. "You went to Brattleboro." Henry looked surprised. He was even more surprised when Hapgood told him whose car he had borrowed, and how he had gone to a diner, and met two women. "You don't know what they said?" he asked in alarm, and Hapgood laughed and said "No, you refused to tell us."[26]

Henry also confirmed that he had arrived home at 2 AM and that the dog had awakened the household.

The implications of these hypnotic experiments are far more startling than those of the others described. Hapgood had argued: "a field is not dependent on the material it organizes. A magnet may attract iron filings and form them into a pattern. If the filings are then thrown out and new filings substituted, the magnet organizes them into the same pattern. The L-field of the body, in the same way, might survive the body and organize other bodies. The T-fields may exist indefinitely, as long as the force that created them exists. And what force can this be but the ultimate creative force?"[27]

A skeptic might reply: "Even if life fields and thought fields exist, they might still be a product of matter, as light and heat are the products of a fire." In other words, they may have no separate existence.

That argument—that matter is the ultimate reality—is almost impossible to refute. Even Hapgood's experiments into hypnotic regression into the past could be explained in material terms—some kind of unconscious memory retained by the cells—or simply imagination.

But that argument cannot be applied to foreknowledge of the future. In materialist terms, the future has not yet happened and therefore cannot be predicted with any accuracy. But for the experiences of Jay at

Keene airport, or Henry at Brattleboro, there can be no "scientific" explanation. If we accept that Hapgood was telling the truth, then we are forced to posit some "T-field"—or whatever—that is free of the limitations of time. And while shamans the world over would accept this as self-evident and find nothing at all odd in being able to describe the future, our modern "way of seeing" prevents us from even beginning to grasp what it means. Still less do we know how to set about changing our way of seeing.

Hapgood would have been excited by the experiments of a contemporary neuropsychiatrist, Dr. Peter Fenwick, of the Institute of Psychiatry in London. In the 1990s, volunteers connected to a polygraph were subjected to a random series of frightening or calming pictures and were found to show fear responses three and a half seconds before the picture was shown.

It was Fenwick who told the British Association Festival of Science at the University of Salford in September 2003 that, "Mind may exist outside the brain, and may be better understood as a field rather than of just the actions in the brain." And he cited cases in which people who had suffered heart failure reported leaving their bodies and watched themselves being resuscitated. He also mentioned the frequency of cases of what he called "deathbed coincidence syndrome" when someone claims to have seen a relative who has just died, or been aware of their presence. And, like Hapgood, he had noted that prayer can have a healing influence, having a "positive effect" on people in the hospital with heart disease or receiving infertility treatment.

Eddie Campbell, the friend who introduced me to the work of Henri Bortoft, offered the following advice: "Shut the door where you work, then sit, bent over your computer keyboard. Put your hands edge-wise on the sides of your head so your line of vision is inside of a tunnel. Stare at the keyboard and let your eyes drift in and out of focus. With a bit of luck you will suddenly find the same sort of 'shift,' which you get when trying these three-dimensional 'dazzle pictures' sold in books. If you are lucky, you'll suddenly find a strange new version of the familiar keyboard. It satisfies Goethe's description of active seeing—'the perception of an object standing in its own depth.'"[28]

The essence of this method seems to be what Narby calls "defocalising." Its aim is the disappearance of normal subject-object perception. Subject and object somehow become one, as described by Stephen Phillips in speaking of his own "mystical" experience.

Eddie Campbell speculates that "there was a line of transmission from a German school, which used active seeing as a means of scientific discovery, perhaps from the early Middle Ages onwards. . . . Copernicus 'saw' his version of the universe in 1543, some three hundred years before the observational data to support it became available."

If he is correct, then it might offer us a clue to how "high levels of science" could be possessed by societies that we would regard as primitive.

<blockquote>
TWELVE
</blockquote>

THE OLD ONES

One morning in July 1989, a group of Israeli archaeologists, led by Professor Naama Goren-Inbar, were excavating in the Jordan valley, and a mechanical digger had carved out two deep trenches to expose the geological profile of the site. Each shovelful of earth was dumped on the ground and searched for bones or artifacts.

But one shovelful contained a wholly unexpected find. It was a part of a planed and polished wooden plank, ten inches long and half as wide. It had obviously been ripped out of a larger plank, and the digger had cracked it across the middle. On its lower side, the plank was slightly convex and had obviously not been planed or polished.

What was so odd about this find? Only that the layer from which it came was half a million years old, the time of Peking Man, who belonged to a species of early man—the first "true man"—called homo erectus. Presumably their brain was about half the size of modern man's. Yet they had made this polished plank, which Professor Goren-Inbar confessed herself unable to explain.

There is a photograph of it in Michael Baigent's book *Ancient Traces*, which is fortunate, since when Baigent rang Dr. Goren-Inbar, there was only one single transparency of it in existence. It was just as well he included the photograph, for the plank has since been destroyed— accidentally, of course—by the Conservation Department of Hebrew University.

This in itself sounds unbelievable. Destroyed?—a piece of wood that could be one of the most important finds in modern archaeology? After all, it could support the suggestion made in the last chapter that if homo erectus could build a raft to carry his family to the island of Flores about 800,000 years ago, he must have been far more intelligent than we give him credit for. Richard Rudgley, of the Pitt Rivers Museum in Oxford, expresses the problem succinctly:

"Preconceived opinions have repeatedly led to the rejection of evidence that does not fit with present dogmas. This has led to the routine acceptance of Upper Palaeolithic engraved bone from the Hayonim Cave in Israel, and the equally routine rejection of an engraved bone of Middle Palaeolithic age from the same site, even though the Middle Palaeolithic bone has more extensive markings than its Upper Palaeolithic counterpart."[1] The Upper Paleolithic dates from 40,000 years ago to 10,000, the Middle Palaeolithic from 200,000 to 40,000.

This sounds like madness—to reject an engraved bone because man is not supposed to have been capable of engraving before 40,000 years ago. Surely it would be more sensible to consider revising the dogma?

Although Rudgley is an orthodox archaeologist, his book *Lost Civilizations of the Stone Age* is full of similar examples. One of the most striking is about the group of stars called the Pleiades or Seven Sisters, in Taurus. These, he points out, are known as the Seven Sisters by native peoples of North America, Siberia, and Australia. This can hardly be coincidence. But if it is not coincidence, then it implies that they were called the Seven Sisters before the peopling of Australia, which is now dated at 40,000 years ago. And this is far too early for most anthropologists.

Even more awkward is the contention of Peter Kershaw, of Monash University, Victoria, that Australia may have been peopled 140,000 years ago. His theory is based on the fact that there was a sudden rise in charcoal levels 140,000 years ago, and an equally sudden decline in pollen levels, both of which Kershaw thinks may have been due to human beings using fire.

A discovery made in 1996 is even more disturbing. A team led by

Dr. Lesley Head, of the University of Woolongong, Western Australia, discovered (according to *The Times* of September 23, 1996) "tools used to make rock art and enormous sculpted boulders believed to be up to 176,000 years old"[2] at a site in Jinmium, Western Australia. In which case, our ancestors may have been calling the Pleidades the Seven Sisters for almost two hundred thousand years.

But even 40,000 years ago is embarrassing enough, for it suggests that our ancestors were studying the stars when they were supposed to be living in caves and hitting animals with clubs. In *Hamlet's Mill*, Giorgio de Santillana and Hertha von Dechend argue that "star lore" predates civilization, and that before history, someone had already named the constellations. But what did Santillana mean by "before history"? He seems to have meant before about 8000 BC, by which time homo sapiens had arrived.

The Seven Sisters also receive a lengthy discussion in Stan Gooch's *Cities of Dreams*, subtitled *The Rich Legacy of Neanderthal Man Which Shaped Our Civilization.*

When I first read *Cities of Dreams* in the year of its publication, 1989, I was rather baffled. Gooch was arguing that Neanderthal man had possessed a complex civilization, but that it was not a civilization of bricks and mortar, but of "dreams." That hardly seemed to make sense. Surely civilization is our defense against nature? Dreams are not much use against a hurricane or a saber-tooth tiger. I was impressed by his observation that Neanderthal man had dug an immense red ocher mine a 100,000 years ago, but surely that alone did not constitute civilization?

But looking at the book more recently, I was struck by the opening lines of the dust jacket blurb: "This book challenges the orthodox view that nothing worth the name of civilization existed prior to the last Ice Age and the subsequent emergence of modern man some 30,000 years ago."[3] This sounded very like Hapgood's assertion about a hundred-thousand-year-old science.

Gooch launches his argument by comparing Neanderthal man with Native Americans:

"Prior to 2000 BC, these varied peoples of North America knew weaving, tent and weapon making, medicine, music and many other skills. . . . They also had by then a complex political life, alongside rich cultural and religious traditions, and great bodies of ancient folklore. . . . Some of the tribes spent much of each day, every day, in complex religious ritual, not unlike orthodox Jews and Moslems of our present day. Yet, we must emphasize, these same complex Indians had no written language, nor did they build any permanent dwellings."[4]

What would have happened, Gooch asks, if they had been exterminated by disease or some catastrophe, and had simply vanished? Archaeologists would find their skeletons and dismiss them as "primitives."

We now know that this "primitiveness" of Native Americans was largely self-chosen. They not only lived close to nature; they believed that they had a symbiotic relationship with nature. In *From Atlantis to the Sphinx* I devoted many pages to the Hopi and the Quiche, whose civilization is as shamanistic as that of Narby's Quirishari. The anthropologist Edward Hall gradually came to understand their way of life, and to recognize that it is a complete alternative to Western civilization. In many ways—the Quiche calendar, for example—it is far more rich and complex than our Western way of life. It would not be inaccurate to call it a "right brain civilization" that has chosen to develop along its own lines.

Speaking of the Seven Sisters, Gooch remarks "The Pleiades are the only constellation noted and named by every culture on earth, past and present, from the most advanced to the most primitive."[5] Then he points out the similarity of the legends of Australian aborigines, Wyoming Indians, and the ancient Greeks.

In the Greek legend, Orion the Hunter pursues the six maidens and their mother through the forest, until Zeus takes pity on them, and changes them all (including Orion) into stars. In the Australian legend, the hunter is called Wurunna, and he captures two of the seven maidens; but these escape up trees that suddenly grow until they reach the sky, where all the maidens live forever. According to the Wyoming Indians, the seven sisters are pursued by a bear and climb up a high rock, which grows until it reaches the sky.

In 1989, Gooch pointed out that there is a 20,000 year gap between the Australian aborigines and the Wyoming Indians—unaware at the time that modern anthropologists would soon extend this to 40,000.

Gooch goes on to mention that the Seven Sisters play an equally important role in the legends of the Aztecs, the Incas, the Polynesians, the Chinese, the Masai, the Kikuyu, the Hindus, and the ancient Egyptians. This worldwide interest in the Pleiades, he argues, surely indicates that it originated in some very early and once central culture.

In Gooch's view, that culture was Neanderthal. We may doubt this and prefer to believe that it was our own ancestor, Cro-Magnon. But Gooch certainly has accumulated some impressive evidence of the intellectual sophistication of Neanderthal man. He speaks, for example, of a find made at Drachenloch in the Swiss Alps, where a 75,000-year-old bear altar was discovered in a cave. In a rectangular stone chest, whose lid was a massive stone slab, archaeologists found seven bear skulls, with their muzzles pointing toward the cave entrance. At the back of the cave, there were niches in the wall with six more bear skulls.

Now seven, as we have seen, is the number associated with shamanism. The Drachenloch cave was clearly a ritual place—in effect, a church. Moreover, as Eliade tells us, there is a worldwide connection between the bear and the moon. And this might have been guessed from the fact that the number of skulls in the cave was thirteen—the number of lunar months in the year. This, and many other clues, led Gooch to infer that the religion of Neanderthal man was based on moon worship, and Neanderthals were the first "star gazers." He argues that, among much else, the knowledge of precession of the equinoxes noted by Santillana probably originated with Neanderthal man.

A "church" implies a priest or shaman. And so another part of the jigsaw puzzle falls into place. Neanderthal man must have had his shamans, "magicians" who played an important part in the hunting rituals, as shamans do worldwide. Is it chance that the moon goddess is Diana the Huntress? Is she perhaps also a legacy from Neanderthal man?

Since Gooch's book came out in 1989, new evidence has accumulated indicating that Neanderthal man also possessed technology. In

1996, it was announced that scientists from Tarragona's Roviri i Virgili University had unearthed fifteen furnaces near Capellades, north of Barcelona. Professor Eudald Carbonell stated that they prove that Neanderthal man possessed a skill level far more advanced than anyone had supposed.

Homo sapiens, he said, were not an "evolutionary leap" beyond Cro-Magnon man, but only a gentle step from Neanderthal. Each of the furnaces served a different function according to its size, some ovens, some hearths, even blast furnaces. The team also discovered an "astonishing variety" of stone and bone tools, as well as the most extensive traces of wooden utensils.[6]

One of Gooch's most amazing statements is that in South Africa, Neanderthal man was digging deep mines to obtain red ocher 100,000 years ago. "One of the largest sites evidenced the removal of a million kilos of ore."[7] Other mines were discovered dated 45,000, 40,000, and 35,000 years ago. In all cases, the site had been painstakingly filled in again, presumably because the earth was regarded as sacred. Neanderthal man seems to have used the red ocher for ritualistic purposes, including burial.

In 1950, Dr. Ralph Solecki, of the Smithsonian Institute, had excavated the Shanidar cave in Iraqi Kurdistan and discovered evidence of ritualistic burial by Neanderthals, in which the dead had been covered with a quilt of woven wild flowers. His book *Shanidar* is subtitled *The Humanity of Neanderthal Man*. He was the first of many anthropologists to conclude that Neanderthal man was far more than an ape.

Gooch points out that red ocher has been in use since at least 100,000 years ago until today, when it is still used by Australian aborigines. He quotes one authority who calls it "the most spiritually rich and magical of all substances."[8]

Red ocher is the oxidized form of a mineral called magnetite, which, as the name suggests, is magnetic. If a small sliver is floated on the surface tension of water, it swings around and points to magnetic north. And in 1,000 BC, the Olmecs were using it as a compass needle, floating on cork, a millennium before the Chinese invented the compass.

Gooch points out that many creatures, including pigeons, have a cluster of magnetite in the brain, which is used for homing, and asks if it is not conceivable that Neanderthal man also had a magnetite cluster in the brain, which may have enabled him to detect hematite under the ground. This, of course, would be simply a variant of the power dowsers have to detect underground water.

For whatever reason Neanderthal man sought red ocher, it seems clear that he must be credited with some kind of civilization.

In January 2002 it emerged that Neanderthal man made use of a kind of superglue. It was a kind of blackish-brown pitch discovered at a lignite mining pit in the Harz mountains, estimated to be 80,000 years old. One of the pieces bore the imprint of fingers and impressions of a flint stone tool and wood, suggesting that the pitch had served as a sort of glue to secure the wooden shaft to a flint stone blade. The pitch, from a birch tree, can only be produced at a temperature of 300–400°C. Professor Dietrich Mania of the Friedrich-Schiller University in Jena said: "This implies that Neanderthals did not come across these pitches by accident, but must have produced them with intent."[9]

Now clearly, all this is revolutionary. We take it for granted that human culture began with Cro-Magnon man, homo sapiens. Our Cro-Magnon ancestors began making drawings in caves about 35,000 years ago, and so, we had always assumed, our civilization had its first beginnings.

But if the Pleiades were recognized 40,000 years ago, and if Gooch's arguments about the Neanderthal religion are sound, then we are speaking of a far more remote period. Of course, if Lesley Head is correct about 176,000-year-old tools and rock sculpture in Australia, it would be even longer ago, and leave little doubt that we were dealing with Neanderthals, and that Neanderthal man studied the heavens—for our Cro-Magnon ancestors, who were still in Africa 176,000 years ago, could not have been responsible.[10]

Again, an 82,000-year-old bone flute discovered by Dr. Ivan Turk, of the Slovenia Academy of Sciences in 1995, demonstrates that Neanderthal man had his own music.[11] It begins to look more and more as if

Gooch's comparison of Neanderthal man to Native Americans is valid. A 26,000-year-old bone sewing needle, complete with a hole for thread, was discovered at another Neanderthal site.

Perhaps the most important proof of Neanderthal man's intelligence came about through discoveries made in the Blombos cave, on the tip of South Africa, beginning in the 1990s. The cave had been used by both Cro-Magnons and Neanderthals, but it was in the specifically Neanderthal levels of the cave that Christopher Henshilwood, of the State University of New York, uncovered quantities of ocher rock decorated with geometric patterns on a prepared flattened surface.

The implications of these discoveries were presented on a BBC Horizon program of February 20, 2005, "The Day We Learned to Think." It began by presenting the theory of Professor Richard Klein that the cave art of 35,000 years ago represented this watershed, and that it was caused by some genetic change that he called "The Human Revolution." But this depended on assumptions about Neanderthals that have been questioned in the last few pages.

A major step in rejecting this view was taken by Jeffrey Laitman, a professor of otolaryngology (the study of the larynx) who pointed out that the larynx in most creatures is higher than in humans, which is why their vocal sounds are higher in pitch than ours. The dropping of the larynx meant a deeper voice, better adapted for speech. But this had already come about in Neanderthals at least two hundred thousand years ago, and it seems unlikely that they possessed the voice box for language without the ability to speak.

The geometric patterns discovered by Henshilwood dated to more than 70,000 years ago. Conceivably, these may not be art, but some form of notation, possibly astronomical, like the dots and line found on the 35,000-year-old piece of antelope bone that David MarShack of the Peabody Institute showed to be a notation of the phases of the moon created by our Cro-Magnon ancestors, and cited by Marshack as an example of the first writing. But the patterns on the Blombos ocher may pre-date by 40,000 years.

All of which may prove to be beside the point if we accept the evidence of a small, carved statue known as the Berekhat Ram figurine, discovered in 1980 by that same Professor Naama Goren-Inbar who found the piece of ancient planking mentioned at the beginning of this chapter.

She found it on the Golan Heights, and its age was established because it was found—along with 7,500 scrapers—between two layers of basalt, known as tuff, that could be dated. And the date was between 250,000 and 280,000 years ago. It resembles a famous Venus of Willendorf but is far cruder. And examination under an electron microscope revealed that it was not just some odd-shaped stone, but that it had been carved—by Neanderthal man. His flint tool had left powder in the grooves.

So Neanderthal man was carving a tiny female figure, probably the moon goddess, more than a quarter of a million years ago. The implication is that he had already developed the religion to which the bear skulls in the Drachenloch cave bear witness—but 200,000 years earlier than we had suspected.[12]

In *Uriel's Machine*, Robert Lomas and Christopher Knight also turned their attention to Neanderthals, and point out that they had larger brain than modern man, adding the startling information that they were around for 230,000 years before they vanished. Neanderthals therefore had plenty of time to acquire a high level of sophistication. They clearly believed in an afterlife, for they buried their dead with every sign of religious ritual, and with tools and meat to supply their needs in the beyond. They buried them in cloaks covered with ornate beads (with buttonholes), decorated caps, carved bracelets, and pendants. They manufactured at least one perfectly circular chalk disc, which is almost certainly a moon disc.

And Lomas and Knight make this important observation:

"It is possible that Neanderthal culture may have reached a level not unlike certain current human groups, such as the Australian Aborigines, who shun technology, preferring their old ways based upon empathy with their environment?"[13]

Speaking of early humans of 100,000 years ago, they add that if a

Neanderthal child could have been snatched up by a time machine, they could have been educated through university to exactly the same level as any person in the modern world.

We think of Neanderthals as apelike creatures who communicated in grunts. But Lomas and Knight quote a scientific paper to the effect that if a Neanderthal man, dressed in modern clothes, walked into a New York subway, no one would give him a second glance. And if Neanderthal man conducted religious rituals, played the flute, studied the heavens, and built blast furnaces, he must have had some form of language other than grunts.

In *From Atlantis to the Sphinx* I was more concerned with Cro-Magnon than with Neanderthal man and consequently overlooked the significance of Neanderthal shamanism. In that book, I argued that shamanism must have played a central part in the development of civilization. If Cro-Magnon cave paintings reveal that shamanic rituals helped the hunters to track and kill their prey, the shaman must have been one of the most important men in the tribe and would inevitably have became a leader. A tradition of priest-kings probably stretches from Cro-Magnon caves to ancient Sumer and Egypt. And ancient Egypt was the last great civilization in which priesthood and kingship were virtually identical. After that, modern man began to divide himself from his instinctive self with his perplexities and doubts.

In an earlier chapter, we saw how "shamanic cultures" seem to take a kind of "group consciousness" for granted. The Amahuaca Indians of Brazil all sat looking at the same visions that Manuel Cordova was seeing: the boa chant brought a gigantic boa constrictor, followed by other snakes, then by birds and animals. For the same reason, Jeremy Narby's Quirishari instructor called their hallucinogen "forest television."

We have all seen a flock of birds wheeling in the autumn sky, and all turning simultaneously, without a single bird lagging behind. We have seen a shoal of fishes in an aquarium do the same thing. Country people are intuitively aware that there is a connection between the individual members of the flock or shoal, just as there is between bees and ants. In flocks or shoals, these creatures are not individuals, but a collective, ruled by a group mind, while the actual cells in the body of the Microstomum worm seems to be governed by a "group mind" that knows more than they do individually.

Incredibly, modern humans can still allow themselves to be governed by a group mind. In *Out of Control*, Kevin Kelly describes a computer conference at Las Vegas in which five thousand people faced a giant television screen in which they could see themselves. They could also exert control over what happened on the screen by means of wands, which were red on one side and green on the other. Now the whole audience was divided into two, reds and greens, and proceeded to play electronic ping-pong, exactly like two individuals. And after other exercises in group activity, a flight simulator appeared on the screen, in which the left half of the audience was placed in charge of the plane's roll, and the right half its pitch. Five thousand minds attempted to bring the plane in to land, and when it became clear that it was not going to make it, caused it to abort the landing and try again. At one point, the whole audience—without any communication—decided spontaneously to make the plane loop the loop.

Obviously, that ancient capacity is still there—even though it has grown rather rusty in our civilized society. We are used to acting as individuals, and when a modern city dweller walks along a crowded street, he feels very little "connectedness" with his fellows, often the reverse. Yet a few hours exercise with a computer screen like the one described above can soon reestablish that sense of connectedness.

According to Schwaller de Lubicz, it was this connectedness that characterized ancient Egyptian society. I summarize his view: "Egyptian science, Egyptian art, Egyptian medicine, Egyptian astronomy, were not seen as different aspects of Egyptian life; they were all aspects of the same thing, which was religion in it broadest sense. Religion was identical with knowledge." Schwaller expressed it: "over four thousand years, ancient Egypt did not 'have' a religion as such; *it was religion in its entirety*" (my italics).[14]

It is impossible for us to grasp the meaning of a society that is a religion in its entirety. Even modern Judaism and modern Islam have moved far from their original roots in which society and religion were the same thing. In ancient societies, it was the very substance of everyday life. Even hunting—and therefore eating—depended on it. Neither Neanderthal nor Cro-Magnon man could have conceived life without religion.

What do we actually know of Neanderthal man? To begin with, he was about a foot shorter than we are, and his large brain made the back of his head bulge out like a squid. (This bulge was due to Neanderthal's much larger cerebellum, a brain organ about which we understand very little, but which is involved in dreaming—hence Gooch's title *Cities of Dreams*.) Moreover, he was almost certainly left handed, since most later cave art was produced by left-handers. Gooch sees that as extremely important. Since physiologists began to study the brain, it has been established that left-handed people are more intuitive than right-handers.

I was suddenly reminded of Gooch's work on Neanderthal man when reading Joseph Needham's Introduction to Robert Temple's book *The Genius of China*. Needham came to research his immense *Science and Civilization* in China when he was in Chunking during the Second World War. The reason no one had ever thought of doing such a thing before was quite simple: "My friends among the older generation of sinologists had thought that we should find nothing"—exactly the same story as with Neanderthal man.[15] Instead, "what cave of glittering treasures was opened up!"[16] He learned that, far from being uninventive, the Chinese had invented practically everything, from binomials to smallpox inoculation, before the west rediscovered it. "Wherever one looked there was 'first' after first."[17]

It was while trying to find out more about the Nineveh number that I wrote to John Michell to ask his opinion, for in his book *The Dimensions of Paradise*, Michell had written: "the ancients regarded numbers as symbols of the universe, *finding parallels between the inherent structure of numbers and all types of form and motion*" (my italics). "They inhabited a living Sacred Science universe, a creature of divine fabrication, designed in accordance with reason."[18]

Michell's reply launched me upon one of the most astonishing stages of this investigation so far.

He pointed out, to begin with, that the Nineveh number is also divisible by the diameter of the sun (864,000 miles) and the diameter of the moon, (2,160 miles) as well as the earth's precessional cycle. He added: "Also by the numbers 1 to 10, and by their product (3,628,800)."[19] He went on to point out: "There are certain nodal numbers, e.g., 86,400, the number of seconds in a 24 hour day, and 864,000 miles, which is the sun's diameter."[20]

He went on to recommend that I read the chapter on "Number and Measure" in *The Dimensions of Paradise*.

I turned to this, and at first found it rather confusing, full of long numbers and decimals, such as the information that the Roman cubit is equal to 1.4598144 English feet, the Greek cubit to 1.52064 English feet, and the Egyptian cubit to 1.728 English feet. All this reminded me of Henry Lincoln's discoveries about earth measurements (see chapter 10), but I could not quite see the relevance of these decimals.

Some of his statements certainly made me pay attention: "dividing the equator into 360 degrees makes each degree equal to 365,243.22 feet, or the number of days in a thousand years."[21]

That certainly is amazing—but then, surely has to be coincidence?

But when I came to the tables relating the Greek, Roman, Hebrew, and Egyptian measures, my hair began to prickle. There could be no doubt that these units are exact divisions of the earth's polar circumference.

This was so startling that I put the book down, to allow my thoughts to settle.

I already knew that, according to Agatharchides of Cnidus, the base of the Great Pyramid was one eighth of a minute of a degree of the earth's circumference, demonstrating that the ancient Egyptians knew the exact size of the earth.

John Michell's figures went further. In showing that Greek, Roman, Egyptian, and Hebrew measurements were all based on the size of the earth, it demonstrated that all were part of the same ancient tradition. But if the sun's diameter in miles is a multiple of the number of seconds in a day, then it looks as if the Sumerians—who invented (or inherited) the second—also knew the sun's exact diameter.

Moreover, in a section on astronomy, John Michell goes on to show that the circumference of the moon, the earth, the sun, the moon's orbit around the earth, and the earth's orbit around the sun, can also be divided precisely by twelve to the power of seven, and concludes that ancient philosophers "established that number in feet as the measure of the moon's circumference, and made it the astronomical standard measure of the universe."[22] (If this is true, it implies—as Henry Lincoln also believes—that the present tendency to get rid of the foot in favor of the meter may be a disastrous mistake.)

I began to see what he meant in his accompanying letter by the statement: "We are dealing here with an entire, organic cosmic code of number which structures the universe, not just odd coincidences."[23]

Now all these numbers cited by Michell belong to what he calls "the canon."[24] And a good starting point for understanding his ideas is a strange work called *The Canon*, by William Stirling, published in London in 1897. Although that remarkable adventurer R. B. Cunningham Graham wrote an Introduction, the book was totally ignored. The author later committed suicide. John Michell was responsible for getting *The Canon* republished in 1974.

At first sight, *The Canon* seems like a typical crank work. It claims that the initiates of ancient mystery religions were taught certain "cosmic laws," upon which the stability of society depends. These laws were expressed in the form of numbers, and these numbers could also be encoded as names—for in Greek and Hebrew, each letter of the alphabet is also associated with a number. (This is known as gematria.)

John Michell insists that all this contains a truth that has been forgotten, and that can be found in many ancient writings.

The starting point of *The Dimensions of Paradise* is Plato's Laws, with its statement that the priests of Egypt possessed a "canon" (or set of laws) of "proportions and harmonies" that was thousands of years old. Plato used this canon in the measurements for his ideal city, which he called Magnesia. But these numbers and proportions were not Plato's invention, for, as Michell shows very convincingly, they are also to be found in the plan of Stonehenge, and later in the New Jerusalem in the *Book of Revelation.*

Perhaps the easiest way of explaining what Michell means by his "canon" of numbers is to refer back to the "Golden Section."

It will be recalled that this springs out of the Fibonacci series, in which every number is the sum of the two preceding numbers: 0, 1, 1, 2, 3, 5, 8, 13, 21, 34, and so on. Every number, divided by its predecessor, comes close to phi—.618—and the bigger the numbers, the closer it gets. What is so amazing is that this simple series turns out to describe all kinds of natural phenomena, from sea shells to spiral nebulae. And when Michell points out that one degree of the earth's equator (in feet) is equal to the number of days in a thousand years, he is citing one of many such "coincidences" that seems to hint at a secret number code of incalculable age.

But the implication—that this has been known for thousands of years—suggests that some ancient cultures with an awesome knowledge of mathematics and astronomy existed at some time in the distant past. Maurice Chatelain's suggestion of 65,000 years no longer seems so absurd.

We also saw, when discussing Berriman's *Historical Metrology* in chapter 10, that the Greek stade implies an exact knowledge of the earth's polar circumference. Yet the Greeks did not know the earth's size until 240 BC, when Eratosthenes made his calculation. Again, it looks as if this knowledge must have come from some far more remote period.

John Michell's observation that the canon can be found in the geometry of Stonehenge again gives rise to a fascinating speculation. Alexander Thom talked about the architects of megalithic circles as "prehistoric Einsteins." But he thought that they simply displayed incredible geometrical talent in constructing their "stone calendars." If Michell is correct, it could be far more than that. It could simply be that the Stone Age Einsteins had inherited an ancient cosmic knowledge that stretches back beyond any known civilization. The Nineveh number and the Quiriga numbers are also part of that "canon."

The "Cosmological Anthropic Principle" was formulated in 1974 by the astronomer Brandon Carter, of the Paris Observatory. It begins by throwing doubt on the assumption of most scientists: that man is merely a biological accident with no "privileged position" in the universe. What Carter pointed out was that whether life is a biological accident or not, one thing is clear: that in creating life, the universe has created observers who can examine it. And that is one respect in which we can regard ourselves as "privileged" without self-deception.

Other scientists entered the debate. The astronomer Fred Hoyle, for example, pointed out in *The Intelligent Universe* that our planet just happens to be suited to the incubation of life. If the sun was a few degrees hotter or colder, there would be no life. Considered from that point of view, the whole universe seems to be oddly well suited to life—almost unreasonably so. For example, to make carbon (which is essential for life) two helium atoms have to collide, and he compared the chance of this happening to two billiard balls colliding on a billiard table the size of the Sahara desert. And then the new atom has to attract a third helium atom to make carbon. But if a fourth helium atom joins the fray, then it converts into oxygen. In theory, all the carbon in our universe ought to have been converted into oxygen, rendering it barren. But this does not happen because the processes involved are subtly out of tune, so only half the carbon gets converted into oxygen.

It looks, as Hoyle once said, as if some "superintendent" has been monkeying with the physics.

Hoyle also pointed out that, if it depended on the laws of chance, life would never have been created—it would have taken billions of times longer than the age of our universe. There is as little chance of life being created by accident, Hoyle says, as of the rusty car parts in a junkyard somehow being blown together to create a new Rolls Royce.

Brandon Carter extended his Anthropic Principle to the statement that not only did the universe create life but—because of the physics involved—it had to create life. And this is not theological wishful thinking, but rigorous scientific logic.

But then, we may feel, (with certain philosophers like Bergson) that the universe did not "create life." Life was already there, so to speak, outside our universe and has spent the past fifteen billion yeas or so somehow "inserting" itself into matter. And we have also noted the discovery of Sir Chandra Bose that even metals exhibit certain properties of living things.

The "anthropic"' principle seems to be implicit in Jeremy Narby's view of the Quirishari, who claim they can enter a visionary state in which they see these properties.

Is it possible that Goethe's description of nature, "God's living garment" is literally true: that the universe is actually alive? In that case, perhaps the universe has a "group mind," which controls us as if we were cells in a living body? Perhaps the whole assumption of science in the past two centuries—that we are living in a purely mechanical universe—is just an immense misconception.

This, according to John Michell, is the principle that underlies the "cosmological canon."

In *Maps of the Ancient Sea Kings*, Hapgood had already concluded it is a mistake to take it for granted that civilization implies steady upward progress. The Anthropic Principle suggests that there is an underlying pattern, both in the universe, and in number itself. And there is also a clear implication that this pattern (or "canon") was known long before the present cycle of civilization that began with Jericho. Therefore our civilization was not the first.

Rand Flem-Ath's study of geodesics led him to the same recognition of an underlying pattern that stretches far back into the past. In *Fingerprints of the Gods*, Graham Hancock had reviewed the evidence that points to a far older civilization and had even speculated on Antarctica as its source. Rand Flem-Ath's "blueprint," with its recognition that so many sacred sites fall into a neat numerical pattern aligned to the Giza meridian, goes far beyond this. Moreover, its use of a grid based on 360 degrees—an invention usually attributed to the Sumerians—seems to leave little doubt that the circle was divided into 360 degrees thousands of years earlier.

If Stan Gooch is correct in his assumption that Neanderthal man had already created his own fairly complex culture, it is even conceivable that the 360 degree circle may have been originally been invented by Neanderthals.

But how could such knowledge come to be lost?

Precession of the equinoxes had to be rediscovered by Hipparchus from old star charts. The Nineveh number and the Quiriga numbers make it quite clear that someone in the remote past knew as much about our solar system as we do. They also knew the precise length of the earth's circumference, which had to be rediscovered by Eratosthenes, the librarian at Alexandria. It is highly probable that much ancient knowledge—of metrology and the cosmological canon—was destroyed when the library was burnt. But the destruction of one single library hardly seems to explain how such an enormous amount of knowledge—including that embodied in the old portolans—was lost.

We have touched on a possible answer several times in this book—for example, the mentally subnormal twins who can nevertheless swap twenty-five-figure primes. According to Oliver Sacks, they can also name what day of the week any date in history fell on; asked what was the 10 December, 50,008 BC, they can reply instantly: "A Tuesday."

It would seem that some brains have an extremely peculiar kind of wiring and storage capacity. And the fact that this is so often found in children and "idiot savants" suggests that it may be a capacity that modern man has allowed to deteriorate. This in turn, suggests it is something to do with our development of left-brain consciousness, with its linear logic. Which in turn implies that we may have lost this ancient knowledge when we developed our dominant left hemisphere.

So when we ask how the Assyrians (or their predecessors) discovered the fifteen-digit Nineveh number, the answer may be: they didn't have to. Their mathematical prodigies may simply have "seen" it as easily as Sacks's twins "see" twenty-five-digit primes. And this could also explain how the pyramid builders knew the exact size of the earth (and probably the moon, sun, and the rest of the planets). It was part of the "canon" everybody took for granted.

The gloomy conclusion would seem to be that modern man, with his highly developed left hemisphere, has simply lost one of the most important parts of his mental abilities.

However, this inference might be premature. It is true that left-brain consciousness is a "pen and paper" mentality. But it is possible to store an enormous amount of knowledge on paper, and to do vast calculations with a pen. With the aid of his pen and paper, man has created the most complex civilization the earth has ever known. What the brain has lost in instant calculating power, he has made up for with computers.

This has one major drawback: that modern life needs an almost obsessive degree of narrow, fixed attention—the "worm's-eye view." We are like blinkered horses, scarcely seeing beyond the end of our noses. And because we are trapped in "close-upness," our civilization has an unprecedentedly high rate of suicide and mental instability—for "close-upness" deprives us of meaning, which is essential to mental health. . . .

In a word, modern man has lost the sense of freedom, which is so natural to a right brainer. Trapped in a round that reduces him to a kind of robot, he has lost the bird's eye view.

This problem has preoccupied western thinkers since Jean Jacques Rousseau, who suggested that the answer was for man to turn his back on civilization and go "back to nature." In the same spirit, the philosopher Heidegger began his career by advocating the rejection of technology. And in the 1980s, a man who called himself the Unabomber, and tried to start his own revolution by sending parcel bombs to industrialists, made it clear to everyone that this kind of response to complexity is dangerously simplistic.

I have always recognized that there is another kind of solution to the problem of the "worm's eye view." It is the real subject of my first book *The Outsider*.

On December 22, 1849, the twenty-seven-year-old novelist Fyodor Dostoyevsky was taken out of prison to the Semyonovsky Square in St. Petersburg, and sentenced to death by firing squad; his offence was circulating "banned" literature. He and his fellow revolutionaries were dressed in coarse linen shirts and lined up opposite the soldiers. Then, as the officer gave the order to fire, a horseman galloped on to the square, to announce that their sentences had been commuted to life in Siberia. Dostoyevsky was untied and taken back to prison. One of his fellow prisoners went insane.

Before this brush with death, Dostoyevsky had been inclined to paranoia and self-pity. Facing a firing squad had the effect of raising him above triviality and turning him into a great writer.

What had happened was simply that he had been made aware of his freedom. To be alive, even in Siberia, was to be free. The "blinkers" had been removed long enough to become aware of the reality behind them. This new insight was reflected in a letter to his brother immediately after the reprieve:

"whatever one's misfortunes, not to despair and not to fall—that is the aim of life."[25]

It was his sense of reality that had been strengthened by his brush with death—what the psychologist Pierre Janet calls his "reality function."

This recognition of choice—of free will—is, oddly enough, the essence of the left-brain mentality. Split-brain physiologists have noted that the left brain is more optimistic than the right. Most ancient peoples—who were natural "right brainers"—saw themselves as "creatures," whose aim is to please their gods or God. When Western man became a left brainer and lost his contact with the gods, he had to learn to stand on his own feet. This can be hard, for he often feels that he is stagnating in a meaningless world, when life seems an endless struggle to stay alive.

But this is counterbalanced by the moments when he experiences a typical left-brain sense of purpose, the sheer optimism of the "spring morning feeling," when anything seems possible. In such moments, he catches a glimpse of the answer: not to return to the less demanding consciousness based on harmony with nature, but of transcending left brain consciousness in a new sense of vital control. The next step in human evolution will be man's discovery of how to open and close the "valve" that enables us to build up greater pressure of consciousness. What we call consciousness is that pressure.

At this stage in our evolution, this is difficult to grasp, because the "worm's eye view" makes us defeat-prone. Yet whenever we experience what one philosopher has called "the source of power, meaning and purpose," we recognize clearly that that is the only way forward, and that this is the path we have to take, whether we like it or not.

However, while a return to the right brain consciousness of the past is neither possible nor desirable, it is impossible to overemphasize the importance of knowledge of this past. It can make us aware of precisely how far we have come, and—more important—where we have to go next.

Certain awkward questions about that past still require answers.

In *Ancient Traces*, Michael Baigent devotes a chapter to "doubts" about how long man has been on earth. For example, he tells how, after the great California gold rush of 1849, miners found themselves unearthing baffling artifacts—such as a stone pestle wedged tightly in a nine-million-year-old level of rock, or an iron nail embedded in a chunk of gold-bearing quartz that was known to be 38 million years old.

If there had been only a few of these "anomalies," they could have been dismissed as hoaxes, or as objects buried in Indian graves that had somehow found their way down to a deeper level. But there were hundreds of them.

In 1874, an archaeologist named Frank Calvert found a mastodon bone engraved with a horned beast and a number of other figures. But that came from a Miocene bed, more that 25 million years old, so the engravings could not have been the work of man.

In June 1891, an Illinois housewife found a fine gold chain when she broke open a lump of coal; half the chain remained in the coal, which was around 3 million years old.

In 1922, a mining engineer named John Reid discovered the fossil of the rear half of a human shoe, with stitching visible. Columbia (New York) professors agreed that the rock was from the Triassic era, more than 213 million years ago; they also agreed that the fossil looked remarkably like a human shoe.

But, for the sake of keeping this argument within boundaries we can all accept, let us assume that the conventional view that man has been on earth perhaps three million years is correct.

According to this view, the first human ancestor, homo erectus, appeared between 2 million and 1.5 million years ago. The polished plank described at the beginning of this chapter may be evidence that he was rather more intelligent than we give him credit for.

One of the main suggestions of the last two chapters is that man probably developed a high level of intelligence long before we came along, and that one of the manifestations of this intelligence was the ability to handle enormous numbers. We have no idea when this evolutionary advance came about. But if homo erectus had developed language and the ability to build rafts, then he may also have been the first true "calculator."

Stan Gooch argues that Neanderthal man possessed this ability, and that Cro-Magnon somehow picked it up from him. Again, we have no way of knowing—except that the evidence of metrology suggests that knowledge of "the cosmological canon" stretches back into the remote past.

So the picture that begins to emerge is of the possibility of highly intelligent human ancestors who lived more than 100,000 years ago. They left behind few signs of their achievement because they were "right brainers" whose technology was primitive. Nevertheless their grasp of cosmology may have been far greater than that of the average educated man of today.

In due course, Cro-Magnon man appeared on the scene—for practical purposes, about forty thousand or so years ago. The evidence he left behind suggests to us that he was a primitive "cave man." In fact, his level of intelligence was probably as great as ours, which would explain why, at the end of the last Ice Age, such men were ready to create the first real (i.e., technological) civilization.

These men also learned of the existence of a "cosmological canon" that seemed to embrace the solar system. Now a 12,000-year-old civilization is one thing; a system of numbers, harmonies, and proportions that embraces the solar system quite another. At which point, I came upon this passage in a book written in 1908:

"Some of the beliefs and legends which have come down to us from antiquity are so universal and deep-rooted that we are accustomed to consider them almost as old as the race itself. One is tempted to inquire how far the unsuspected aptness of some of these beliefs and sayings . . . is the result of mere chance or coincidence, and how far it may be evidence of a wholly unknown and unsuspected ancient civilization of which all other relic has disappeared."[26]

The writer of these words was not some follower of Madame Blavastsky or Rudolf Steiner, but the physicist Frederick Soddy (1877–1956), a colleague of Ernest Rutherford who is best known for his discovery of isotopes in 1913.

In *The Interpretation of Radium*, Soddy goes on to talk about the philosophers' stone, "which was accredited with the power not only of transmuting metals, but as acting as the elixir of life."[27] And he asks: "Was then this old association of the power of transmutation with the elixir of life merely a coincidence? I prefer to believe it may be an echo from one of the many previous epochs in the unrecorded history of the world, of an age when men which have trod before the road we are treading today, in a past possibly so remote that even the very atoms of civilization literally have had time to disintegrate."[28]

It is odd that in 1908, a scientist of Soddy's eminence felt no embarrassment at suggesting ideas that no contemporary scientist would dare to utter. But then, he was living at a time before there was an impassable gulf between science and imagination. Nowadays such speculations must be left to those with no academic reputation to lose.

One such is John Michell, who concluded an article on the canon— and may be left to conclude this book—with the words: "This is not just a vague prescription; you can study the mathematical proofs for yourself, and the more you do so, the more clearly you see the truth in Plato's reassurance: 'things are far better taken care of than we can possibly imagine.'"[29]

ATLANTIS IN CYPRUS?

In August 2004 I received a phone call from a travel agent named Roy Bird, who organizes trips to exotic places. He told me that an American named Robert Sarmast was about to set out on an expedition from Limassol, Cyprus, with the aim of trying to locate Atlantis. He asked me what I thought of the notion that Atlantis might be found in that area, and I replied that I could think of nothing less likely. Plato had said that Atlantis was "beyond the Pillars of Hercules,"[1] which are generally accepted to be the Straits of Gibraltar. Professor Galanapoulos, the chief advocate of the theory that the island of Santorini (midway between Crete and the mainland to the north) argued that two capes of southern Greece, Maleas and Taenarum, were also known as the Pillars of Hercules. But as far as I could see, there was no possible way in which the island of Cyprus, in the extreme eastern Mediterranean, could be "beyond" the Pillars of Hercules on either interpretation.

That, said Roy Bird, was not quite true. According to Sarmast, the ends of the Bosphorus were also known as the Pillars of Hercules. And if you were looking at these from Greece, you would be looking due east, and Cyprus would indeed be "beyond" them.

I had to admit that if Atlantis was in the Mediterranean, it would explain another puzzle: Plato's assertion that the Atlanteans had been at war with the Athenians. If Atlantis had been somewhere out in the Atlantic Ocean—or even, as my fellow author Rand Flem-Ath had suggested, on the continent of Antarctica—there could be no remote possibility of a war between nations so far apart.

The reason Roy Bird was ringing me was that he hoped I might interest the *Daily Mail* in the story, and tempt a few hundred tourists to pay cash to join the expedition. I rang a friend on the *Mail* features, who liked the idea, and asked me to write an article about it. Which is what I did. However, the newspaper decided not to print the address of my website, giving details of how potential customers could pay their money. And so, from Roy Bird's point of view, the whole exercise was a waste of time.

But by then, I had got hold of Sarmast's book *The Discovery of Atlantis: The Startling Case for the Island of Cyprus* and was so intrigued by his theory that I decided to take a holiday in Cyprus with my wife and look into it myself. We had a friend who had retired to Limassol—the psychic Robert Cracknell—and this would give us an opportunity to go and visit him. He obligingly booked us into a beach hotel in Limassol, and so in September we flew to Larnaca, and were met off the plane by Bob and his wife Jenny. From our hotel we rang Sarmast, who was staying in Limassol, and invited him to dinner the following day.

We had already been told that the expedition would not sail on time, due to various problems to do with obtaining permits. So we did not expect to be able to sail on the ship. In fact, it had begun to look as if it might be months before it set out. But the following evening, when Sarmast arrived at our hotel for an early drink, he told us that things had suddenly improved dramatically, and that it now looked as if they would be leaving that weekend.

Sarmast was a good-looking man in his late thirties, born in Iran, but having spent most of his life in America, where his family had fled to escape the rule of the Ayatollah Khomeini. As we sat on the terrace overlooking the swimming pool and drank cold beer, he told me about his background, and how he had become interested in Atlantis.

When he left university, he had felt that his priority was to "find himself," and he had taken a one-way ticket to India, to avoid the temptation of changing his mind. There he found various gurus, but ended by feeling basically dissatisfied. His story reminded me of so many "religious Outsiders" I have written about—for example, Peter. D. Ouspensky who went to India before the First World War in search of a guru who could teach him the meaning of life, but failed to find him until he returned to Russia and met Gurdjieff.

In Robert Sarmast's case the search continued after his return to America. One of the things he came across was a teaching that identified Atlantis with the Biblical Eden. And it was in pursuing this odd clue that he came to feel that Eden had been to the east of Lebanon, in the days when the Mediterranean was far lower than it is today, and when the island of Cyprus had been joined to the mainland.

Like Galanapoulos, he had concluded that Plato's figures had been exaggerated by the copyist (even Plato expresses doubts about them) by mistaking the symbol for ten for the very similar symbol for a hundred, and were around ten times too large. He goes on to point out:

1. Plato says that the fertile plain was used by farmers to grow food for the Atlanteans. But that is about half the size of England and would certainly provide more food than any city could eat, even London.
2. Plato says there was a rectangular ditch around the whole plain, into which several rivers were diverted to collect drinking water. But that would provide enough water for ten cities.
3. Plato says that the plain contained a harbor consisting of concentric circles of canals, all 100 feet deep and 300 feet wide. But who would want to dig a canal that deep? A 100 feet is the size of five average houses piles on top of one another, and no ship would have that much draught, or even a quarter of it. As to that enormous width, it would take half a dozen aircraft carriers.

So anyone can see that these figures would be more convincing if divided by ten.

Besides, said Sarmast, maps show a vast undersea plain 23 miles long by 34 miles wide. Knock off two noughts from Plato's Atlantis plain and you have these exact dimensions.

He managed to persuade some French oceanographic project to let him have a small section of their recent survey of the sea bed covering that area and found a hill in the exact spot where Plato's Acropolis Hill should have been, and what appeared to be a long wall at its foot—again, as Plato described. In fact, as Plato said, the whole hill seemed to be boxed in by walls, as far as one could judge from surveys taken a mile deep.

Later, in the restaurant, Robert showed us a computer simulation of the sea breaking through the mountain barrier that once separated Gibraltar from North Africa.

Now it was during the 1960s that geologists first learned that the earth's surface is not a continuous sheet, like the skin of an orange, but consists of tectonic plates that move about separately. Then scientists learned that that the Mediterranean is a fairly young sea that was created about seven million years ago, when the plate containing Africa drifted north, and collided with Europe. The sea was trapped into a kind of gigantic pond, which extended from Gibraltar to Lebanon. Gradually, this pond evaporated in the hot sun until the floor of the basin was covered with gleaming salt flats.

Geologists have always assumed that the Atlantic began to break through a gap near Gibraltar five million or so years ago, as stated earlier in this book. But since salt beds cannot be carbon dated, no one knows exactly when. All we know is that the last great Ice Age began about 115,000 years ago, and came to an end about 15,000 years ago. But we do know there have been many tremendous floods sine it ended, as vast northern lakes melted and poured billions of gallons of fresh water into the sea.

Plato, of course, stated that Atlantis was submerged nine thousand years before his own time, which would make it about 9400 BC. Sarmast suggests that this was when the melting ice caused the Atlantic to force a new gap in the mountain barrier between Gibraltar and North Africa, and into the island-dotted salt lake we now call the Mediterranean. But at first the sea broke through only in one place, and the lake remained lower than the Atlantic.

It was, according to Sarmast, during this period, while the Mediterranean was still protected by a range of low mountains, and the peninsula we now call Cyprus had turned into a huge island, about twice its present size, that a new civilization began to flourish in the eastern Mediterranean—Atlantis.

The day after our dinner, Sarmast was having a press conference on board the ship, the *Flying Enterprise*, and we were invited—together with Bob and Jenny Cracknell. A television crew interviewed Sarmast on the bridge, and I later did a short interview to camera (for the local news) explaining why I thought it conceivable that this search for Atlantis, which was being partly financed by the government of Cyprus, (partly for its anticipated effect on the tourist trade) might well produce interesting results. We also looked at the robot camera that could be used to scan at a depth of a mile.

That weekend, Joy and I returned home. In fact, the *Flying Enterprise* failed to leave Limassol the day it was supposed to, apparently still on account of permits. And I had more-or-less given up wondering when the expedition would set out when, on Sunday, November 14, 2004, Bob Cracknell rang me from Cyprus, to tell me that Sarmast had sailed the previous Monday, and was now back in Limassol, announcing that he had found Atlantis—or something very like it. I lost no time in ringing Sarmast, who told me he had a press conference in an hour, but would ring me back later in the day. He kept his promise, and I recorded the conversation.

It seemed that, in spite of initial difficulties, the *Flying Enterprise* had reached the area of the "temple mount," then released the sonar device on three miles of steel cable, which was towed behind the ship, about fifty feet above the sea bed. Then the winch releasing the cable broke down, and took a whole night to repair. (This was done by technicians, one of whom had just returned from working on the Titanic.) After another long day, making long sweeps over the area of the "temple hill," the team went to bed very tired. Robert was awakened with the discouraging news that the generator, which provided the energy for the winch, had failed.

It looked at the point as if the expedition was over, and there was nothing to do but return to Limassol. But there was a problem: the cable was trailing three miles behind the ship, and without the winch, could not be wound in. There was only one thing to do—to get another generator.

This had to be brought from Limassol and was even bigger than the one that had broken down (which was about the size of a small room). And, of course, the ship had to keep moving, otherwise the sonar device would sink down to the seafloor, and might well get snagged on some obstacle. So they continued to steam ahead, waiting for the arrival of the ship (*The Ares*) with the new generator.

When this finally happened, both ships had to steer a parallel course side by side, while the new generator was transferred to the deck of the *Flying Enterprise* on a steel cable. Sarmast said that he was terrified that, if the cable snapped while the generator was swinging aloft, it would fall and sink the ship.

Finally, the transfer was made and the new generator—even bigger than the old one—installed. *The Ares* sailed back to Limassol, while the *Flying Enterprise* turned in a huge circle, with its trailing cable, and went back over the mound that they thought to be Plato's Acropolis hill.

What they were doing, in effect, was using the sonar to "film" long strips of sea bed. But as Sarmast looked at the first results, he was discouraged. They seemed to show very little. When he went to bed that night, he had come to accept that the whole expedition had been a failure, and that he was still no nearer to proving that the undersea mound was Plato's Acropolis hill.

He awoke to good news. While he had been asleep, the technicians had been working on the long "strips" of map, placing them side by side. And what had finally emerged was a great hill, about three kilometers long, with a plateau on top, and unmistakeable signs of a great wall that surrounded it. He had recognized the signs of a wall at the southern foot of the hill on the original sonar maps provided by the French, but "experts" he had consulted had told him it was probably a mud slide. He had replied that a mud slide that long, and in a straight line, was unlikely, but they had declined to be convinced. Now he had been proved right.

I asked whether it might be possible to film the walls with the robot camera, but he pointed out that at that depth—around a mile—it would be pitch black, and that everything would be covered in a layer of mud.

Two weeks later, Robert came to London, and he and I appeared together in a television interview about his discovery. As we ate dinner together in Bertorellis in Soho, I asked him what happened now. "Now," he said, "we start the long, slow business of raising millions of dollars for an expedition that can get down there on the sea bed, and see what we've really found."

Have they, in fact, found Plato's sunken city? An element of skepticism in me suggests that this would be too good to be true. But whatever it is, Sarmast has found an unknown bit of human history.

Postscript

In August 2005, the BBC Web site published a recent discovery that seemed to confirm that Sarmast is correct.[2]

The story begins: "A submerged island that could be the source of the Atlantis myth was hit by a large earthquake and tsunami 12,000 years ago, a geologist has discovered."

It goes on:

"Spartel Island now lies 60m under the sea in the Straits of Gibraltar, but some think it once lay above water.

"The finding adds weight to a hypothesis that the island could have inspired the legend recounted by the philosopher Plato more than 2,000 years ago.

"Evidence comes from a seafloor survey published in the journal *Geology*.

"Marc-Andre Gutscher of the University of Western Brittany in Plouzane, France, found a coarse-grained sedimentary deposit that is 50–120cm thick and could have been left behind after a tsunami.

"Dr. Gutscher said that the destruction described by Plato is consistent with a great earthquake and tsunami similar to the one that devastated the city of Lisbon in Portugal in 1755, generating waves with heights of up to 10m.

"The thick 'turbidite' deposit results from sediments that have been shaken up by underwater geological upheavals.

"It was found to date to around 12,000 years ago—roughly the age indicated by Plato for the destruction of Atlantis, Dr. Gutscher reports in Geology.

"Spartel Island, in the Gulf of Cadiz, was proposed as a candidate for the origin of the Atlantis legend in 2001 by French geologist Jacques Collma-Girard.

"It is 'in front of the Pillars of Hercules,' or the Straits of Gibraltar, as Plato described. . . . Sedimentary records reveal that events like the 1755 Lisbon earthquake occur every 1,500 to 2,000 years in the Gulf of Cadiz."

The report concludes:

"But the mapping of the island carried out by Dr. Gutscher failed to turn up any manmade structures and also showed that the island was much smaller than previously believed."

This is only to be expected. Spartel Island is too small to have been Plato's Atlantis. But if, in 10,000 BC, it exploded like the island of Santorini eight and a half millennia later, then it would have triggered a tsunami that would have devastated the southern part of the island of Cyprus. Sarmast understandably regards it as an extremely powerful piece of evidence for his Cyprus theory of Atlantis.

NOTES

Chapter One: Hapgood's Unsolved Mystery

1. Personal correspondence with the author.
2. Personal correspondence with the author.
3. Plato, *Timaeus and Critias* (New York: Penguin Classics, 1972).

Chapter Two: A Trip Down the Nile

1. Joseph Jochmans, *The Hall of Records* (privately printed, 1980).
2. Charles Hapgood, *Maps of the Ancient Sea Kings* (Philadelphia: Chilton Books, 1966).
3. David Elkington and Paul Howard Ellson, *In the Name of the Gods: The Mystery of Resonance and the Prehistoric Messiah* (Green Man Publishing Ltd., 2001).
4. Maurice Chatelain, *Our Cosmic Ancestors* (Sedona, AZ: Temple Golden Publications, 1988).
5. Ibid.
6. Ibid.
7. E. W. H. Myers, *Human Personality and Its Survival of Bodily Death*, edited by Susy Smith (New Hyde Park, NY: University Books, 1961).
8. Robert Graves, "The Abominable Mr. Gunn," from *The Shout and Other Stories* (New York: Penguin Books, 1971).
9. Ibid.

Chapter Three: Ancient Technologies

1. Charles Hapgood, *Maps of the Ancient Sea Kings* (Philadelphia: Chilton Books, 1966).

2. Ibid.

3. Colin Wilson and Rand Flem-Ath, *The Atlantis Blueprint* (London: Little Brown, 2000).

4. Jules Verne, *The Mysterious Island* (New York: Charles Scribner and Sons, 1876), 2:153.

5. Personal correspondence with the author.

6. www.Freeenergynews.com/directory/essays/suppression_bird.htm.

7. Ibid.

8. Ibid.

9. Ibid.

10. Zeharia Sitchin, *The Lost Realms, Book IV of the Earth Chronicles* (New York: Avon, 1990).

11. Ibid.

12. Ibid.

13. Ibid.

14. Ibid.

15. Ibid.

16. *Quest for the Lost Civilization. Heaven's Mirror* / an Independent Image production for Channel 4 Television and The Learning Channel; series director, Timothy Copestake; producers, David Wickham, Stefan Wickham; written and presented by Graham Hancock, 1998.

Chapter Four: The Flood

1. Alan L. Kolata, *The Tiawanaku: Portrait of an Andean Civilization* (Cambridge, MA: Blackwell, 1993).

2. Arthur Posnanky, *Tiahunanacu: The Cradle of American Civilization* (New York: J. J. Augustin Publisher, 1945).

3. Plato, *Timaeus and Critias* (New York: Penguin Classics, 1972).

4. *The Epic of Gilgamesh* (New York: Penguin Classics, 2003).

5. Ibid.

6. Ibid.

7. Sir Charles Leonard Woolley, *Ur of the Chaldees: A Record of Seven Years of Excavation* (New York: Penguin Books, 1940).

Chapter Five: More Catastrophes

1. Simon Lang and David Singleton, *Earth Story, the Shaping of Our World* (BBC, 1999).

2. Alexander Tollman and Edith Tollmann, *Und die Sinflut gab es doch: vom*

Mythos zur Historischen Wahreit (1993). Also "The Flood Came at 3 O'clock in the Morning," *Austria Today*, April 1992.

3. Ibid.

4. Rand and Rose Flem-Ath, *When the Sky Fell: In Search of Atlantis* (New York: St. Martin's Press, 1995).

5. *Natural History*, March 1987.

6. Stephen Oppenheimer, *Eden in the East, the Drowned Continent of Southeast Asia* (London: Phoenix, 1999).

7. Alexander Tollman and Edith Tollmann, *Und die Sinflut gab es doch: vom Mythos zur Historischen Wahreit* (1993).

8. Ibid.

9. Stephen Oppenheimer, *Eden in the East, the Drowned Continent of Southeast Asia* (London: Phoenix, 1999).

Chapter Six: The Mystery of the Maya

1. Robert Temple, *The Crystal Sun: The Most Secret Science of the Ancient World* (London: Century, 2001).

2. Jose Arguelles, *The Mayan Factor: The Path Beyond Technology* (Rochester, VT: Bear & Co., 1987).

3. Robert Temple, *The Crystal Sun: The Most Secret Science of the Ancient World* (London: Century, 2001).

4. David Keys, *Catastrophe, An Investigation into the Origins of the Modern World* (New York: Ballantine, 2000).

5. Ibid.

6. Delia Goetz and Sylvanus G. Morley, trans., *Popul Vuh: The Sacred Book of the Ancient Quiche Maya,* (London: William Hodge & Company, 1951).

7. Ibid.

8. Ibid.

Chapter Seven: The Shamanic Vision

1. Ross Salmon, *My Quest for El Dorado* (London: Hodder and Stoughton, 1979), 75–76.

2. Ibid.

3. Rand Flem-Ath, *When the Sky Fell* (New York: St. Martins Paperbacks, 1997).

4. Ross Salmon, *My Quest for El Dorado* (London: Hodder and Stoughton, 1979).

5. Ibid.

6. Ibid.

7. Ibid.

8. Percy Harrison Fawcett, *Exploration Fawcett* (London: Arrow Books, 1968).

9. Ibid.

10. Colin Wilson, *The Psychic Detectives* (London: Pan Books, 1984).

11. Percy Harrison Fawcett, *Exploration Fawcett* (London: Arrow Books, 1968).

12. Ibid.

13. Ibid.

14. Ibid.

15. Ibid.

16. Ibid.

17. Ibid.

18. Ibid.

19. Mircea Eliade, *Shamanism: Archaic Techniques of Ecstasy* (New York: Bollingen Foundation, 2004).

20. F. Bruce Lamb and Manuel Cordova-Rios, *Wizard of the Upper Amazon* (New York: Atheneum, 1971).

21. Harry B. Wright, *Witness to Witchcraft* (New York: Funk & Wagnalls, 1957).

22. Geoffrey Ashe, *Dawn Beyond the Dawn: A Search for the Earthly Paradise* (New York: Henry Holt & Co., 1992).

23. Jacquetta Hawkes, *Man and the Sun* (New York: Random House, 1962), 49–50.

24. Ibid.

25. Colin Wilson, *From Atlantis to the Sphinx* (New York: Fromm International, 1997).

26. Jeremy Narby and Francis Huxley, eds., *Shamans through Time: 500 Years on the Path to Knowledge* (New York: Tarcher/Putnam, 2000).

27. Mircea Eliade, *Shamanism: Archaic Techniques of Ecstasy* (New York: Bollingen Foundation, 2004).

28. Ibid.

29. Jeremy Narby and Francis Huxley, eds., *Shamans through Time: 500 Years on the Path to Knowledge* (New York: Tarcher/Putnam, 2000).

30. Ibid.

31. Ibid.

32. Ibid.

33. Ibid.

34. Ibid.

35. Arthur Rimbaud, *Season in Hell* (Norfolk, CT: New Directions, 1945).

36. Jeremy Narby and Francis Huxley, eds., *Shamans through Time: 500 Years on the Path to Knowledge* (New York: Tarcher/Putnam, 2000).

37. Ibid.

Chapter Eight: A More Powerful Reality

1. Jeremy Narby and Francis Huxley, eds., *Shamans through Time: 500 Years on the Path to Knowledge* (New York: Tarcher/Putnam, 2000).

2. Michael Harner, *The Way of the Shaman: A Guide to Power and Healing* (San Francisco: Harper & Row, 1980).

3. Ibid.

4. Jeremy Narby, *The Cosmic Serpent: DNA and the Origins of Knowledge* (New York: Jeremy P. Tarcher/Putnam, 1998).

5. Ibid.

6. Ibid.

7. Jeremy Narby and Francis Huxley, eds., *Shamans through Time: 500 Years on the Path to Knowledge* (New York: Tarcher/Putnam, 2000).

8. Jeremy Narby, *The Cosmic Serpent: DNA and the Origins of Knowledge* (New York: Jeremy P. Tarcher/Putnam, 1998).

9. Ibid.

10 Ibid.

11. Ibid.

12. Ibid.

13. Ibid.

14. Carl Jung, *Memories, Dreams, Reflections* (New York: Vintage, 1989), ch. 8.

15. Michael Harner, *The Way of the Shaman: A Guide to Power and Healing* (San Francisco: Harper & Row, 1980).

16. Mircea Eliade, *Shamanism: Archaic Techniques of Ecstasy* (New York: Bollingen Foundation, 2004).

17. Jeremy Narby and Francis Huxley, eds., *Shamans through Time: 500 Years on the Path to Knowledge* (New York: Tarcher/Putnam, 2000).

18. Ibid.

19. Ibid.

20. Ibid.

21. Ibid.

22. Ibid.

23. Ibid.

24. Ibid.
25. Ibid.
26. Jeremy Narby and Francis Huxley, eds., "Interview with a Killing Shaman," *Shamans through Time: 500 Years on the Path to Knowledge* (New York: Tarcher/Putnam, 2000).
27. Ibid.
28. Fernando Payaguaje, *The Yage Drinker or El bebedor de Yaje* (Shusufindi-Rio Aguarico, Ecuador: Vicariato de Aguarico, 1990).
29. Ibid.
30. Jeremy Narby and Francis Huxley, eds., *Shamans through Time: 500 Years on the Path to Knowledge* (New York: Tarcher/Putnam, 2000).
31. Ibid.
32. Ibid.
33. Ibid.
34. Ibid.
35. Max Freedom Long, *The Secret Science Behind Miracles* (Los Angeles: Kosmon Press, 1948).
36. Christian Jacq, *The Empire of Darkness: A Novel of Ancient Egypt* (New York: Atria Books, 2001).
37. Ibid.
38. David St. Clair, *Drum and Candle* (New York: Doubleday, 1971).
39. Ibid.
40. Ibid.
41. Ibid.

Chapter Nine: Enoch's Burning Mountain

1. Christopher Knight and Robert Lomas, *Uriel's Machine* (Rockport, MA: Element Books, 2000).
2. Christopher Knight and Robert Lomas, *The Hiram Key: Pharaohs, Freemasons and the Discovery of the Secret Scrolls of Jesus* (Rockport, MA: Element Books Ltd., 2000).
3. Charles Guignebert, *The Jewish World in the Time of Jesus* (New York: University Books, 1959).
4. Arkon Daraul, *A History of Secret Societies* (New York: Citadel Press, 1962).
5. Christopher Knight and Robert Lomas, *The Hiram Key: Pharaohs, Freemasons and the Discovery of the Secret Scrolls of Jesus* (Rockport, MA: Element Books Ltd., 2000).

6. Rupert Furneaux, *The Other Side of the Story: The Strange Story of Christianity, the Dark Spot of History* (London: Cassell, 1953).

7. Percy Seymour, *The Birth of Christ—Exploding the Myth* (London: Virgin, 1998, 1999).

8. Colin Wilson, *A Criminal History of Mankind* (London, New York: Granada, 1984).

9. Peter Bamm, *Early Sites of Christianity*, translated by Stanley Godman (New York: Pantheon Books, 1957).

10. Christopher Knight and Robert Lomas, *The Hiram Key: Pharaohs, Freemasons and the Discovery of the Secret Scrolls of Jesus* (Rockport, MA: Element Books Ltd., 2000).

11. Christopher Knight and Robert Lomas, *Uriel's Machine* (Rockport, MA: Element Books Ltd., 2000).

12. Michael Baigent and Richard Leigh, *The Dead Sea Scrolls Deception* (New York: Summit Books, 1991).

13. Ibid.

14. Christopher Knight and Robert Lomas, *The Hiram Key: Pharaohs, Freemasons and the Discovery of the Secret Scrolls of Jesus* (Rockport, MA: Element Books Ltd., 2000).

15. Christopher Knight and Robert Lomas, *The Second Messiah: Templars, the Turin Shroud and the Great Secret of Freemasonry* (Rockport, MA.: Element Books Ltd., 1998).

16. Christopher Knight and Robert Lomas, *Uriel's Machine* (Rockport, MA: Element Books Ltd., 2000).

17. Ibid.

18. Ibid.

19. Michael Baigent and Richard Leigh, *The Temple and the Lodge* (London: J. Cape, 1989).

20. Ibid.

21. Christopher Knight and Robert Lomas, *The Hiram Key: Pharaohs, Freemasons and the Discovery of the Secret Scrolls of Jesus* (Rockport, MA: Element Books Ltd., 2000).

22. Ibid.

Chapter Ten: The Magic Landscape

1. Michael Baigent, Richard Leigh, and Henry Lincoln, *The Holy Blood and the Holy Grail* (New York: Delacorte, 1982). Also Colin Wilson and Damon Wilson, *Encyclopedia of Unsolved Mysteries* (London: Harrap, 1987).

2. Ibid.

3. Ibid.

4. Ibid.

5. Henry Lincoln, *The Key to the Sacred Pattern: The Untold Story of Rennes-le-Château* (New York: St. Martin's Press, 1998).

6. Ibid.

7. Ibid.

8. Ibid.

9. Maurice Chatelain, *Our Cosmic Ancestors* (Sedona, AZ: Temple Golden Publications, 1988).

10. Christopher Knight and Robert Lomas, *The Hiram Key: Pharaohs, Freemasons and the Discovery of the Secret Scrolls of Jesus* (Rockport, MA: Element Books Ltd., 2000).

11. Henry Lincoln, *The Key to the Sacred Pattern: The Untold Story of Rennes-le-Chateau* (New York: St. Martin's Press, 1998).

Chapter Eleven: Primal Vision

1. Keith Critchlow, *Time Stands Still* (London: Gordon Fraser, 1979).

2. *The Boy with the Incredible Brain,* produced by Martin Weitz for Focus TV, 2005.

3. Robert Graves, "The Abominable Mr. Gunn," in *The Shout and Other Stories* (New York: Penguin Books, 1971).

4. Peter D. Ouspensky, *A New Model of the Universe* (New York: Knopf, 1931).

5. R. A. Schwaller De Lubicz, *Sacred Science: The King of Pharaonic Theocracy* (Rochester, VT: Inner Traditions, 1982).

6. William James, *The Writings of William James* (New York: Random House, 1967).

7. Henri Bortoft, *The Wholeness of Nature: Goethe's Way toward a Science of Conscious Participation in Nature* (Hudson, NY: Lindisfarne Press, 1996).

8. Ibid.

9. Johann Peter Eckermann, *Conversations with Goethe* (London: Dent, New York: Dutton, 1971).

10. William Blake, *Marriage of Heaven and Hell*, edited and with an introduction by Harold Bloom (New York: Chelsea House, 1987).

11. Gottfried Benn, *Primal Vision: Selected Writings of Gottfried Benn*, edited by E. B. Ashton (London: Bodley Head, 1961).

12. William Wordsworth, *Intimations of Immortality: An Ode* (Portland, ME: Thomas B. Mosher, 1908).

13. Personal correspondence with the author.

14. Personal correspondence with the author.

15. T. E. Lawrence, *The Seven Pillars of Wisdom* (London: J. Cape, 1952).

16. Peter Tompkins and Christopher Bird, *The Secret Life of Plants* (New York: Harper & Row, 1973).

17. Ibid.

18. Charles H. Hapgood, *Voices of Spirits: Through the Psychic Experiences of Elwood Babbitt* (New York: Delacorte Press/S. Lawrence, 1975), introduction.

19. Ibid.

20. Ibid.

21. Ibid.

22. Ibid.

23. M. J. Morwood, "Early hominid occupation of Flores, East Indonesia, and its wider significance," in I. Metcalfe, I. Smith, I. Davidson, and M. J. Morwood, eds., *Faunal and Floral Migrations and Evolution in SE Asia-Australasia* (Lisse, Netherlands: Swets and Zeitlinger, 2001).

24. Charles H. Hapgood, *Voices of Spirits: Through the Psychic Experiences of Elwood Babbitt* (New York: Delacorte Press/S. Lawrence, 1975), introduction.

25. Ibid.

26. Ibid.

27. Ibid.

28. Henri Bortoft, *The Wholeness of Nature: Goethe's Way toward a Science of Conscious Participation in Nature* (Hudson, NY: Lindisfarne Press, 1996).

Chapter Twelve: The Old Ones

1. Richard Rudgley, *Lost Civilizations of the Stone Age* (New York: Free Press, 1999).

2. *The Times of London*, September 3, 1996.

3. Stan Gooch, *Cities of Dreams: The Rich Legacy of Neanderthal Man Which Shaped Our Civilization* (New York: Century Hutchinson, 1989).

4. Ibid.

5. Ibid.

6. *Sunday Times (of London)*, November 3, 1996.

7. Stan Gooch, *Cities of Dreams: The Rich Legacy of Neanderthal Man Which Shaped Our Civilization* (New York: Century Hutchinson, 1989).

8. Ibid.

9. Ananova website, January 6, 2002, "Neanderthal clever enough to make Superglue."

10. Studies of "mitochondrial DNA"—DNA inherited only from the mother—are said to indicate that our common ancestor, "mitochondrial Eve," can be traced back about 200,000 years.

11. *Sunday Times (of London)*, November 3, 1996.

12. Peter Watson, "Mankind's Golden Stone of Destiny," *The Sunday Times*, February 6, 2000.

13. Christopher Knight and Robert Lomas, *Uriel's Machine* (Rockport, MA: Element Books Ltd., 2000).

14. R. A. Schwaller de Lubicz, *Sacred Science: The King of Pharaonic Theocracy* (Rochester, VT: Inner Traditions, 1982).

15. Robert Temple, *The Genius of China: 3,000 Years of Science, Discovery, and Invention* (New York, Simon & Schuster, 1986).

16. Ibid.

17. Ibid.

18. John Michell, *Dimensions of Paradise: The Proportions and Symbolic Numbers of Ancient Cosmology* (New York: HarperCollins, 1988).

19. Ibid.

20. Ibid.

21. Ibid.

22. Ibid.

23. Ibid.

24. Ibid.

25. Fyodor Dostoyevsky, *Crime and Punishment*, translated by Constance Garnett (New York: Bantam, 1984).

26. Frederick Soddy, *The Interpretation of Radium and the Structure of the Atom* (New York: Putnam, 1922).

27. Ibid.

28. Ibid.

29. John Michell, *Dimensions of Paradise: The Proportions and Symbolic Numbers of Ancient Cosmology* (New York: HarperCollins, 1988).

Appendix: Atlantis in Cyprus?

1. Plato, *Timaeus and Critias* (New York: Penguin Classics, 1972).

2. http://news.bbc.co.uk/1/hi/sci/tech/4153008.stm

INDEX